MOBILE AND WIRELESS NETWORKS

Prentice Hall Series in Advanced Communications Technologies

Emerging Communications Technologies, *Uyless Black*

ATM: Foundation for Broadband Networks, *Uyless Black*

Mobile and Wireless Networks, *Uyless Black*

Other Books by Uyless Black

Computer Networks: Protocols, Standards, and Interfaces, 2/E, © 1993, 450 pp., cloth, ISBN: 1-13-175605-2

OSI: A Model for Computer Communications Standards, © 1991, 640 pp., cloth, ISBN: 0-13-637133-7

Data Networks: Concepts, Theory, and Practice, © 1989, 877 pp., cloth, ISBN: 0-13-198466-7

Data Communications and Distributed Networks, 3/E, © 1993, 448 pp., cloth, ISBN: 0-13-203464-6

Data Link Protocols, © 1993, 271 pp., cloth, ISBN: 0-13-204918-X

Emerging Communications Technologies, © 1994, 428 pp., cloth, ISBN: 0-13-051500-0

ATM: Foundation for Broadband Networks, © 1995, 426 pp., cloth, ISBN: 0-13-297178-X.

MOBILE
AND WIRELESS
NETWORKS

UYLESS BLACK

For book and bookstore information

http://www.prenhall.com

Prentice Hall PTR
Upper Saddle River, New Jersey 07458

Library of Congress Cataloging-in-Publication Data

Black, Uyless D.
   Mobile and wireless networks / by Uyless Black.
     p. cm.
   Includes bibliographical references and index.
   ISBN 0-13-440546-3
   1. Wireless communication systems. 2. Mobile communication
systems. I. Title.
   TK5103.2.B53 1996
   384.5—dc20   96-11741
                                        CIP

Acquisitions editor: Mary Franz
Cover designer: David Levavi
Cover design director: Jerry Votta
Manufacturing manager: Alexis R. Heydt
Compositor/Production services: Pine Tree Composition, Inc.

 © 1996 by Prentice Hall PTR
Prentice-Hall, Inc.
A Simon & Schuster Company
Upper Saddle River, New Jersey 07458

The publisher offers discounts on this book when ordered in
bulk quantities.

For more information, contact:
        Corporate Sales Department
        Prentice Hall PTR
        One Lake Street
        Upper Saddle River, New Jersey 07458

        Phone: 800–382–3419
        FAX: 201–236–7141
        email: corpsales@prenhall.com

Printed in the United States of America
10 9 8 7 6 5 4 3 2 1

ISBN: 0-13-440546-3

Prentice-Hall International (UK) Limited, *London*
Prentice-Hall of Australia Pty. Limited, *Sydney*
Prentice-Hall Canada, Inc., *Toronto*
Prentice-Hall Hispanoamericana, S.A., *Mexico*
Prentice-Hall of India Private Limited, *New Delhi*
Prentice-Hall of Japan, Inc., *Tokyo*
Simon & Schuster Asia Pte. Ltd., *Singapore*
Editora Prentice-Hall do Brasil, Ltda., *Rio de Janeiro*

In our ongoing activities, we come across many experiences that demonstrate that life imitates art, or that art imitates life. For the subject matter of this book we can take these ideas to another plane and state: Science imitates nature.

In our day-to-day lives, we are witness to many examples of my statement. For this book, an example of this imitation is the lowly frog and, specifically, the diminutive coqui (36 millimeters in length). This amazing amphibian displays many of the sophisticated features we find in mobile and wireless communications, which in effect, imitate the frog's communications skills.

In the tropical rain forests of Puerto Rico, where the coqui makes its home, there are many frogs in each part of the forest. Because of this population density, the coqui must share the audible frequency spectrum with other frogs. To ensure that a frog communicates effectively with another, each frog uses a variety of different frequencies when it croaks to its intended listener. In the technical words of the telecommunications industry, this little animal is capable of spectrum sharing and frequency division multiplexing. The listener is capable of filtering the extraneous signals and processing those signals that are relevant to the communications.

What is equally extraordinary, these frogs exhibit time division multiplexing capabilities. Different species "place calls" (emit croaks) at particular times of the day in order to make better use of the limited frequency spectrum, and to reduce "co-channel interference."

The coqui uses these time slots not only during a particular time of day (as just described), but during each moment of the day. Each frog knows when (and when not) to croak in order to reduce or eliminate possible interference with a neighbor in the same area of the forest. In mobile and wireless jargon, this capability is called a talk spurt. Perhaps we can dub the time division multiplexing capabilities of these frogs as "croak spurts."

In an array of experiments, scientists have used machines to simulate (in a random fashion) the sending of frog croaks within an area of the rain forest. During these experiments, it was discovered that the coqui can avoid transmitting its call when certain tones are generated by the machine. The frog dynamically adjusts its croaking rate to randomized periods of silence or nonsilence, and sends its messages in the silent periods only. If humans were so polite!

As if this adjustment to potential bandwidth "hogging" were not amazing enough, some frogs add redundancy to their transmissions just as we do in some wireless systems. Certain species of frogs can produce a "periodic stereotyped" call that exhibits redundancy in the "signals." The end result of this redundancy is that if certain frogs happen to be interfering with each other's croaks, extra information is provided in the signal to help the listener figure out the information contained in the croak.

Finally, certain frogs, such as the coqui, are tuned to the tone and characteristic periods of a specific croak. In case some frog is croaking at the same time as its neighbor, the listener can discern the desired signal from the undesired signal. In other words, these little animals have selective coders and decoders so that they can glean the relevant information in a composite accumulation of croaks.

If we pause and think for a moment about my description of this frog's communications abilities, its capabilities can be rather humbling. Our society has invested extensive research and committed an immense amount of money in developing the sophisticated technology called mobile wireless communications. Yet, in the reaches of a primitive rain forest we find that the frog has been developing and refining these communications capabilities for millions of years.

So, with all due respect to certain special people in my life to whom I normally dedicate my books, the dedication for this book is not meant to slight them. Nonetheless, this book is dedicated to that wonderful little amphibian, the frog.

As I have done in the preface to each book to this series, I issue a word of caution. Let us remember one other aspect of our journey through the mobile and wireless world and down the so-called "information highway." So much information permeates our lives—some of it useful and helpful, but much of it trivial and banal. We can benefit from observing the behavior of other creatures on this planet. The coqui has learned to filter extraneous information, and receive only what it needs.

At the risk of oversimplification, we can use this idea to observe that a "filtering" capability is one of the major challenges we face as the world accelerates its pace to provide information to us. In this information age, deciding which information is or is not important may be one of the most challenging problems we face in our quest for knowledge and understanding.

Contents

CHAPTER 5   **Channel Utilization Schemes**   **91**

CHAPTER 8   **Global System for Mobile
                    Communications (GSM)**   **176**

CHAPTER 10   **Satellite-Based Systems**   **243**

CHAPTER 11   **Data over the Mobile Link**   **258**

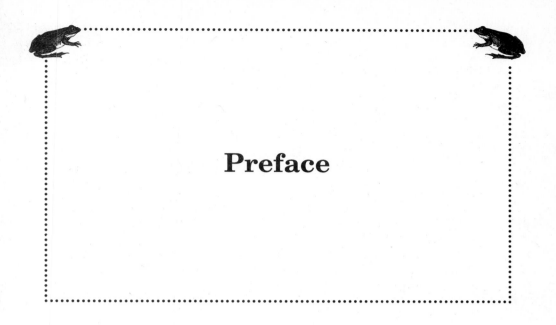

Preface

This book is the third in a series of books in the Prentice Hall series titled, "Advanced Communications Technologies." It is designed to complement the other books in this series.

I recognize that many books are available on the topic of mobile and wireless networks. After studying the offerings that are available, I concluded that most of the books in this industry concentrate on the physical aspects of the subject, such as spectrum management and cell reuse. But most of the offerings are quite terse in the descriptions of the protocols that exist to support a mobile call across the air interface.

Therefore, I decided to amplify this literature with a book that explains the physical layer, but emphasizes other aspects of mobile communications, principally the operations at the data link and network layers. I also explain in more detail the TDMA burst structures for the various technologies (DECT, GSM, PCS, etc.).

I have also devoted a full chapter to the mobile and wireless communications infrastructure that exists in the United States and a summary of the recent FCC auctions.

Mobile and wireless systems are one of the most dynamic industries in telecommunications, and their story is far from complete. However, I have attempted to bring you an up-to-date description of this technology.

I wish to thank several organizations and individuals for their support during the time that I wrote this book. LaVerne Johnson and her staff at the International Institute for Learning (ILL) in New York have sponsored several of my lectures on this subject in the United States. IBC in Europe also provided me a podium during my work "across the pond." Nortel and Nortel Technologies (formerly BNR) provided some excellent ideas and material on GSM, and I thank these organizations for their support. Bellcore's PCS views, and Pete Arnold's ideas on multi-path propagation have been quite helpful and are reflected in the PCS and channel utilization chapters respectively. The writings of George Calhoun are prerequisites for any serious reader on this subject, and I have used several of his ideas in Chapter 5 to explain channel utilization schemes.

I also wish to thank Peter M. Narins, whose article about frog communication (*Scientific American,* August 1995) provided the inspiration that led to the dedication of this book.

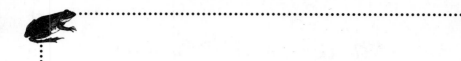

Notes for the Reader

In several chapters, I show a number of detailed examples of traffic flow between machines. I maintain consistency in the depiction of the relative positions of the mobile station and land stations. The mobile station is placed on the right side of the page, and the other stations (base station, etc.) are placed to the left. There is one exception to this practice. Since the various standards and recommendations vary on the placement of these components, I defer to their depictions in the introductory part of each chapter. In case the reader uses my book and also refers to these specifications, my approach will make it easier for you to correlate this introductory information. But for the detailed illustrations, I had to draw the line somewhere, and I think you will find this consistent format easier to follow from chapter to chapter.

Most of the material in this book (as with my other books) is based on the original specifications that deal with the subject matter, such as the ANSI, Bellcore, EIA/TIA, ITU-T, and ETSI standards/recommendations.

IS-41 (Chapter 7) cites the use of the Remote Operations Service Element (ROSE) and the Transaction Capabilities Port (TCAP). Both protocols provide transaction-based operation with invoke and result messages. As a general practice these ROSE operations are mapped into the TCAP message header. For simplicity, only the ROSE operations are depicted in the Chapter 7 figures.

After this book was completed, the draft specifications for PCS 1900 were issued by the Telecommunications Industry Association (TIA). These standards are being used for the North American deployment of PCS. They are based on the Global System for Mobile Communications (GSM) standards (Chapter 8) and define the same interfaces as GSM (see Table 8–2).

1

Introduction to Mobile and Wireless Networks

INTRODUCTION

This chapter introduces the subject of mobile and wireless systems, and provides an overview of the major systems in place today. The pros and cons of mobile and wireless systems are explained and we review several milestones in the technology. The transition to mobile systems is described in the context of paradigm shifts and the S-curve. As a prelude to other chapters, the concepts of a cell and cell reuse are introduced.

MOBILE COMMUNICATIONS—A PARADIGM SHIFT

The term paradigm has come into vogue today. It was used in the past as a scientific term, but is used today to mean a view, a perception, or a frame of reference about something [COVE89]. I have found the term to be useful in describing the ascendancy of mobile networks. Like any new popular term or concept, it risks being misused, overused, or both. Nonetheless, it applies to the subject matter of this book. The movement from fixed, wire-based communications to mobile communications surely represents a paradigm shift.

This shift should not be interpreted in the technical context alone, for it reflects profoundly how we humans communicate with each other—surely one of the more important aspects of our lives.

How did this shift come about? Simply put, it is a manifestation of our mobile information society, and the need of many individuals (sometimes real, sometimes perceived) to be in touch instantly with others.

We indeed have become "information dependent." Much of our society depends on the rapid reception and dissemination of information. Decisions on stock market purchases, dispatching emergency vehicles, responses to contractual bids, and so on, all require rapid access to automated information. In the past, fixed communications systems served all the needs of these applications. Not any longer.

The continued use of fixed wire-based communications systems as the exclusive way for making telephone calls does not meet the needs of the information society marketplace. Furthermore, in many situations, mobile systems are more effective, both from a business and a financial standpoint. To illustrate this point, we shall use the well known S-curve [ASTH95] and correlate it with the concept of the paradigm shift.

The S-curve has been used for over twenty-five years to keep track of a technology as a function of research and development (R&D) effort and time. It is also used to make decisions on whether an enterprise should continue the use of a technology or replace the technology with something else (usually a new technology). In addition, it is used to plot the effectiveness of a technology in relation to its market penetration. In effect, it is used to determine if the continued use of an ongoing technology needs to be reassessed, if a new frame of reference or model is in order; that is, if a paradigm shift is needed.

We will use the S-curve and the idea of the paradigm shift to describe why mobile communications are successful and why they will continue to be successful—at the expense of wire-based communications systems. Be aware that the initial part of this discussion is focused on the wireless air interface between the user's handset and a public switched telephone network (PSTN). We are not discussing communications within a PSTN, which is wire-based (optical fiber, etc.). Later, I will focus on the PSTN.

Figure 1–1 is a plot of three S-curves reflecting the fixed, wire-based, and mobile, wireless user handset interfaces into the PSTN. The effectiveness of wire-based handsets (for many users' needs) has reached the flat part in the S-curve, labeled A. The curve's changing from concave to flat (or even convex) means that (1) a new technology is needed, or (2) users and implementators must be content with the old technology.

By the way, some organizations would choose option (2) due to the uncertainty of committing to a new technology, and some individual consumers are beginning to resist the continued movement to other (and sometimes harder to use) products.

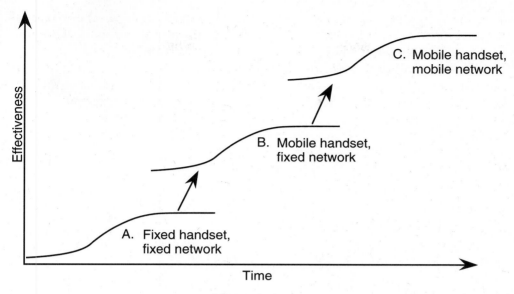

Figure 1–1
The S curves.

The arrow in Figure 1–1 between A and B represents a paradigm shift that occurred in the early 1980s with the introduction of commercial cellular systems. For a large segment of our society, the emergence and subsequent use of these mobile systems has provided a better means of communications. By jumping to this new S-curve, people have faster access from a mobile phone to other communications networks, notably the PSTN.

The shift to mobile communications also reflects the human race's immutable quest for convenience. Since the first tool was invented, we have continued to populate our lives with more tools to make our existence easier. Mobile phones are a good example of this quest.

With mobile communications, we no longer have to "go to the phone"—the phone comes to us. We no longer have to install phone jacks every few feet in our homes and business—there is no jack. We no longer need a phone in every room—one mobile phone acts for many fixed phones.

The previous phrase—"one mobile phone acts for many fixed phones"—is good news and bad news. It is good news for the consumer, who buys phones. It is bad news for the vendor, who sells phones, and here is where the S-curve comes into play once again. In several affluent, industrialized countries, the fixed-phone market sales has flattened out. Sales for phones and fixed network switches are becoming less profitable.

As a consequence, prescient manufacturers are moving their plants, R&D efforts, and sales forces to other countries (notably China and India) where the S-curve for mobile (and fixed systems) is still rising.

But in the United States, resting on the fixed-phone S-curve for too long may spell doom for a company. It is well-understood that in today's fast-moving and highly competitive environment, the company that rests for too long on its technical laurels may discover that it is technically obsolete and irrelevant to the information society.

What Comes after Mobile Phones?

If we assume the S-curve labeled B in Figure 1–1 will flatten or become convex, then what is next? Shall we witness someday "technology-saturation" with a shift to a reverse S-curve? I think not, but no one knows.

At any rate, some companies have already shifted to a new S-curve, labeled C in Figure 1–1. Instead of using mobile handsets that are connected to the fixed telephone network (PSTN), these companies believe another paradigm shift is needed: mobile handsets connected to mobile networks, with the network operations residing in mobile, orbiting satellites. In essence, the fixed telephone network is bypassed completely. Chapter 10 explains this subject in more detail.

Where will it end? Will the "handset" prove to be too heavy, too inconvenient? Perhaps a fourth S-curve will be to a microchip-based phone strapped to our wrist or attached to our head [VISO95].

I was discussing this subject with an acquaintance who delights in putting her own spin on most conversations. Her response was that the "ultimate" S-curve for mobile communications is not phone at all—but what the mystics have long held to be true: mental telepathy!

My prosaic mind is not able to make so great a leap, but it is interesting to contemplate.[1] On a more serious plane, whatever the outcome, mobile communications will continue to alter and shape our professional and personal lives.

With this background in mind, let us take a look at some earlier mobile and wireless systems and then examine today's modern wireless communications infrastructure.

---

[1]While writing this part of the book, I saw a delightful TV commercial sponsored by IBM. It shows a group of contemplating monks exercising their mental telepathy powers in their communications with each other. One monk complains that some others are "contemplating too hard or too 'loudly'," and disturbing his thoughts.

SOME HISTORICAL MILESTONES

It may surprise the reader to know that commercial mobile systems appeared on the horizon some time ago. Indeed, they are over fifty years old. On April 7, 1928, the first mobile radio system went into operation in Detroit. It was used by the Detroit Police Department and is considered the world's first successful system.

By 1935, frequency modulation (FM) had been developed and tested (by Edmond H. Armstrong). It proved to be a much superior technology to amplitude modulation (AM) because it was robust in handling noise problems. AM suffers from impulse noise (noise spikes), which is quite common in electromagnetic-based systems.

The early systems (around the 1950s) required enormous bandwidth. A 120 kHz spectrum was required to transmit a voice circuit that consisted of only 3 kHz. However, by the 1960s the FM receiver design had been improved and the required bandwidth was reduced to 30 kHz. Obviously, the reduction of bandwidth requirements meant that more channels could be utilized across the limited spectrum space.

During World War II, extensive use was made of FM technology, and mobile radios were used throughout the war zones for mobile FM communications. Immediately after the war, AT&T developed and introduced the Improved Mobile Telephone Service (IMTS) (Figure 1–2). It consisted of a broadcast system with a high-power transmitter. Typically, the system was set up to operate in a metropolitan area. This system was followed shortly with limited cellular networks and the implementation of the first mobile radio system to connect with a fixed telephone number.

In the 1950s, paging systems began to appear. During this period, Bell Labs continued to test the cellular techniques, which came to fruition in 1970 when the Federal Communication Commission (FCC) allocated spectrum space for cellular systems. At this time, AT&T proposed the cellular system that is now known as the Advanced Mobile Phone System (AMPS). The technology of cellular service (also see Figure 1–2) as we know it today in the United States actually began in 1983 with services implemented commercially in Chicago and Baltimore.

MAJOR SYSTEMS

As shown in Figure 1–3, the wireless communications industry in the United States is very diverse. It consists of systems such as microwave, satellites, mobile phones, and infrared-based local area networks. One

**From this:**

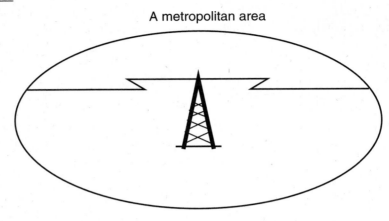

**To this:**

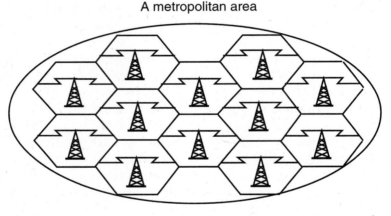

Figure 1–2
Improved Mobile Telephone Service (IMTS) and cellular service.

of the biggest challenges is finding a way to analyze these diverse systems. With this in mind, Figure 1–3 depicts one method to classify wireless systems. It is based on the FCC classification scheme, and will be used throughout this book.

In cellular radio-telephone service, also called commercial mobile radio service, geographic areas are split into smaller areas, called cells (see the lower part of Figure 1–2). Within noncontiguous cells, allo-

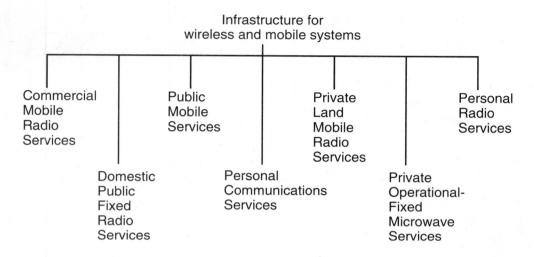

Figure 1–3
Classification of mobile services.

cated frequencies can be reused. These systems are implemented in many parts of the world (and especially in the United States and Canada) with the well-known AMPS that was installed throughout North America in the early 1980s. However, the world's first cellular mobile service was implemented in Japan in 1979.

Domestic public fixed radio services are point-to-point microwave radio services, such as conventional microwave systems, satellite systems, TV systems, and systems for U.S. government departments/agencies. In the United States, the FCC establishes many rules and guidelines on the use of public fixed radio services. As one example, frequency assignments to common carriers are described as part of this FCC operation. Also, since the frequency spectrum is limited and must be managed with care, public fixed radio services are often shared with earth and satellite systems. So, this part of the U.S. wireless infrastructure includes FCC rules on how the frequencies are shared with stations supporting fixed-satellite and private-operational fixed microwave services.

The term public mobile services might mean to the reader that it includes conventional cellular services, but it does not. I just explained where conventional cellular services fit into the U.S. wireless infrastructure. Public mobile services in the United States include paging systems, rural radio-telephone service, air-to-ground service, and offshore service.[2]

Perhaps the best-known aspect of public mobile services are paging services, which entail the use of short coded signals that are sent to a small receiver. The receiver is activated by a signal with its specific code.

Personal communications service (PCS) is a relatively new addition to the wireless services. PCS is a broad concept, but generally, the service operates at low power and uses small cells to accommodate a mobile unit that is slow-moving (a person). Interestingly, the term "service" in PCS is not defined concisely by the FCC (or for that matter most anyone). In practice, PCS is a wireless telephone service, much like our current cellular telephone system. However, while its implementation and use may not be discernible from current mobile systems to the end user, it uses different and more effective technologies. In the United States, frequencies for PCS have been allocated for the narrowband and broadband spectrum. These allocations are explained later in this book (see Chapter 3), and Chapter 9 is devoted to a full explanation of PCS.

Private land mobile radio (PMR) services include industrial radio services, such as the power, petroleum, forest products, film and video production, and newspaper industries. These closed community systems have provided low-cost, two-way support to meet the specific needs of these types of industries, mainly for dispatch operations. Taxis, couriers, utility companies, and so on have reaped many benefits from the PMR systems. Other countries have established PMR systems (which are also called specialized mobile radio [SMR] in some of these countries).

Private operational-fixed microwave services (OFS) are the well-known private wireless systems that operate point-to-point, or point-to-multipoint. Microwave systems operate in the 900 MHz to 31 GHz bands,

---

[2]It is fruitless to question the rationale for the classification of the U.S. wireless infrastructure. Much of it rests on the evolution of the industry, its technical innovations, and the political climate at the time the rules were made. Nowhere is this more evident than in public mobile services, where we see restrictions/freedoms on local exchange carriers (LECs): They may be "state-certified." In some situations, they are allowed to hold authorizations for these licenses.

depending on the type of system installed. Usually, operators are given licenses based on a first-come, first-served basis. They are widely used by banks, utility companies, schools, alarm companies, and the like due to their prices and flexibility. Initially, these systems were limited to "not-for-profit" use. The spectrum space and system can now be treated as an asset by the owner and resold on a profit basis.

Personal radio services, more commonly known as interactive video and data service (IVDS) is a relatively new regulated service. The FCC created this service in 1992. It is intended that IVDS will provide the basis for a wide variety of services, such as video-on-demand, interactive participation in polling activities, on-line shopping, and interactive banking. The allocation of the frequency spectrum for IVDS is also part of the FCC auctions and is explained in Chapter 3.

THE CELLULAR INDUSTRY

All cellular systems employ the use of fixed cells, which is a defined geographical area in which a relatively low-power transmitter is employed to send signals to receivers operating within the cell. The principal differences between cellular systems are in their use of the frequency spectrum and the spacing between the channels. Table 1–1 provides a summary of the more widely used systems and their subscriber bases. The AMPS is implemented in over forty countries, with the main subscriber base in the United States. The Total Access Communications System (TACS) has its largest subscriber base in the United Kingdom, and operates in twenty other countries. The Nordic Mobile Telephone system (NMT) is implemented as NMT450 and NMT 900 and found mostly in the Nordic countries, although it has presence in thirty-one countries. The 450 system is installed mainly in Germany.

The digital systems are relatively new, but are experiencing wide and rapid acceptance. The Global System for Mobile Communications (GSM) has seen the most use because of its acceptance in Europe. The PDC (Personal Digital Cellular) system is being deployed in Japan. The Digital Cellular System-1800 (DCS-1800) uses GSM protocols, but operates in the 1800 MHz spectrum. Finally, time division multiple access (TDMA) is experiencing very rapid growth. (GSM uses TDMA techniques; TDMA is broken out separately here because it is another standard).

Table 1–1   Cellular Systems

A. World Subscriber Growth (millions of subscribers) 1994–1995

	6/95	*12/94*
Europe	18.5	14.7
Asia-Pacific	15.6	11.1
North America	28.2	26.0
South/Central America	3.0	2.4
Middle East	0.5	0.4
Africa	0.6	0.3
Total	66.4	54.9

B. Technology Use (millions of subscribers): 1994–1995

	6/95	*12/94*
Analog		
AMPS	35.5	32.4
TACS	12.3	9.5
NMT-450	1.4	1.4
NMT-900	3.0	2.7
NTT	2.3	1.9
Others	0.9	1.0
Subtotal	55.4	49.3
Digital		
GSM	7.4	4.6
PDC	1.5	0.5
DCS-1800	0.6	0.4
TDMA	1.5	1.0
Subtotal	11.0	6.0
Total	66.4	54.9

Source: European Mobile Communications (EMC), PCS-1900 Conference, 12/95, Washington, DC.

WHAT WAS IT LIKE BEFORE MOBILE PHONES?

Let us pause for a moment and reflect on the technical innovations that have occurred in the last few years that span say, five generations. I will use my family as a model. You may be older or younger than I, but this model fits most family pedigrees.

Consider that (1) as youths, my great-grandparents did not have access to the radio; (2) for my grandparents, the telephone was not available to them until they were old; (3) my parents did not have television until they were in their later years (and when available, it was not allowed into our home until all their children were gone. One of my cultural gaps is my lack of knowledge about the Mouseketeers); (4) I grew up without mobile phones; and (5) my son takes them for granted.

It will be interesting to learn how my son replies to his children when they ask, "Daddy, what was it like before mobile phones?"[3]

This brief interlude was made to make a point: Technology is changing rapidly, and each succeeding generation is consuming one or more new "revolutionary" approaches to communications. Thus, our society seems to be shifting with increasing frequency from one S-curve to another and embracing technologies more quickly. Let us take a look at some statistics depicted in Figure 1–4 that support this claim.

TECHNOLOGIES IN THE MARKETPLACE

The birth of new technologies and the rate of their acceptance in the marketplace is occurring at an accelerating rate. Mobile communications systems are no exception.

New consumer electronics technologies are being accepted in a much shorter timeframe than earlier systems. Figure 1–4 shows the number of years it took for several "new" technologies to reach the 500,000 and one million user range. It took almost twenty years for the consumer population to purchase one million black and white television sets. But, it took only eight years, after the introduction of the color TV, for one million color TVs to be sold. And, it took a much shorter period of time for the number of users to reach one million for VCRs, personal computers, and cellular telephones. According to market researchers, it will take less than one year to sell one million PCS systems, and Bellcore projections indicate that PCS users will number about 46 million by the year 2005 [SHER95].

---

[3]Several years ago I asked my Dad (a cattle rancher in New Mexico who worked the herds as far back as 1915) what it was like before the phone. His reply was interesting: Sudden on-a-whim conversations did not happen between neighbors who lived some ten miles away. No one in their right mind rode a horse or walked this distance to say, "Hello, I thought I would drop by for a chat." On the other hand, when the neighbors did meet, I gathered the "information content" of the conversations was pretty high.

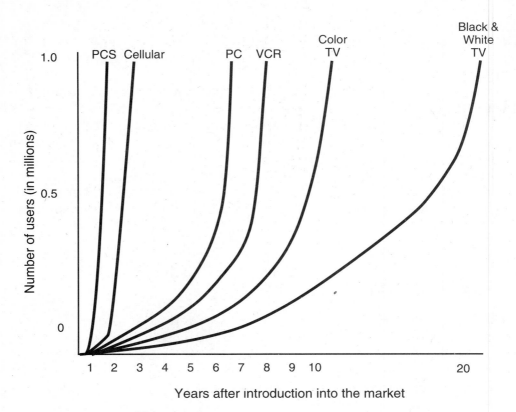

Figure 1–4
Consumer acceptance of technologies.

Predictions for use of wireless services vary, depending upon who is doing the predicting. As another example, the BIS Strategic Decisions' projections for the wireless service revenues in the United States are depicted in Figure 1–5. At the end of 1993, analog cellular systems were tracked; at the end of 1994, digital cellular (large cell) systems were added, and beginning in 1995, PCS (small cell) systems will be added. The study is projected through 1998 and shows a gradual decrease in the use of analog technology.

Other industry predictions on the projected growth of PCS are less modest, and predict that revenues could at least double the figures projected in this early analysis. Only time will tell, but all forecasts point to rapid acceptance of the technology.

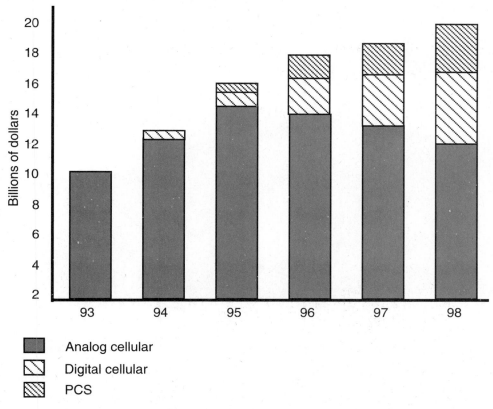

Analog cellular
Digital cellular
PCS

Figure 1–5
Ongoing use and an early projection of wireless service revenues.

We have discussed some reasons for the ascendancy of the mobile communications systems. Let us now take a more detailed look at their advantages (and disadvantages).

The growth of cellular usage during the last four years has been almost exponential, with the market almost doubling each successive year. Figure 1–6 shows the growth curve, plotted since 1989.

At year end 1994, there were 55 million cellular subscribers. At year end 1995, there were 87 million subscribers. Many forecasts have been made about what the subscriber base may be by the end of the century. The forecasts vary by an order of magnitude, because no one knows how deeply the technology will penetrate into the population in each country.

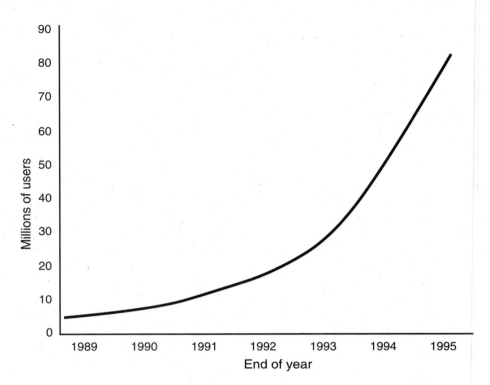

Figure 1–6
World cellular subscriber growth   (Source: European Mobile
Communications (EMC), PCS-1900 Conference, 12/95, Washington, DC).

In some countries, the penetration rate is very low. In others it is quite
high. Sweden has the highest penetration rate, about 25 percent of its
population are cellular subscribers—an extraordinary number when we
consider that 1 in 4 Swedes have a cellular phone.

ADVANTAGES AND DISADVANTAGES OF MOBILE SYSTEMS

Figure 1–7 summarizes some of the principal benefits derived from mobile systems as well as some of the problems entailed in using them.
First, users are not constrained to fixed locations when using mobile sys-

Pros:
- Users are not constrained to fixed locations
- Immediate access to services, regardless of person's location
- Physical cabling (trenches, access lines, digging, physical rights-of-way) are not an issue:

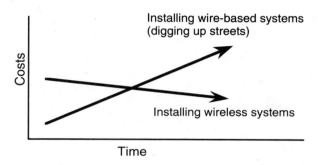

Cons:
- Limited frequency spectrum
- Complex technologies
- Security/privacy issues and authentication requirements
- Power supply for the small portable units
- Quality of signals ("hostile" environment)

Figure 1–7
Mobile systems: pros and cons.

tems. Since the handset can be carried anywhere for use where there is an access node to the mobile network, a user has immediate access to services. (This is also a disadvantage. In many instances, the ubiquitous mobile telephones are an annoyance and a nuisance in certain environments.) Perhaps one of the most important benefits that accrues to the use of mobile systems is the fact that the immense expense and inconvenience of physically cabling systems through and under streets, across byways, across rights-of-way are simply not an issue. In the long run, this latter feature leads to dramatically reduced costs in the ongoing installation and maintenance of communications systems.

There are disadvantages to almost all aspects of life, and mobile systems are no exception. The technologies are quite complex due to the hostile environments of open space (air interfaces) and the somewhat unpredictable terrain and topology over which the signals must travel. Wireless systems must accommodate to a wide array of conditions, both from the standpoint of weather and physical layouts. Of course, all radio technologies are constrained by the use of limited frequency spectrums. Only so much bandwidth is available in the wireless frequency range. Therefore, careful conservation and management of the bandwidth is essential for the effective use of the technology.

It is evident that the installation of wire-based systems is quite labor intensive. In addition, very few enterprises can venture into the wired-world because of the necessary restrictions on installing wires or cables in most geographical areas. Therefore, unless one has rights-of-way through a city or countryside, wire-based systems are usually owned by public telecommunications operators (PTOs), such as telephone companies. Even with these companies, the costs of installing wire-based systems is very high.

Figure 1–8 represents one of many studies made on the costs of wire-based installations vs. wireless installations [MASO94]. It shows that the costs are related to the distance from the telephone company's central office (CO) for wire-based systems. Of course, for wireless systems, distance is not a factor as long as the communicating units are reachable.

While other studies vary in the exact ratio of cost versus distance, they all support the supposition that wire-based systems are more expensive to install and maintain than wireless systems.

THE AUCTIONS

In the past, the Federal Communications Commission (FCC) has released spectrum space to public and private enterprises without compensation, or with small compensation. The spectrum was considered to be rented temporarily, while remaining in the ownership of the government (the public). This approach has changed and beginning in 1994, the FCC established programs to sell spectrum space to the highest bidder. This operation is known collectively as the FCC auctions.

While the auctions are bringing in substantial amounts of money, many of the companies that won a bid have failed to raise the necessary capital and their licenses have been placed back in the pool. The FCC has not actually "deposited" all the money that is listed in the auction figures (in Chapter 3).

In addition, the auction provides preferences for small businesses, minorities, and female-owned firms. These groups have been successful in bidding on some (but not all) of the licenses because of this preferen-

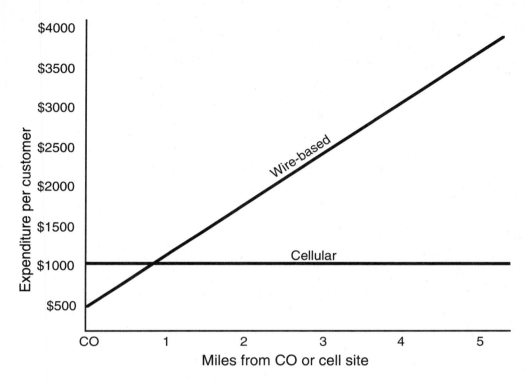

Figure 1–8
Capital expenditures per customer for wired and wireless systems. [MASO94]

tial program. This program policy has come under fire recently due to changes in the political and social climate.

After extensive planning and debating, the FCC began the auctioning of PCS spectrum space in July 1994. During that month, auctions were completed for Interactive Video and Data Services (IVDS). This was a first auction; others followed. The FCC granted two licenses in the 218-219 MHz band in 734 service areas. The FCC reaped $216 M in this first auction of 297 markets.

Also in July 1994, the first auction was conducted for the National Narrowband PCS (advanced national two-way paging) service. Ten licenses were granted in the 901-941 MHz band. In October 1994, auctions were conducted for Regional Narrowband PCS (advanced regional paging, covering one-fifth of the United States). A total of thirty licenses were sold. The auctions for Broadband PCS began in December 1994, and continued into 1995. A total of 74 applicants bid for these licenses. Chapters 3 and 9 provide more detailed information on the auctions.

INTRODUCTION TO MAJOR WIRELESS MOBILE SYSTEMS

This section provides an introduction to the major mobile systems that are in operation, or that will be installed during the next few years. Subsequent chapters will expand considerably on this brief overview.

AMPS was developed by AT&T after the FCC allocated spectrum space for cellular systems. It was implemented in 1983, when providers in Chicago and Baltimore got their systems on line. AMPS is an analog-based technology, and defines the operations between the mobile station and the land station, which is usually called a base station.

IS-41 is widely used in the United States. It defines operations on the network side of a cellular system (it is comparable to GSM's MAP). It is a partner to AMPS, in that it manages all the cellular operations from the base (land) station back to various control stations, location registers, and the fixed-wire exchanges.

The Global System for Mobile Communications (GSM) is a new-generation standard that is being deployed in several parts of the world, notably Europe and the Far East. It is also beginning to be accepted in North America as well, and some providers have selected GSM to support PCS services in the United States. Unlike AMPS, which is an analog technology, GSM uses digital technology.

CT2 is a cordless telephony system that has seen varying degrees of success (failure in UK, success in Hong Kong). Some companies are using CT2 or CT2 Plus inside their buildings. DECT is a similar technology to CT2, and in some countries is viewed as a "competitor" to CT2. Like CT2, it has seen limited (but growing) success, and has been implemented in some parts of the world. CT3 is another cordless system that has seen limited use. In contrast to CT2, which is based on analog technology, CT3 uses digital time division multiplexing techniques (TDMA).

IS-54 is a cellular time division multiple access (TDMA) standard, that has seen some deployment (beginning in 1993). It has more capacity than AMPS, and will eventually replace some of the AMPS systems. IS-136 is also a TDMA specification. It is new and has not yet seen wide use. It is an enhanced IS-54 system, and is intended to supersede IS-54.

IS-95 is a relatively new specification for dual-mode code division multiple access (CDMA) radio systems. IS-54, IS-136, and IS-95 are candidates for use in the PCS arena.

INTRODUCTION TO THE CELL CONCEPT

Many of the systems covered in this book are implemented with the cell technology. As explained earlier, a cell is a geographical area with a low-power transmitter. The mobile telephone in the automobile, truck, or on a person communicates with the transmitter through an "air interface," which in turn communicates with a unit that is an extension of the telephone central office.

As the mobile station passes through the network, the user is assigned a frequency for use during the transit through each cell. Since each cell has its own low-power transmitter, the signals are distance-limited. Consequently, signals in nonadjacent groups of cells do not interfere with each other. So, a group of non-contiguous cells can use (reuse) the same frequencies.

As Figure 1–9 shows, one attractive aspect of cellular technology is that the frequency reuse pattern permits a more efficient allocation of the limited spectrum space. A system that uses small cells can provide more circuits per square mile than a system that uses no cells (or large cells). The reuse pattern is noted as N, where N represents the frequency reuse pattern; that is, how many cells are associated with a group. Within a group, each cell uses different frequencies, but these frequencies can be reused in the cells of another group. In this figure, N = 7.

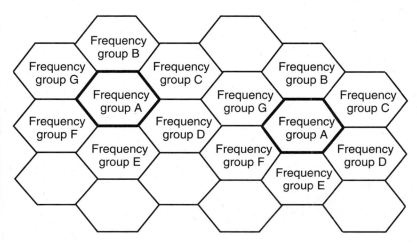

Figure 1–9
Concepts of cells and cell reuse. (N cells in a group = 7).

SUMMARY

Commercial mobile wireless systems are a recent entry into the telecommunications world. Wireless systems are complex, but have significant cost advantages over wire-based systems. In the United States, the Federal Communications Commission (FCC) controls the allocation of the wireless spectrum space. Recent auctions are intended to open new vistas for "personal" communications services, and interactive voice and data services.

2

Basics of Mobile
and Wireless Systems

INTRODUCTION

This chapter provides a basic tutorial on key aspects of mobile and wireless systems. In addition, wire-based systems are explained and compared to wireless systems. The characteristics of voice, analog, and digital signals are compared, and the frequency spectrum is explained. The more advanced reader can skip this chapter and not suffer any ill effects.

WIRE-BASED SYSTEMS

The telephones in our homes and offices are connected through local loops to a local facilities network that consists of switching gear located at office centers. The actual building is called a wire center, which services a wire center area. The customers in a wire center area communicate with each other through the wire center.

Typically, the telephones in our homes and offices transmit the voice, data, and other images to and from the telephone network in the format of analog signals. Increasingly, digital techniques are being used both within the telephone network and at the local loop interfaces.

Telephone users, either in homes or offices, connect through the telephone system into the central office (CO), local exchange, or end office. Thousands of these offices may be installed around a country.

Connection is provided to the CO through a pair of copper wires (or four wires) called the local loop or subscriber loop.

The use of direct or indirect connections between offices with tandem trunks or other tandem switching systems depends on several factors: distances between offices, the traffic volume between offices, and the potential for sharing facilities among the customers within the geographical area. In the case of intermediate traffic volumes or longer distances, the telephone system generally establishes a combination of direct and tandem links.

The system is built around high-usage trunks (or high-volume trunks), which carry the bulk of the traffic. High-usage trunks are established when the volume of calls warrants the installation of high-capacity channels between two offices. Consequently, trunk configurations vary depending on traffic volume between centers.

The local loops emanating from businesses and buildings that have many tenants are configured for either analog or digital transmission. Typically, the lines are analog if for conventional dial-up services and digital if dedicated lines are leased from the local exchange carrier. Twisted pair cable is gradually being replaced with optical fiber in many buildings.

With very few exceptions, the long-haul trunks that comprise the media between telephone switching facilities use digital transmission technology. In addition, optical fiber has become the preferred method for sending traffic, due to its large information carrying capacity. Microwave is also widely used for long-haul transmissions between the switching facilities.

Increasingly, the "local loops" are being enhanced (or replaced) with wireless media, which is the subject of this book.

WIRELESS SYSTEMS

Wireless systems use the atmosphere for the transmission media. Radio signals are sent across this media through an electromagnetic signal. Electromagnetic radiation is created by inducing a current of sufficient amplitude into an antenna whose dimensions are approximately the same as the wavelength of the generated signal. The signal can be generated uniformly (like a light bulb) or can be directed as a beam of energy (like a spotlight).

The radio signals are radiant waves of energy transmitted into space. The signals are similar to that of heat or light. In a vacuum, they travel at the speed of light (186,000 miles or 297,000 kilometers per sec-

Table 2–1   Radio Frequency Bands

Classification Band	Initials	Frequency Range
Extremely low	ELF	Below 300 Hz
Infra low	ILF	300 Hz–3 kHz
Very low	VLF	3 kHz–30 kHz
Low	LF	30 kHz–300 kHz
Medium	MF	300 kHz–3 MHz
High	HF	3 MHz–30 MHz
Very high	VHF	30 MHz–300 MHz
Ultra high	UHF	300 MHz–3 GHz
Super high	SHF	3 GHz–30 GHz
Extremely high	EHF	30 GHz–300 GHz
Tremendously high	THF	300 GHZ–3000 GHz

ond). Due to the resistance of media, (such as cable, air, or water) signal waves travel at a rate slower than the theoretical maximum. The radio frequency spectrum is divided and classified by frequency bands as shown in Table 2–1.

As depicted in Figure 2–1, the radio wave and transmitting antenna are designed around the following operations: (1) ground or surface wave, (2) space wave, (3) sky wave, or (4) satellite-based wave.

The surface or ground wave is characterized by its propagation along the lower edge of the earth's surface. In effect, it follows the curvature of the earth. This signal is used generally in the low frequency bands (30 kHz–300 kHz). It is also used for broadcasting in the medium frequency band (300 kHz–3MHz).

The long wavelengths of ground waves are relatively immune to terrestrial topography. For example, a 30-kHz signal has a wavelength of 6.2 miles (10,000 meters). Buildings or mountains do not affect the signal very much. However, a higher frequency signal will experience distortion and breakup from trees, mountains, and large buildings.

The space wave travels in a straight line between the transmitting and receiving antenna. It is considered to be a line of sight transmission (a direct wave). In addition, it has a component that travels by reflecting from the earth. This type of signal is used principally in TV broadcasting operation in the VHF/UHF/SHF frequency bands.

The sky wave is transmitted upward into the ionosphere. Based on the ionospheric conditions, the signal or a portion of it is returned to

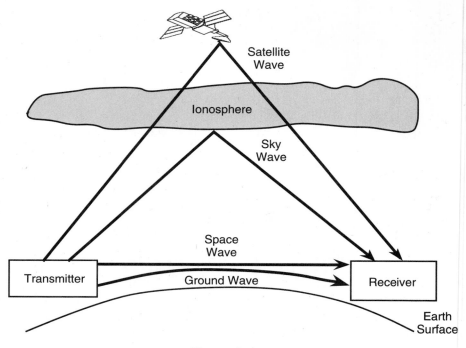

Figure 2–1
Radio waves.

earth and received at the ground station. This type of transmission is commonly used for high frequency radio communications devices (3 MHz–30 MHz). It has seen rather extensive use in radio broadcasting and long distance telephone operations.

The satellite wave method uses a radio frequency transmitted to a satellite station that is amplified and then transmitted back down to earth at a different frequency. This technique is discussed in more detail later in this chapter and in Chapter 10.

Microwave is a directed line-of-sight radio transmission (see Figure 2–2). It is used for radar and wideband communications systems and is quite common in the telephone system. In fact, many long-distance telephone trunks use microwave transmission. The first commercial microwave system was used across the English Channel. In 1931 in Dover, England, the International Telephone Company implemented this microwave system.

Microwave covers a wide range of the frequency spectrum. Typically, frequencies range from 2 to 40 GHz, although most systems

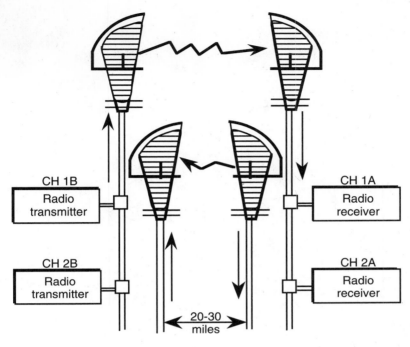

**Figure 2–2
A microwave system.**

operate in the range of 2 to 18 GHz. The data rate is greater at the higher frequencies. For example, a data rate of 12 Mbit/s can be obtained on a 2 GHz band microwave system, yet a data rate of 274 Mbit/s is possible on a 18 GHz band system.

Television transmission also utilizes microwave transmission, because microwave provides the capacity required for video transmission. The high bandwidth gives a small wavelength and the smaller the wavelength, the smaller one can design the microwave antenna. Microwave is very effective for transmission to remote locations. For example, Canada has one of the most extensive systems in the world, and the former Soviet Union has placed microwave systems in such remote areas as Siberia. Several U.S. carriers' primary product line is the offering of voice-grade channels on their microwave facilities.

Satellite communications are unique from other media for several reasons (see Figure 2–3). The technology provides for a large communica-

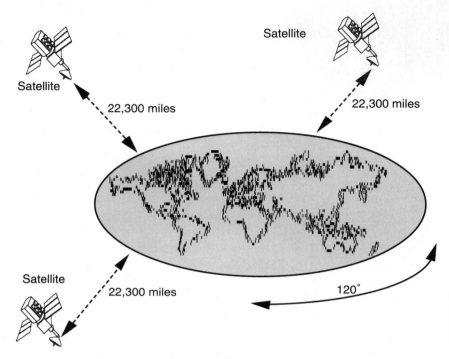

Figure 2–3
Geosynchronous satellites.

tions capacity. Through the use of the microwave frequency bands, several thousand voice grade channels can be placed on a satellite station.

The satellite has the capacity for a broadcast transmission. The transmitting antenna can send signals to a wide geographical area and any station tuned to the proper frequency can receive the signal. Applications such as electronic mail and distributed systems find the broadcast capability quite useful.

Transmission cost is independent of distance between the earth sites. For example, it is immaterial if two sites are 100 or 1000 miles apart as long as they are serviced by the same communications satellite. The signals transmitted from the satellite can be received by all stations, regardless of their distance from each other.

The stations experience a significant signal propagation delay. Since some satellites are positioned 22,300 miles above the earth, the transmission has to travel into space and return. A round trip transmission requires a minimum of about 240 milliseconds (ms), and could be greater as the signal travels through other components. This may affect certain applications or software systems.

The broadcast aspect of satellite communications may present security problems, since all stations under the satellite antenna can receive the broadcasts. Consequently, transmissions are often changed (encrypted) for satellite channels.

Many satellites are in a geosynchronous orbit. They rotate around the earth at 6900 miles/hour and remain positioned over the same point above the equator. Thus, the earth stations' antenna can remain in one position since the satellite's motion relative to the earth's position is fixed. Furthermore, a single geosynchronous satellite with nondirectional antenna can cover about 30 percent of the earth's surface. The geosynchronous orbit requires a rocket launch of 22,300 miles into space. Geosynchronous satellites can achieve worldwide coverage (some limited areas in the polar regions are not covered) with three satellites spaced at 120-degree intervals from each other.

INFRARED SYSTEMS

The use of infrared frequencies for short-haul transmission is another option that has proved quite successful for some applications (see Figure 2–4). The system is built around optical transceivers that transmit and receive at relatively short distances (approximately one mile maximum).

Infrared has several attractive features. First, the signals are not subject to microwave interference, and the FCC does not require the

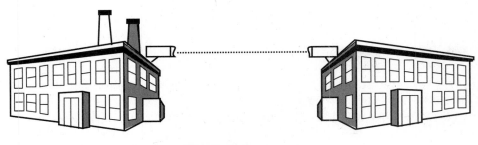

Figure 2–4
Infrared systems.

users to obtain permission to use the frequency spectrum. Second, unlike hardwire systems, infrared requires no cable-pulling, and consequently, the user may not have to obtain rights-of-way for the infrared installation. Third, the systems are relatively inexpensive and easy to install. Fourth, the systems operate at relatively high data rates, typically in the Mbit/s range.

However, the distance is limited to about one mile due to a myriad of factors. The signal experiences scattering due to fog, smog, and dust. It can also experience shimmer due to air temperature variations that change the reflective index of the air. Rain will also cause a distortion of the signal. Notwithstanding, infrared works quite well for special, short-distance applications.

CELLULAR RADIO

Cellular radio was conceived as a terrestrial voice telephone network. Its purpose is to upgrade the existing mobile radio-telephone system. The idea goes back to 1972 when the FCC recognized that the demand for mobile telephones was exceeding the frequencies available.

The FCC then opened up frequencies, initially in the 800-900 MHz band, and schemes were developed to reuse the same frequencies in the same geographical vicinity. In 1979, a prototype network was built in Chicago by AT&T. In a few short years, cellular radio has grown to reach all metropolitan areas, and systems are being developed for nationwide service.

As depicted in Figure 2–5, a cellular radio network is structured around the concepts of "cells." Each cell is a geographical area with a low power transmitter. The mobile telephone in the automobile, truck, or whatever communicates with the transmitter, which in turn communicates with the Mobile Telephone Switching Office (MTSO). The MTSO is an extension of the telephone central office, and the mobile channel appears to be the same as a wire line to the stored program control (SPC) logic at the telephone office.

As the mobile unit passes through the network, the user is assigned a frequency for use during transit through each cell. Since each cell has its own transmitter, the signals for nonadjacent cells do not interfere with each other. As a consequence, the noncontiguous cells can use the same frequencies. The base station operates with a transmitter of about 10 W to the mobile station (the forward path), but the mobile station op-

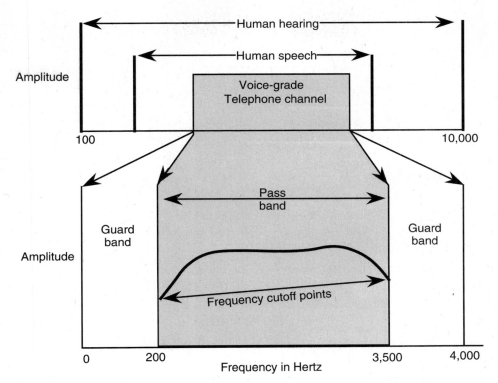

Figure 2–9
Hearing, speech, and voiceband channels.

THE FREQUENCY SPECTRUM

The greater the bandwidth, the greater the capacity. As seen in Figure 2–10, the frequency spectrum ranges from the relatively limited ranges of the audio frequencies through the radio ranges, the infrared ranges, the visible light frequencies, and up to the x-ray and cosmic ray band. The importance of the higher frequencies can readily be seen by an examination of the bandwidth of the audio-frequency spectrum and that of radio. The bandwidth between 10^3 and 10^4 is 9,000 Hz (10,000 − 1,000 = 9,000), which is roughly the equivalent to three voice-grade bands. The bandwidth between 10^7 and 10^8 (the HF and VHF spectrum) is 90,000,000 Hz (100,000,000 − 10,000,000 = 90,000,000), which could support several thousand voice-band circuits.

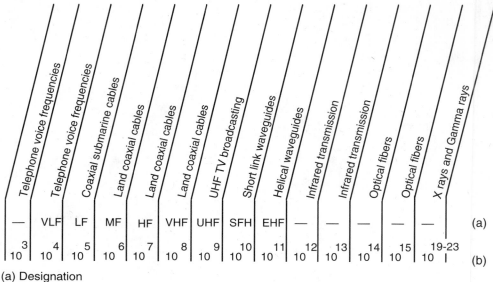

(a) Designation
(b) Frequency

Figure 2–10
The frequency spectrum (another view).

THE DIGITAL SIGNAL

In contrast to analog signals that convey voice transmissions, digital signals represent discrete signal states of one and zero, ON/OFF, true/false. Since computer signals use binary schemes where the bits are coded as one or zero, digital signalling is an ideal scheme for the transmission of computer traffic. Figure 2–11 shows an example of one form of digital signaling.

In the simplest digital systems and interfaces, a zero is represented by a positive voltage of (for example) at least +3 volts and a 1 is represented by (for example) a negative voltage of at least −3 volts. This convention is used in EIA-232-E. This simple scheme is sufficient to provide the digital signals to create codes such as the binary code for NAK or the binary code for EOT simply by altering the voltage level within a computer or on a transmission media.

However, since many of the transmission media are telephone circuits designed for analog transmission, it is obvious that using a digital signal on a basically analog medium presents a rather interesting chal-

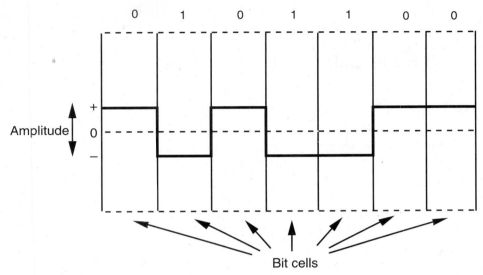

- Discrete signals
- "Abrupt" signal changes (voltage shifts)
- Well-suited for data transmission

Figure 2–11
Digital signal: major characteristics.

lenge. This situation is certainly the case for wireless systems, which must make use of airwaves to send information.

We shall have more to say about using the digital signal on analog circuits later in this book.

BROADBAND AND BASEBAND SIGNALS

Signals are usually categorized as either broadband or baseband. A broadband signal is identified as an analog signal that has a large bandwidth (typically in the megahertz-to-gigahertz range). The analog signal uses analog modulation and often uses frequency division multiplexing for channel sharing.

A baseband signal is a digital signal with limited bandwidth that does not use analog modulation. A signal in the form of positive or negative voltage changes are placed on the line. A baseband signal may use time division multiplexing for channel sharing.

Many people use the term baseband to describe an unmodulated signal. A baseband signal may be used to modulate an analog carrier signal but the carrier need not be a broadband carrier; it may be a voice-band carrier, which is not considered a broadband signal.

SUMMARY

The physical layer is responsible for sending and receiving the physical signals between mobile stations, base stations, and other components in the mobile, wireless network. Wireless systems can operate with either analog or digital signals, although at the air interface, digital signals must be modulated over an analog carrier. For data signals, modems are employed to translate the digital signal to a form that is acceptable to the analog communications link.

3

U.S. Mobile and Wireless Systems Infrastructure

INTRODUCTION

This chapter expands on the introductory material in Chapter 1 on the mobile and wireless systems infrastructure in the United States. The focus of our discussion is on both mobile-wireless and fixed-wireless systems.

FCC's ORGANIZATION OF THE INDUSTRY

The mobile wireless infrastructure in the United States is determined to a great extent by the FCC. Because of the importance of the FCC's rules and regulations, this chapter examines this infrastructure, as well as the organization of the FCC. Figure 3–1 was introduced in Chapter 1, and will be used throughout this chapter to explain the fixed and mobile wireless infrastructure in the United States.

Commercial Mobile Radio Services

For the reader who must deal with the FCC rules, it is a good idea to review its Part 20, which are the rules for providing mobile radio services to commercial providers. Generally, it provides background information for its other regulations, so it is also a useful basic document. The rules in Part 20 set forth the requirements and conditions for commercial

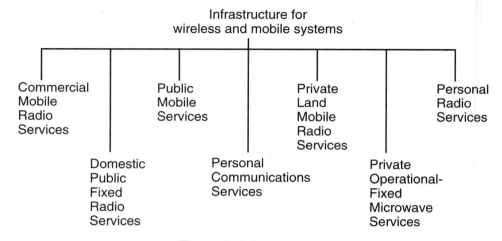

Figure 3–1
FCC operational areas.

providers. In addition (for the newcomer) this document provides definitions and descriptions of commercial mobile radio services.

It also describes procedures (generally) for connections into local exchange carrier (LEC) facilities, and establishes the procedures for states who wish to petition the FCC to regulate the rates for these services within their state.

Domestic Public Fixed Radio Services

The regulation of domestic public fixed radio services are set forth in Part 21. This part provides a description of operations and frequencies for point-to-point microwave radio service. It establishes the rules for sharing frequencies with satellite systems, TV systems, and government departments and agencies.

Bandwidth Allocations.   Table 3–1 lists the frequency allocations for point-to-point microwave radio service. A legend describing the frequency allocations is provided in Table 3–2.

Public Mobile Services

Part 22 of the FCC rules defines the operations for carriers that provide public mobile services. Included in these rules are the requirements the carrier must meet to design, build, and provide the public service.

Table 3–1   Point-to-Point Microwave Radio Service

From	To	Note
932.5	935	17
941.5	944	17, 18
2,110	2,130	1, 3, 7, 20
2,160	2,180	1, 2, 20, 21
3,700	4,200	8, 14
5,925	6,425	8, 14
6,525	6,875	14
10,550	10,680	19
10,700	11,700	8, 9, 18
13,200	13,250	4
17,700	18,820	5, 10, 15
18,920	19,160	5, 10, 15
19,260	19,700	5, 10, 15
21,200	22,000	11, 12, 13
22,000	23,600	4, 11, 12
27,500	29,500	5
31,000	31,300	16
38,600	40,000	4

All frequencies in MHz.

This document also contains specifications (with formula) for computing distances, terrain elevations, and other parameters.

As the reader might expect, frequency spectrum ranges are defined as well as the bandwidth requirements within each spectrum. Also, as with all the FCC rules in all the Parts, effective radiant power limits are defined based on a concept of the effective radiated power (ERP), which defines the maximum ERP in watts based on the frequency range.

FCC rules for Part 22 provide specifications for a wide variety of services. Paging services are defined including one-way, two-way, point-to-point, and point-to-multipoint. All of the operations in this part contain clauses regarding the operations of mobile transmitters across the U.S.-Canada border, as well. In effect, any mobile stations that are licensed by the Canadian government may also receive two-way service in the United States from stations licensed under this Part. The intent is to allow mobile stations to obtain services across the border.

Rules are also established for licensing and operating of stations for what is known as rural video telephone service. Only local exchange car-

Table 3–2   Point-to-Point Microwave Radio Service Legend

1. Frequencies in this band are shared with control and repeater stations in the Domestic Public Land Mobile Radio Service and with stations in the International Fixed Public Radiocommunication Services located south of 25° 30′ north latitude in the State of Florida and U.S. possessions in the Caribbean area. Additionally, the band 2160-2162 MHz is shared with stations in the multipoint Distribution Service.
2. Except upon a showing that no alternative frequencies are available, no new alternative frequencies will be made in the band 2160-2162 MHz for stations located within 80.5 kilometers (50 miles) of the coordinates of the cities listed in §21.901(c).
3. Television transmission in this band is not authorized and radio frequency channel width shall not exceed 3.5 MHz.
4. Frequencies in this band are shared with fixed and mobile stations licensed in other services.
5. Frequencies in this band are shared with stations in the fixed-satellite service.
6. These frequencies are not available for assignment to mobile earth stations.
7. Frequencies in the band 2110-2120 MHz may be authorized on a case-by-case basis to Government or non-Government space research earth stations for telecommand purposes in connection with deep space research.
8. This frequency band is shared with station(s) in the Local Television Transmission Service and, in the U.S. possessions in the Caribbean area, with stations in the International Fixed Public Radiocommunications Services.
9. The band segments 10.95-11.2 and 11.45-11.7 GHz are shared with space stations (space to earth) in the fixed-satellite service.
10. This band is co-equally shared with stations in the fixed services under Parts 21, 74, 78, and 94 of the Commission's Rules.
11. Frequencies in this band are shared with Government stations.
12. Assignments to common carriers in this band are normally made in the segments 21.2-21.8 GHz and 22.4-23.0 GHz and to operational fixed users in the segments 21.8-22.4 GHz and 23.0-23.6 GHz. Assignments may be made otherwise only upon a showing that no interference free frequencies are available in the appropriate band segments.
13. Frequencies in this band are shared with stations in the earth exploration satellite service (space to earth).
14. Frequencies in this band are shared with stations in the fixed-satellite and private-operational fixed microwave services.
15. Stations licensed as of September 9, 1983 to use frequencies in the 17.7-19.7 GHz band may, upon proper application, continue to be authorized for such operation.
16. Frequencies in this band are co-equally shared with stations in the Auxiliary Broadcasting (Part 74), Cable Television Relay (Part 78), Private Operational-Fixed Microwave (Part 94), and General Mobile Radio (Part 95) services.
17. Frequencies in these bands are shared with government fixed stations and stations in the Private Operational-Fixed Microwave service (Part 94).
18. Frequencies in the 942 to 944 MHz band are also shared with broadcast auxiliary stations (Part 74).
19. Frequencies in this band are shared with stations in the private-operational fixed microwave service.
20. New facilities in these bands will be licensed only on a secondary basis. Facilities licensed or applied before January 16, 1992, are permitted to make modifications and minor extensions and retain their primary status.
21. Any authorization of additional stations to use the 2160-2162 MHz band for Multipoint Distribution Service applied for after January 16, 1992 shall be secondary to use of the band for emerging technology services.

riers that have been state-certified to provide basic exchange telephone service are allowed to hold authorizations for these licenses.

Air-ground radio telephone service is also provided with the frequency established from ground-to-air and air-to-ground. The reader might wish to refer to the FCC document relating to this operation titled, "Technical Reference, Air-Ground Radio Telephone Automated Service (AGRAS) System Operational Equipment Characteristics," dated April 12, 1985.

Radio telephone service is defined as well. Channels and bandwidth requirements are specified. Also included are ERP, antennae height limitations, and guidance on transmitter locations.

Finally, Part 22 establishes the rules for the use of cellular radio telephone service. Rules are established for the carriers that can operate within the cellular area, designated as the cellular geographic service area (CGSA). CGSA is actually the composite of all the services of all the cells in a system within the market boundary defined by the FCC.

Bandwidth allocations.   Channels for mobile systems are allocated based on two "blocks" designated as channel block A and channel block B. The two blocks are assigned to the two cellular system providers in each geographical area. Channels have a bandwidth of 40 kHz and are designated by their cellular frequencies in MHz. Each channel block is assigned exclusively to one licensee for the use in the licensee-to-cellular geographic service area (accorded specifically from the FCC rules). Table 3–3 shows the allocation for the cellular service for channel block A and channel block B.

Personal Communications Services (PCS)

Part 90 documents the rules for the assignments of frequencies for broadband and narrowband PCS, rules for ownership and use, as well as rules for the auctions of the frequency spectrum.

After several revisions, the final frequency allocations for broadband are in the 1850-1890, 1930-1970, 2130-2150, and 2180-2000 MHz bands. The allocations for narrowband are in the 901-902, 930-931, and 940-941 MHz bands.

Many people think that "personal communications services" mean that these specifications describe the types of services that will operate over these frequencies. This is not the case. Indeed, the FCC is rather vague in its definition of PCS. The following is FCC's definition of PCS: "Radio communications that encompass mobile and ancillary fixed com-

Table 3–3   Channels for Cellular Service

Channel Block A

   416 Communication channel pairs

base	mobile		base	mobile
869.040 ....824.040			890.010 .... 845.010	
869.070 ....824.070			890.040 .... 845.040	
879.990 ....834.990			891.480 ....846.480	

   21 Control channel pairs

base	mobile
834.390 ....879.390	
834.420 ....879.420	
834.990 ....879.990	

Channel Block B

   416 Communication channel pairs

base	mobile		base	mobile
880.020 ....835.020			891.510 ....846.510	
880.050 ....835.050			891.540 ....846.540	
889.980 ....844.980			893.970 ....848.970	

   21 Control channel pairs

base	mobile
835.020 ....880.020	
835.050 ....880.050	
835.620 ....880.620	

Note: All channels have a bandwidth of 40 kHz and are designated by their center frequencies in MHz.

munication that provides services to individuals and business and can be integrated with a variety of competing networks." In other words, the services are not defined, and each PCS provider will decide what is a marketable service.

The services that emerge for PCS will be much the same as with any communications system: voice services, fax, e-mail, and so on. We will examine this idea later in this chapter and in Chapter 9.

Specialized Mobile Radio Service

In 1974, the FCC established a specialized mobile radio service to accommodate demand for a wide variety of services and to meet the requests of industries providing those services. Part 90 establishes the rules for these services, the allocation of spectrum space, and other related areas. Although this part of the U.S. mobile wireless infrastructure is intended for private systems, the services can be provided for profit.

Recently, the FCC made major changes to Section 232 of the Communications Act, and now provides a structure to regulate all mobile radio services in a more uniform manner. This includes common carrier, PCS, and private services. Hereafter, any "private" specialized mobile service company that provides interconnected services will be regulated under Part 20. Others are regulated under Part 90.

The industries that are covered are quite broad. The major categories are (with many subcategories not listed here): power, petroleum, forest products, film and video production, relay press (newspapers), special industrial (mainly rural: breeding, spraying, and construction), business, manufacturers, and telephone maintenance radio services (for common carriers only).

Private Operational-Fixed Microwave Service

Originally, the FCC established the private operational-fixed microwave service (OFS) for organizations that wished to have their own system for their private uses. Now, OFS is broadened to allow OFS providers to offer their system to others on a for-profit basis. OFS is documented in Part 94.

OFS allows the transmission of voice, video, or data on a point-to-point or point-to-multipoint basis. The latter topology is referred to as either multiple address systems (MAS) or digital termination systems (DTS).

In effect, OFS permits user and provider to bypass the telephone local exchange carrier (LEC). OFS is widely used by banks, utility companies, schools, and alarm companies because they are inexpensive and flexible to use.

Personal Radio Services or Interactive Video and Data Service (IVDS)

Personal radio service, more commonly known as interactive video and data service (IVDS), is a relatively new regulated service. The FCC created this service (actually, the allocation of spectrum space) in 1992. It is intended that IVDS will provide the basis for a wide variety of services, such as video-on-demand, interactive participation in polling activities, online shopping, and interactive banking.

Although IVDS is in its infancy, the FCC perceives a system to consist of cellular technology. One or more cell transmitter stations (CTS) are operated by the IVDS provider, and will communicate with subscribers through a response transmitter unit (RTU) located at the subscriber's site. For example, the subscriber sees the services on the TV screen and interacts much like a typical handheld remote control unit. The system is different from current offerings in that it is wireless and does not require expensive landline facilities.

Currently, the FCC has allocated 1 MHz in the 218-219 MHz band for the service. Two providers are licensed per market, with the local service areas defined by the current cellular structure. As of this writing, licenses have been granted for nine major metropolitan areas in the United States. The next section provides more information on IVDS.

THE AUCTIONS

In the Omnibus Budget Act of 1993, the U.S. Congress authorized several auctions of the electromagnetic frequency spectrum in the United States. The auctions began in 1994 and continue into 1996. The most interest has centered on the PCS auctions, but auctions also were held in the interactive video and data service (IVDS) area.

Broadband PCS Frequency Spectrum Plan

The initial declarations of the FCC on the PCS spectrum did not please many segments of the industry because of the separate bands. The new FCC rules on the allocation of spectrum space is simpler, and allocates one continuous band (instead of two bands, with the former allocation). Figure 3–2 shows the revised allocations.

The total spectrum allocation does not change. It remains at 120 MHz. In addition, the allocation of the spectrum blocks have changed. Instead of the "old" two 30-MHz and one 20-MHz blocks, the new FCC plan allocates three 30-MHz blocks.

Philosophy of Auctioning Spectrum Space

Some people are against the auctions. These opponents dislike the idea of a government selling off what they consider a natural monopoly (the people's property). I conducted a lecture in Europe last year and was explaining the auctions to my audience. One person made the comment that it was only a matter of time before the Americans started auctioning

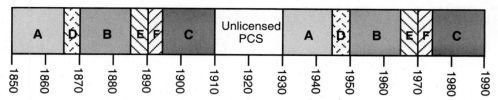

Blocks A, B based on Rand McNally's Major Trading Areas (MTA)
Blocks C, D, E, F based on Rand McNally's Basic Trading Areas (BTA)
Unlicensed PCS is nationwide

**Figure 3–2
Spectrum allocation plan.**

off the air. Another delegate said, "It is the American way: If it is sell-able, sell it!"

Proponents believe the auctions will effectively jump start a new generation of mobile and wireless systems. These individuals state that if the companies who buy the licenses are publicly held, the public still "owns" the spectrum if they are willing to purchase ownership in the company.

Auction Results

The remainder of this chapter reflects the latest information on the results of the auctions. I have delayed writing this book until the initial auctions were finished, and this section reflects this approach. We shall see that other auctions will be undertaken in the near future.

For numerous reasons (insufficient capital, FCC is too harsh in its requirements, etc.), some of the initial bids (and the companies that were granted licenses) have been rescinded or the licensee has defaulted. I shall concentrate on what has happened so far, with the caveat that some of the licensees and bidders cited in this discussion may not be the final vendors. In some contentious cases, the process will snake its way through the judicial system, which might take a long time to resolve.

Interactive Video and Data Services (IVDS)

In July 1994, the FCC completed the first of two auctions on band-width for IVDS licenses. A total of $216 million resulted from the auctions. The FCC allocated 1 MHz of spectrum operating in the 218-219 MHz band. Two licenses are rented in each of 734 service areas. Each license will be granted 500 kHz for two channels.

Table 3–4   The IVDS Auctions

MSA Segment	Block	Winner	Bid Amount ($)	Adjusted Bid Amount ($)
5	A	Commercial Realty St. Petersburg, Inc. 1333 Monterey Blvd. N.E., St. Petersburg, FL 33704	1,150,000	362,500
5	B	Interactive Video and Data Networks 606 N. Second Street, Jena, LA 71342	1,200,000	1,200,000
11	A	Commercial Realty St. Petersburg, Inc. 1333 Monterey Blvd. N.E., St. Petersburg, FL 33704	1,500,000	1,200,000
11	B	IVDS Auction Consortium Ltd. Pts. 640 Broadway, Sonoma, CA 95476	1,500,000	1,500,000
12	A	Commercial Realty St. Petersburg, Inc. 1333 Monterey Blvd. N.E., St. Petersburg, FL 33704	4,300,000	3,225,000
12	B	Panamerican Interactive Corp.. 6701 Hanley Road, Tampa, FL 33634	3,100,000	3,100,000
13	A	Commercial Realty St. Petersburg, Inc. 1333 Monterey Blvd. N.E., St. Petersburg, FL 33704	1,900,000	1,425,000
13	B	Vision TV Inc. c/o Joseph Randaza, New York, NY 10022	1,000,000	1,000,000
14	A	Commercial Realty St. Petersburg, Inc. 1333 Monterey Blvd. N.E., St. Petersburg, FL 33704	2,200,000	1,850,000
14	B	Whitehall Wireless Corporation 712 Holly Drive North Annapolis, MD 21401	1,500,000	1,500,000
15	A	Commercial Realty St. Petersburg, Inc. 1333 Monterey Blvd. N.E., St. Petersburg, FL 33704	1,900,000	1,425,000
15	B	IVDS Auction Consortium Ltd. Pts. 640 Broadway, Sonoma, CA 95476	1,500,000	1,500,00
16	A	KMC Interactive TV Inc. 705 Melvin Avenue, Suite 101 Annapolis, MD 21401	1,150,000	1,150,000
16	B	WCI Partners 440 E Huntington Drive, #300, Arcadia, CA 91006	1,200,000	900,000

MSA Segment	Block	Winner	Bid Amount ($)	Adjusted Bid Amount ($)
17	A	Commercial Realty St. Petersburg, Inc. 1333 Monterey Blvd. N.E., St. Petersburg, FL 33704	3,100,000	2,325,000
17	B	IVDS Auction Consortium Ltd. Pts. 640 Broadway, Sonoma, CA 95476	3,000,000	3,000,000
18	A	Interactive America Corporation 10817 Tuxform Street, Sun Valley, CA 91352	3,400,000	2,550,000
18	B	Commercial Realty St. Petersburg, Inc. 1333 Monterey Blvd. N.E., St. Petersburg, FL 33704	2,600,000	2,500,000
19	A	Commercial Realty St. Petersburg, Inc. 1333 Monterey Blvd. N.E., St. Petersburg, FL 33704	1,600,000	1,200,000
19	B	IVDS Auction Consortium Ltd. Pts. 640 Broadway, Sonoma, CA 95476	1,800,000	1,300,000

IVDS is a short distance service operating either on a point-to-multipoint or multipoint-to-point basis. When developed, it will provide services to individual subscribers such as pay-for-view programming, homemaking, and educational services.

The July 1994 auction is the first of two planned services. The first auctions, shown in Table 3–4, cover 297 markets. The markets listed in Table 3–4 pertain to the following market areas:

- 5   Detroit/Ann Arbor
- 11   St. Louis
- 12   Miami/Ft. Lauderdale-Hollywood
- 13   Pittsburgh
- 14   Baltimore
- 15   Minneapolis/St. Paul
- 16   Cleveland
- 17   Atlanta
- 18   San Diego
- 19   Denver/Boulder

The FCC gave away several licenses in 1993 before Congress ordered the FCC to establish auction procedures. Over 94 percent of all the bidders for the first auction consisted of minorities, women, and small businesses. Over half the licenses were awarded to women, 33 percent went to minorities. The preferences set up for minorities and women included installment financing for the auction fee as well as a 25 percent bidding credit that allowed these groups to have a competitive edge in the bidding process.

Nationwide Narrowband PCS

In July 1994, the FCC conducted an auction for nationwide narrowband PCS licenses. This auction raised over $617 million and the auction winners were a wide array of companies from the communications and wireless industry. Bidder applications totaled 67 organizations with 29 bidders actually participating in the auction rounds. The PCS narrowband services will focus principally on nationwide paging services. Since two frequencies are allocated to each license, the service will provide two-way paging capacity.

Applications for narrowband PCS have not been defined but they will likely also include (in addition to paging) image and data transmission, locator services, electronic mail, and directory services.

Table 3–5   Nationwide Narrowband PCS Auction

Market Number	Company	Winning Bids
Type:	**50-50 kHz paired**	
N-1	Paging Network of Virginia	$80,000,000
N-2	Paging Network of Virginia	$80,000,000
N3	KDM Messaging Co. (Mainly owned by McCaw Cellular)	$80,000,000
N4	KDM Messaging Co. (Mainly owned by McCaw Cellular)	$80,000,000
N5	Nationwide Wireless Network Corp. (Mtel)	$80,000,000
Type:	**50-12.5 kHz paired**	
N6	Airtouch Paging	$47,001,001
N7	BellSouth Wireless	$47,505,673
N8	Nationwide Wireless Network Corp. (Mtel)	$47,500,000
Type:	**50 kHz unpaired**	
N-10	Paging Network of Virginia	$37,000,000
N-11	Pagemart II, Inc.	$38,000,000
	Total	**$617,006,674**

(Mtel was awarded 50 kHz unpaired pioneer's preference license for market N-9.)

As depicted in Table 3–5, the McCaw Cellular and Paging Network Inc. won two licenses and telephone companies also were winners. BellSouth Wireless (a subsidiary of BellSouth Industries) and Airtouch Paging (part of Pacific Telesis) both won licenses. Mtel was awarded a one-way paging license as a pioneer preference as well as a two-way license.

The FCC also established preference for women-owned and minority-owned companies; however, due to the extremely high bidding, these companies were unable to win any of the licenses.

Table 3–6 provides a summary of the requirements established by the FCC for the narrowband PCS services.

As with all FCC rules, power and radiation limits are specified in various parts of the FCC dockets. Table 3–7 provides a summary of the FCC rules on RF radiation limits for licensed PCS devices.

Regional Narrowband PCS

In October 1994, the FCC auctioned thirty regional narrow-band PCS licenses. The FCC received over $400 million for these licenses. The regional licenses were divided into major trading areas (MTAs). Another thirty licenses were won by four designated organizations, being small

Table 3–6   Narrowband PCS Construction Requirements

	Nationwide	Regional	Major Trading Area	Basic Trading Area
Area to be covered in 1000 km²:				
after 5 years	750	150	75	1 base station
after 10 years	1500	300	150	in 1 year
Percent of area's population reachable:				
after 5 years		37.5		—
after 10 years		75		
Maximum number of channels[a], each 50 kHz:				
paired with 12.5 kHz	3	4	3	2
paired with 50 kHz	5	2	2	—
unpaired	3	—	2	—

[a]Only two 12.5 kHz response channels are allowed in any one geographic area. The maximum amount of spectrum will range from 150-300 kHz.

Source: FCC, *Memorandum, Opinion and Order*, General Docket 90-314 and ET Docket 92-100, released March 4, 1994.

Table 3–7   RF Radiation Limits for Licensed PCS Devices

Frequency Block	Central Frequency MHz	Maximum power density permissible, mW/cm^{2a}	. . . at Minimum distance from transmitter, in meters[b]
A	1857.5	1.238	0.802
B	1872.5	1.248	0.798
C	1885.0	1.257	0.795
D	2132.5	1.422	0.748
E	2137.5	1.425	0.747
F	2141.5	1.428	0.746
G	2147.5	1.432	0.746

[a]Averaged over any 30-minute period. The values normally apply to an antenna's far-field region, where electromagnetic field has a predominantly plain-wave character.

[b]The distance from a PCS transmitter at which power density first falls off to a level deemed harmless; applies to uncontrolled environments, where people may be unwittingly exposed.

Source: FCC, *Second Report and Order*, General Docket 90-314, Sept. 23, 1993, Appendix E: Compliance with ANSI/IEEE RF Guidelines.

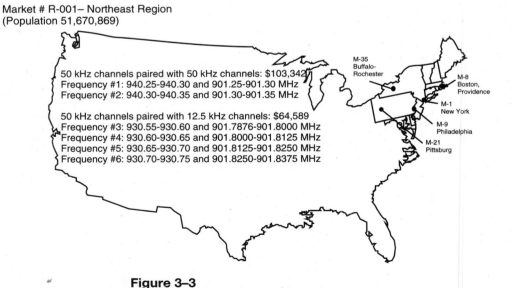

Market # R-001– Northeast Region
(Population 51,670,869)

50 kHz channels paired with 50 kHz channels: $103,342
Frequency #1: 940.25-940.30 and 901.25-901.30 MHz
Frequency #2: 940.30-940.35 and 901.30-901.35 MHz

50 kHz channels paired with 12.5 kHz channels: $64,589
Frequency #3: 930.55-930.60 and 901.7876-901.8000 MHz
Frequency #4: 930.60-930.65 and 901.8000-901.8125 MHz
Frequency #5: 930.65-930.70 and 901.8125-901.8250 MHz
Frequency #6: 930.70-930.75 and 901.8250-901.8375 MHz

M-35 Buffalo-Rochester
M-8 Boston, Providence
M-1 New York
M-9 Philadelphia
M-21 Pittsburg

Figure 3–3
Regional narrowband PCS auctions.

businesses, women-owned businesses, and minority-owned businesses. The bandwidth for these licenses are in the 900 MHz range, with the licenses divided into five regions across the United States. The regions shown in the following figures as well as the channel allotment and the initial payment required to participate in the bidding.

Figures 3–3 through 3–7 show how the various parts of the United States were divided for purposes of spectrum allocation and the granting of licenses. Each figure illustrates the MTA, which is identified with an

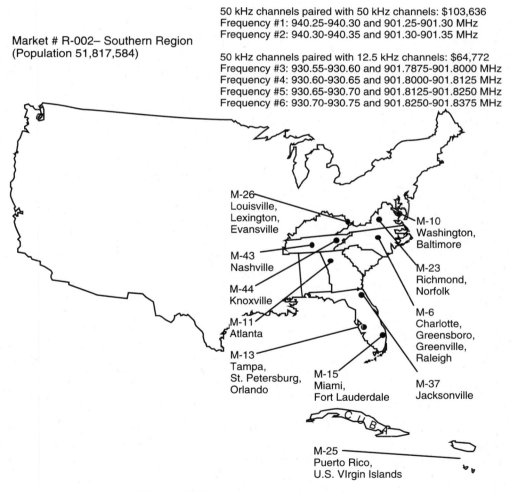

50 kHz channels paired with 50 kHz channels: $103,636
Frequency #1: 940.25-940.30 and 901.25-901.30 MHz
Frequency #2: 940.30-940.35 and 901.30-901.35 MHz

50 kHz channels paired with 12.5 kHz channels: $64,772
Frequency #3: 930.55-930.60 and 901.7875-901.8000 MHz
Frequency #4: 930.60-930.65 and 901.8000-901.8125 MHz
Frequency #5: 930.65-930.70 and 901.8125-901.8250 MHz
Frequency #6: 930.70-930.75 and 901.8250-901.8375 MHz

Market # R-002– Southern Region
(Population 51,817,584)

M-26
Louisville,
Lexington,
Evansville

M-10
Washington,
Baltimore

M-43
Nashville

M-23
Richmond,
Norfolk

M-44
Knoxville

M-6
Charlotte,
Greensboro,
Greenville,
Raleigh

M-11
Atlanta

M-13
Tampa,
St. Petersburg,
Orlando

M-15
Miami,
Fort Lauderdale

M-37
Jacksonville

M-25
Puerto Rico,
U.S. VIrgin Islands

Figure 3–4
Regional narrowband PCS auctions.

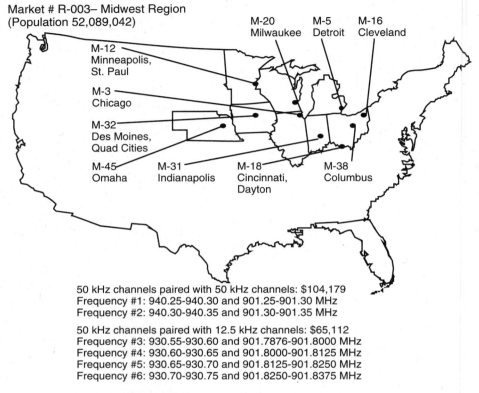

Market # R-003– Midwest Region
(Population 52,089,042)

M-20 Milwaukee   M-5 Detroit   M-16 Cleveland

M-12 Minneapolis, St. Paul

M-3 Chicago

M-32 Des Moines, Quad Cities

M-45 Omaha   M-31 Indianapolis   M-18 Cincinnati, Dayton   M-38 Columbus

50 kHz channels paired with 50 kHz channels: $104,179
Frequency #1: 940.25-940.30 and 901.25-901.30 MHz
Frequency #2: 940.30-940.35 and 901.30-901.35 MHz

50 kHz channels paired with 12.5 kHz channels: $65,112
Frequency #3: 930.55-930.60 and 901.7876-901.8000 MHz
Frequency #4: 930.60-930.65 and 901.8000-901.8125 MHz
Frequency #5: 930.65-930.70 and 901.8125-901.8250 MHz
Frequency #6: 930.70-930.75 and 901.8250-901.8375 MHz

Figure 3–5
Regional narrowband PCS auctions.

M-n designation. Each figure also shows the fees required for each license in each market area. With this explanation, the reader can study each figure. I provide no more explanation as each figure is self-explanatory. Table 3–8 lists each winner, the bidding area, and the amount of the bid.

Broadband PCS

On June 9, 1994, the FCC allocated the PCS spectrum into the 1850–1990 MHz band, with 1910-1930 MHz allocated for unlicensed PCS systems. As shown in Table 3–9, (and Figure 3–2) blocks A, B, and C are allocated 30 MHz; blocks D, E, and F are allocated 10 MHz. The A and B blocks are licensed for the fifty-one MTAs. The D, E, and F blocks are licensed for the basic trading areas (BTAs).

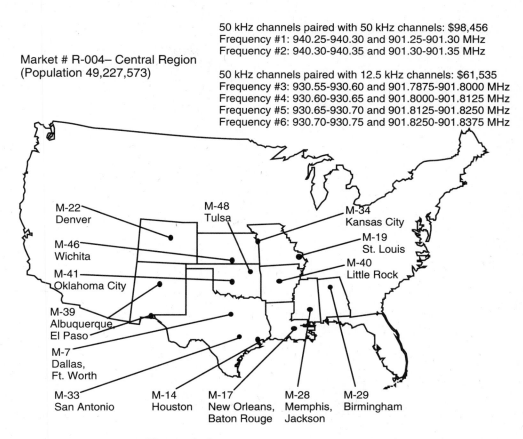

50 kHz channels paired with 50 kHz channels: $98,456
Frequency #1: 940.25-940.30 and 901.25-901.30 MHz
Frequency #2: 940.30-940.35 and 901.30-901.35 MHz

50 kHz channels paired with 12.5 kHz channels: $61,535
Frequency #3: 930.55-930.60 and 901.7875-901.8000 MHz
Frequency #4: 930.60-930.65 and 901.8000-901.8125 MHz
Frequency #5: 930.65-930.70 and 901.8125-901.8250 MHz
Frequency #6: 930.70-930.75 and 901.8250-901.8375 MHz

Market # R-004– Central Region
(Population 49,227,573)

Figure 3–6
Regional narrowband PCS auctions.

The PCS broadband auction was based on 1990 U.S. Census population figures. The United States and territories were divided into fifty-one market areas, called MTA. Ninety-nine licenses were to be auctioned. The most populous area, New York, was market 1 (M-1). It was based on a population figure of 26,410,597. The least populated area, was American Samoa (M-51), with a population of 47,000. Frequency blocks A and B were auctioned. As discussed earlier, block A is 1850-1865 MHz paired with 1930-1945 MHz, and block B is 1870-1885 MHz paired with 1950-1965 MHz.

PCS bidders were required to submit an upfront payment and (of course) to fill in the required FCC form (Form 159). The payment was

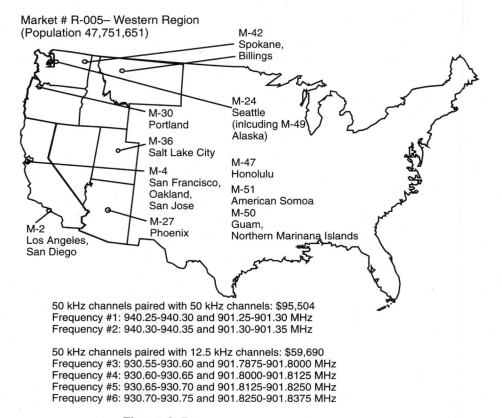

Market # R-005– Western Region
(Population 47,751,651)

M-42
Spokane,
Billings

M-24
Seattle
(inlcuding M-49
Alaska)

M-30
Portland

M-36
Salt Lake City

M-4
San Francisco,
Oakland,
San Jose

M-27
Phoenix

M-47
Honolulu

M-51
American Somoa
M-50
Guam,
Northern Marinana Islands

M-2
Los Angeles,
San Diego

50 kHz channels paired with 50 kHz channels: $95,504
Frequency #1: 940.25-940.30 and 901.25-901.30 MHz
Frequency #2: 940.30-940.35 and 901.30-901.35 MHz

50 kHz channels paired with 12.5 kHz channels: $59,690
Frequency #3: 930.55-930.60 and 901.7875-901.8000 MHz
Frequency #4: 930.60-930.65 and 901.8000-901.8125 MHz
Frequency #5: 930.65-930.70 and 901.8125-901.8250 MHz
Frequency #6: 930.70-930.75 and 901.8250-901.8375 MHz

Figure 3–7
Regional narrowband PCS auctions.

based on the following formula: population × block size (in MHz) × $.02 (and rounded to nearest dollar). With this formula, the M-1 area's upfront payment was $15,846,359; the M-51 area was $28,000. Figure 3–8 shows the top ten PCS markets.

On March 13, 1995 the broadband PCS auction came to an end. As expected, the large companies emerged as the top bidders for the licenses. Sprint and its three cable partners bid $2.11 billion for licenses in twenty-nine markets, including the New York City market. AT&T was the next highest bidder, committing $1.68 billion for licenses in twenty-one markets. The next highest bidder was PCS Primeco, which is a consortium of Nynex, US West, Bell Atlantic, and Airtouch. This group bid $1.11 billion for eleven markets, including the Chicago market. Pacific

Table 3–8   Regional Narrowband PCS License Winners

Market No.	Frq. Block No.	License Description (Paired)	Name	Bid Amount* ($ in Mill.)
Northeast R001	01	50/50	Pagemart II, Inc.	17.5
R001	02	50/50	PCS Development Corp.	24.75
R001	03	50/12.5	Mobilemedia PCS, Inc.	9.47
R001	04	50/12.5	Advanced Wireless Messaging, Inc.	8.95
R001	05	50/12.5	Air Touch Paging	8.68
R001	06	50/12.5	Lisa-Gaye Shearing	17.09
South R002	01	50/50	Pagemart II, Inc.	18.40
R002	02	50/50	PCS Development Corp.	31.30
R002	03	50/12.5	Mobilemedia PCS, Inc.	11.80
R002	04	50/12.5	Advanced Wireless Messaging, Inc.	11.54
R002	05	50/12.5	Insta-Check Systems, Inc.	8.00
R002	06	50/12.5	Lisa-Gaye Shearing	18.77
Midwest R003	01	50/50	Pagemart II, Inc.	16.81
R003	02	50/50	PCS Development Corp.	28.93
R003	03	50/12.5	Mobilemedia PCS, Inc.	9.29
R003	04	50/12.5	Advanced Wireless Messaging, Inc.	10.06
R003	05	50/12.5	Ameritech Mobile Svcs., Inc.	9.50
R003	06	50/12.5	Lisa-Gaye Shearing	17.09
Central R004	01	50/50	Pagemart II, Inc.	17.34
R004	02	50/50	PCS Development Corp.	28.56
R004	03	50/12.5	Mobilemedia PCS, Inc.	8.25
R004	04	50/12.5	Advanced Wireless Messaging, Inc.	8.79
R004	05	50/12.5	Air Touch Paging	8.26
R004	06	50/12.5	Benbow P.C.S. Ventures, Inc.	17.48
West R005	01	50/50	Pagemart II, Inc.	22.55
R005	02	50/50	PCS Development Corp.	22.55
R005	03	50/12.5	Mobilemedia PCS, Inc.	14.86
R005	04	50/12.5	Advanced Wireless Messaging, Inc.	14.28
R005	05	50/12.5	Air Touch Paging	14.28
R005	06	50/12.5	Benbow P.C.S. Ventures, Inc.	18.20

*Total bid amount $488,772,800

Table 3–9   Broadband PCS Allocation

Frequency Block	Amount of Spectrum	Geographic Scope	Frequency Range (MHz)	Number of Licenses
A	30 MHz	MTA	1850–1865/1930–1945	51
B	30 MHz	MTA	1870–1885/1950–1965	51
C	30 MHz	MTA	1895–1910/1975–1990	493
D	10 MHz	BTA	1865–1870/1945–1950	493
E	10 MHz	BTA	1885–1890/1965–1970	493
F	10 MHz	BTA	1890–1895/1970–1975	493
Unlicensed	20 MHz	Nationwide	1910–1930	—

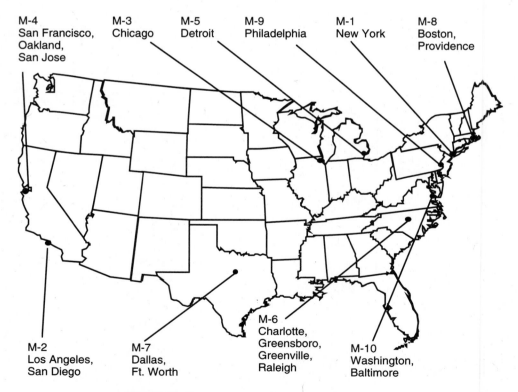

Figure 3–8
Top ten broadband PCS auction markets.

4

Fundamentals
of Cellular Systems

INTRODUCTION

This chapter continues the introductory discussions on cellular systems that began in Chapters 1 and 2. The first part of the chapter highlights early cellular systems. Next, mobile cellular components, such as the mobile station and base station, are described.

Discussions also focus on cell design issues, such as cell shape and size. In this part of the chapter, the concepts of cell splitting, cell reuse, and cell sectoring are introduced. The chapter concludes with an examination of roaming and handoff operations.

Be aware that one overriding factor permeates almost all cellular design considerations: making the most efficient use of the limited bandwidth. The constant concern is achieving "good spectrum efficiency."

EARLIER SYSTEMS

Earlier wireless systems utilized what are called nontrunk radio systems, where a user was assigned to a fixed transmit and receive frequency. Therefore, each radio channel was dedicated to a specific user or perhaps a group of users. With groups of users, the system looked very much like a party line. Newer systems have migrated to trunk radio systems where channels are made available to all users. If a channel is in use, the next available channel will be assigned to the user. Therefore, no channel is fixed or dedicated to any one user. The advantage of this approach is the increased efficiency of spectrum usage, but it does translate into more complex equipment by requiring the systems to be frequency agile.

TYPICAL CELL LAYOUT

Figure 4–1 shows a typical topology for a cellular radio system. The principal components of this system are the Mobile Telephone Switching Office (MTSO), the cell and its base transceiver station (BTS), and a mobile unit or mobile station. I use the generic term MTSO in this discus-

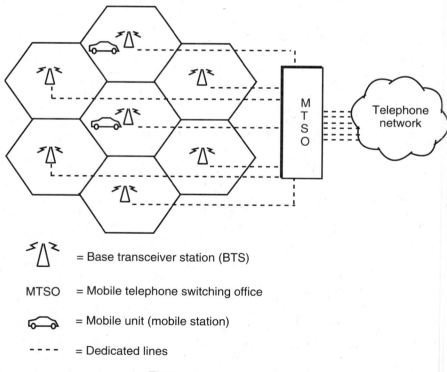

= Base transceiver station (BTS)

MTSO   = Mobile telephone switching office

= Mobile unit (mobile station)

- - - -   = Dedicated lines

Figure 4–1
Cellular radio topology.

sion. Later chapters will use other terms that are cited in specific standards, such as land station, mobile switching center, etc. The term BTS is also known as the base station or the land station.

The MTSO is the control element for this system. It is responsible for switching the calls to the cells, providing for backup, interfacing with telephone networks, monitoring traffic for charging activities, performing testing and diagnostic services, and managing the overall network.

The mobile station (or mobile unit) is actually the mobile transceiver that is installed in an automobile, truck, etc. It contains a frequency-agile machine that allows it to change to a particular frequency designated for its use by the MTSO.

The cell site contains the BTS, which is the air interface between the mobile station and the MTSO. By receiving signals and directions from the MTSO, the BTS sends and receives traffic to/from the mobile station.

DEALING WITH THE CELL SIGNALS

The cellular system must be designed for the receiver to accommodate to a wide variety of signal characteristics. We will examine these characteristics in this section, and explain the factors that can cause signal distortions. Our discussion is centered around research performed at Bellcore [ARNO95].

Path Loss

Figure 4–2 shows the typical loss of signal strength (path loss) as the receiver (a vehicle, a person) moves away from the base station (assuming an antenna of about 25 feet in height). The path loss in dB represents the ratio of the strength of the transmitted signal to the received strength. The distance is a log measurement of the distance between the sender and receiver.

The loss somewhat resembles a straight line, but with wide fluctuations. The reasons for these fluctuations are due to factors discussed shortly. The immediate point to be made with regard to Figure 4–2 is the rapid loss of signal strength that occurs as the mobile station moves away from the transmitting antenna. Therefore, the cellular system must be able to detect when the signal loss requires the handover of the

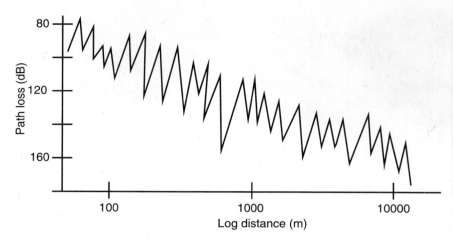

Figure 4–2
Path loss (conceptual view).

mobile station to a different antenna (a different cell). Handover is de-scribed in the last section of this chapter.

Multipath Propagation Delay

A radio signal can be reflected from various objects such as build-ings, walls, or mountains. Indeed, a direct line-of-sight path between the mobile and base station may be infrequent.

One effect of multipath propagation is that the multiple signals will arrive at the receiver at slightly different times, as seen in Figure 4–3 (for purposes of simplicity, only two signals are shown). These received signals exhibit the qualities of vector addition: The resulting signal (vec-tor) is the result of the successive application of the two signals (vectors). If the two signals are in phase with each other, they reinforce each other; if they are out of phase, they cancel each other.

The multipaths on each channel are created by (1) reflections (as in Figure 4–3), (2) absorptions, (3) diffractions (bending of the waves around obstacles), and (4) an unobstructed signal.

Several aspects of Figure 4–3 are noteworthy. First, signal 1 arrives sooner at the receiver than signal 2, which was reflected off a building. As the mobile station moves, the path from the base station changes, which results in phase changes of the signals at the receiver. These

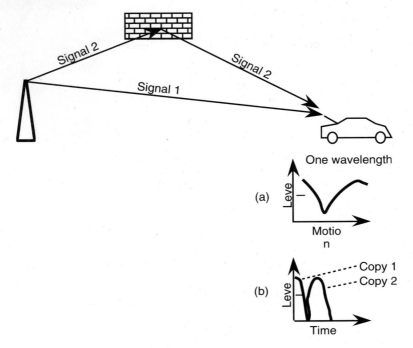

Figure 4–3
Multipath propagation delay.

phase changes are occurring differently for each received signal. Thus, the large fluctuations of the received signal (refer back to Figure 4–2) is due to the out-of-phase, in-phase relationship of the two signals when they are received at the mobile station as the interpreted waveform. In Figure 4–3(a), the signal exhibits considerable fluctuation over one wavelength.

The scenario is changed slightly in Figure 4–3(b). The transmitter is sending a pulse to the mobile station. Due to multipath propagation delay, two copies of the pulse are detected at the receiver. Since the signal is traveling at the speed of light (~1 foot per nsec.), the paths length differ by 100 feet, which means the pulses arrive at the receiver 100 nsec apart. This problem is called time dispersion or time delay spread.

The effect displayed by a single frequency seen in Figure 4–3(a) is similar to a system in which a wider range of signals is employed, or in a system where a signal is spread over a wider range of frequencies, which are the situations for most cellular systems. Like time dispersion, this effect (called frequency selection) is a function of path length, but is also due to the following properties of signal propagation.

The phase of a signal is proportional to the product of its frequency and the length of the path. In addition, as the frequency varies, the phase of the signal on the longer path changes more rapidly than the signal on the shorter path. This phenomenon means that as frequencies change, so do the phases. The receiver might detect an in-phase signal on one frequency and out-of-phase signal on another. The effect can be such that the reflected signal may be 180° out-of-phase with the other signal. Still, they might not cancel each other entirely because the reflected signal is not as strong as the nonreflected signal. Well, maybe. The nonreflected signal may have been partially attenuated by absorption.

Multipath Fading

For fixed point-to-point systems, multipath delay can be predicted and the components can be designed to handle the problem, or only the simple moving of an antenna may be required. For mobile systems, the situation is more complex. Figure 4–4 illustrates the problem. As the mobile station moves through a cell, the multipath signals abruptly and rapidly add to and subtract from each other. The effect is called a Rayleigh fade (named after Lord Rayleigh, a famous physicist).

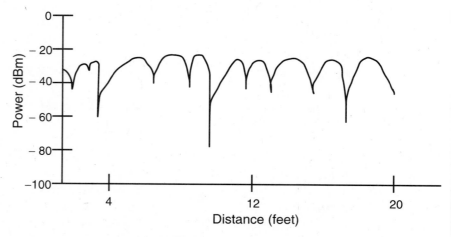

Figure 4–4
Multipath fading.

Several aspects of the signal in Figure 4–4 are of interest. The signal peaks are broad and fairly consistent with regard to loss. The signal fades are narrower and very deep, as much as −80 dBm in this figure. So, in mobile systems, wide "good" signals are interspersed with narrow, but "very poor" signals.

It is possible to describe the Raleigh fade on a statistical basis, but it is impossible to predict when they will occur, since the mobile unit encounters so many different path combinations. In essence, the various combinations of the additive vectors is impossible to know.

Dealing with the Problems

What can be done to compensate for these problems? In many cellular systems, the base station uses two separately located antenna to take advantage of the fact that the deep fades occur at different times relative to each antenna. Consequently, the base station selects the best signal at a given instant.

For the mobile station, the physical unit may not accommodate two separately located antennas. For example, in the PCS environment, at 2 GHz the antennas should be separated by one-half half wave length, which is three inches. This poses ergonomic challenges.

Multipath and polarization effects. Another solution takes advantage of the properties of radio waves, which contain electrical and magnetic fields. The polarity state of the fields is described by the direction of the electrical field, either vertical (V) or horizontal (H). In many systems, the antenna are designed to send and receive with V polarization only. However, in a PCS handset, the components can be designed where the send side uses V only, but the receive side has co-located V and H antennas. It so happens that the fades occur at different times with colocated antennas, which means that the overall power is about equal across the V and H receivers. The end result is the elimination of the deep troughs in a Rayleigh fade.

This means that physical diversity is not needed; diversity is achieved with two cross-polarized antenna. This approach permits diversity reception in a PCS handset, and it is the approach recommended by Bellcore [ARNO95].

As the reader can see, mobile signaling is orders of magnitude more complex than fixed signaling, and there are other aspects to the subject that are beyond this general text. Let us now turn our attention to the cell itself and learn why and how it is employed in mobile systems.

SIZE AND SHAPE OF CELL

We learned earlier that the basic premise of cell technology is the provision for the reuse of frequencies. This section explains how frequency reuse is determined and how cell size is computed.

It is not practical to generate signals that stay within the boundaries of the hexagonal (six-sided) cell, but it is used because the hexagon resembles a circle, which is an ideal shape for signal coverage. Additionally, the hexagons can be placed together (tessellated) side-by-side to yield nonoverlapping cells. Even if circles are used, they are still not reflective of the actual signal coverage, which is more irregular, due to terrain and antenna location. The hexagonal shape also is useful because directional antennas can be installed at the base station and transmit within sectors of a cell.

Frequency Reuse

Frequency reuse depends on a number of factors: (1) the power of the transmitted signal, (2) the frequencies used, (3) the type of antenna, (4) the height of the antenna, (5) weather, and (6) the terrain over which the signal is sent.

Frequency reuse is computed on the reuse distance D as:

$$\frac{D}{R} = \sqrt{3N}$$

where D is the distance between cells using same frequency (see Figure 4–5), R is cell radius, and N is the reuse pattern (the cluster size).

Therefore, for a 7-cell group that has 3-mile radius cells, D is 13.74 miles. For 2-mile radius cells, D is 9.16 miles. Obviously, an increased D reduces the chances of co-channel interference from cells using the same frequencies. But this means the number of channels assigned to each cell becomes smaller, resulting in inefficiencies in managing the spectrum and the trunks.

However, as the radius of the cell decreases, dramatic increases in capacity can be realized. Calhoun correlates the reuse factor in relation to the radius of the cell (in miles)[CALH92], and establishes a measure for comparing the number of circuits per MHz (CIR/MHz) of available spectrum:

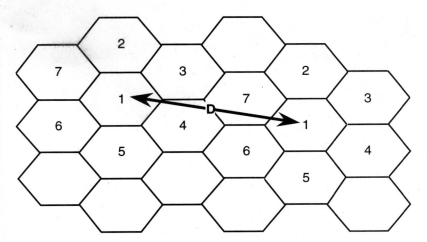

Figure 4–5
The reuse distance D.

$$CIR / MHz = ((C / B \times (RA + 1)) \times (1000(MHz) / 2))$$

where C = number of channels per carrier, B = channel bandwidth (total, including unusable guardband), RA = number of restricted adjacent channels (frequencies between adjacent channels that cannot be used due to antenna design in some systems).

Spectrum Efficiency

Based on this scheme, Table 4–1 compares the spectrum efficiency of several prominent systems. The figures cited for the column labeled "Circuits per MHz" are more realistic than some other studies I have reviewed, because Calhoun has factored into variable C the total channel bandwidth, including the guardband and the coding/modulation technique. This latter operation is an important consideration because systems code the traffic into either 64, 32, 16, or 8 kbit/s transmissions, and use different modulation schemes (2, 3, 4, etc. bits per baud). The information contained in the column titled "Channel Utilization Scheme" is explained in Chapter 5.

It is obvious that small cells yield more capacity. The tradeoff is the increased overhead of handing off calls across cells, and the overhead of keeping the user location accurate.

Table 4–1   Spectrum Efficiency Comparisons

Name	Channel Utilization Scheme	Circuits per MHz
IMTS	Analog FDMA	20
AMPS	Analog FDMA	5.5
Digital AMPS-full rate	TDMA	16.7
Digital AMPS-half rate	TDMA	33.3
Digital AMPS	E-TDMA	~80
Microwave	Single-channel TDMA	2–8[1]
BETRS	TDMA	80
GSM	TDMA	~7

[1]Different microwave systems vary.
[CALH92]

The N = 7 arrangement is a common practice in analog cellular systems, due to the arrangement yielding better performance in relation to fading and co-channel interference. Such a cluster with a cell radius of two miles (for example) means the cell centers are about 9.2 miles away from each other.

TRANSMISSION INTERFERENCE

It is evident that considerable thought must be given to the design of the cell and the cell groups in order to prevent adjacent channel interference (interference from adjacent channels in the same cell) as well as co-channel interference (interference between cells).

The goal is to find an adequate frequency reuse distance to reduce co-channel interference as much as possible. Fortunately, a fixed size cell means that co-channel interference is independent of the transmitted signal in each of the cells. Therefore, the cell size is a function of the signal strength of the signal in the cell. Co-channel interference is calculated as follows:

$$q = \frac{D}{R}$$

where q = co-channel interference reduction factor, D = reuse distance, and R = radius. When q increases, co-channel interference decreases. The effects of interference can be demonstrated with a carrier-to-interference ratio (CI) computed as follows:

$$C/I = \frac{C}{\sum\limits_{k=1}^{k_I} I_k}$$

where C/I = carrier-to-interference ratio at the desired mobile receiver, k = number of co-channel interfering cells.

CELL CAPACITY TO HANDLE CALLS

In order to expand our discussion on cellular operations, it is necessary to take a diversion and discuss the concepts of traffic demand, and the ability of a cellular system to meet that demand. Some of the examples pertain to traffic demand and channel capacity at the air interface; others pertain to operations at a switch or a gateway MTSO. The reader who is familiar with the topic of Erlangs can skip this section.

Cellular networks are demand-driven systems. At any time, the user can request (demand) service from the system. In this regard, a cellular system is like the telephone network, because both systems assume that a user must wait for the availability of the service. The wait may be short (a few milliseconds), or it may be long (a few minutes, with call-waiting), but it entails a wait.

In any situation where waiting for a service is a part of the process, the common feature is the demand on the system. Demand is called the offered load (or subscriber demand) and it could be in the form of cellular calls or, for that matter (to take a familiar example), it could be customers waiting in a queue in a bank for a bank teller to handle their deposit.

Whatever the type of load that exists in a service system, offered load is defined by two random processes: (1) the average arrival rate of the callers who are requesting the service (average arrival), λ; and (2) the average length of time the subscriber requires the service (average holding time), T.

The cell site cannot always service the customer immediately. For example, a customer experiences a wait when the system is servicing other calls. In some systems, the customer waits for the service by joining a line or queue, but not in a cellular system, unless the system supports call-waiting. The queue length is somewhat unpredictable because the customers ask for service on a random basis.

A perfect system with respect to time entails no delay (no queues). If n subscribers are connected to a network, a "no delay" system would require n(n − 1)/2 direct connections—clearly an impossible task. Consequently, a cellular system is designed to provide a reasonable delay during normal traffic conditions, yet refuse (block) calls during periods of heavy traffic.

Naturally, what is reasonable and normal is subjective. A user's view of unavailable channels may differ from the view of the network provider. But all parties have the same idea: A channel should be available when needed. Cellular network providers continuously monitor their system to ascertain traffic loads and potential call saturation, and modify their systems to accommodate increases in traffic. This topic is covered later in this chapter.

For any service system with enough servers to service customers immediately upon their request, the average number of busy servers is always the product of λ and T. This relationship is independent of the patterns of arrivals and variations of holding time [COOP81]. As a result of this supposition, the offered load (a) is defined as:

$$a = \lambda \times T$$

For example, if 300 customers need to be serviced per minute during an hour, and each customer requires 2 minutes of service, then offered load a = 600. However, this simple result does not tell the whole story. If peak periods exist beyond the average (which certainly is the case in most service systems, such as a cellular network), then the network provider must accommodate the additional traffic by having additional service facilities. For cellular systems, this translates to additional bandwidth and more channels at the air interface.

The offered load expressed in a hour of calls is called traffic intensity. In the previous example, the traffic intensity is 300/60 minutes = 5 hour calls. Traffic intensity represents the average number of simultaneous calls.

Traffic intensity is not the same as traffic density. This latter term refers to the number of simultaneous calls in a given instant. Traffic intensity describes the average traffic density during a length of time (typically a one-hour period). Also, the offered load is usually different from the carried load since the system does not carry (service) all requests.

Average arrival rates and average holding times are generally expressed in the same unit of time. This means the value *a* is a dimensions quantity. Its values are expressed as Erlangs (after the Danish mathematician A. K. Erlang, one of the founders of traffic theory). One Erlang represents a service facility occupied for one hour.

As an example, assume 200 callers generate 60 requests during a busy hour [KLEI86]. The average holding time for the calls is 240 seconds. The arrival rate is:

$$60 / 3600 = 1 \text{ request per second}$$

The Erlang is calculated as:

$$\frac{60 \text{ calls}}{3600 \text{ seconds}} \times \frac{240 \text{ seconds}}{\text{Call}} = 4 \text{ Erlangs}$$

In addition to the Erlang, telephone systems measure the load in one hundred call seconds (CCS) per hour. CCS is calculated as:

$$\text{CCS} = \text{NCBH} \times \text{HT} / 100$$

where NCBH = number of calls during a busy hour; HT = holding time. One hour consists of 3600 seconds. Therefore, a continuous traffic load of one hour represents 36 CCS or 1 Erlang. The CCS unit is a common, widely used term of measurement for telephone system traffic engineering. To continue our example, the number of 100 call seconds is:

$$\frac{(60 \times 240)}{100} = 144 \text{ CCS}$$

The traffic per caller is:

$$144 / 200 = .72 \text{ CCS} / \text{caller}$$

A single server has a capacity of 1 Erlang. This means the server is always busy. The maximum capacity (in Erlangs) is equal to the number of servers. However, the actual activity must be less than the maximum server capacity because a telephone loss system experiences infinite blocking probability when the traffic intensity is equal to the server capacity. In our example, more than four links are required to adequately serve the callers.

In the public telephone network and in a cellular system, even though loads vary from hour to hour, historically they vary in predictable and recognizable patterns. As a consequence, the network provider can utilize these historical measures to more effectively accommodate peak periods.

Of course, the public telephone system does not always service customers to their satisfaction. During Mother's Day and other notable events, the traffic is simply too much for the system to handle, and we experience the familiar busy signal during such holidays. Nonetheless, during most times, even though the exact number of calls that must be serviced is not known, it can be determined (historically and statistically) that there will be some number of them. The probability that a call will be serviced and leave the system can also be estimated. These same ideas can be applied to cellular systems as well.

The concepts involved in the design of the cellular network are founded on a common assumption that the probability (P) of an arrival of a call at the cell during some small interval (T, T + t) is proportional to the length of this small interval; that is, t. Furthermore, the portionality constant is average arrival rate (λ); therefore:

$$P(T, T + t) = \lambda \times t$$

This important yet simple assumption has been used to develop many traffic theory techniques.

Poisson Distribution Process

One of the most widely used equations for studying practically any kind of user service situation is the Poisson distribution process. This equation describes a large independent number of potential users such that the community of users may have only a small number requesting service at any one time. It is defined as:

$$P(K, t) = \frac{(\lambda t)^k}{K!} e^{-\lambda t}$$

where P(K,t) = probability that k calls arrive in any interval of fixed length t.

It should also be noted that the arrivals of the calls are memory-less: They are independent of each other. The probability of the event at time (T, T + t) depends on the probability of time only—which is one case of a Markov process [PAPO84].

In any service system such as a bank, the telephone system, or cellular network, traffic engineering must also consider that the customer will eventually leave the system (in a bank, walking out the door, and in a cellular system, hanging up the handset). Consequently, we can make the assumption that during the interval length (t) each customer or call will terminate with probability "μt" where "μ" is the departure rate. The following formula describes the probability that a given arrival requires service for t seconds or less.

$$H(t) = 1 - e^{-\mu t}$$

Referring to Figure 4–8, we assume cell 1 uses frequencies X. Cell 1 is running out of bandwidth, so it borrows frequencies Z from cell 6. We assume cell 6 has frequencies Y remaining. Cells 8 and 9 also use frequencies Y and Z. In order to ensure that these frequencies do not interfere with each other, the following rules apply: For cell 1, Z frequencies used only in sector a, but they are not used in sectors b or c. For cells 8 and 9, only frequencies Y are used in sector a.

EXAMPLE OF A MOBILE CELLULAR CALL

Figure 4–9 shows how a mobile station establishes a call with an MTSO. It is a generic example that pertains to several systems in operation worldwide. Specific examples of particular systems (AMPS, IS-51, GSM, etc.) are covered in other chapters.

As depicted in Figure 4–7, when a cellular set in the mobile station is turned on, a handshake takes place between this unit and the MTSO that is controlling the cell in which the mobile station is located. Unknown to the person using the unit, the handshake validates the unit (through the exchange of pre-established identifiers). As part of this handshake, the MTSO registers the unit's location. In the United States, the handshake also determines if system A or system B is to be used.

During the initialization phase, the mobile station will scan the paging channels and tune to the strongest channel. The unit then monitors control channels, and goes into an idle state, but will continually listen for signals addressed to the unit. The mobile station must monitor the control channels at all times (even when no call is taking place). It continues to lock onto the best (strongest) channel in order to receive control messages (paging, etc.) from the base station.

During idle conditions, the mobile station must be able to respond to an MTSO's ongoing control messages, such as responses to paging or periodic verification of identifiers.

When the person in the mobile station wishes to make a call, the user enters a telephone number into a keypad. The unit finds an available access channel and sends a call request. The MTSO receives the request, selects an available frequency, and returns a message to the user containing the assigned channel.

The call then takes place through the MTSO, which may entail con-

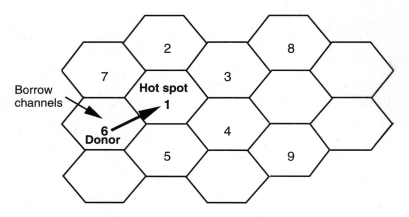

(a) Channel Borrowing

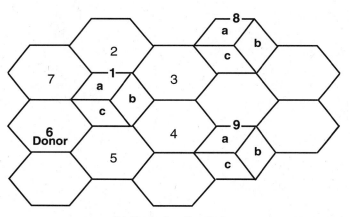

(b) Sectoring the Cells

Cell 1 uses frequencies X
Cell 1 borrows frequencies Z from cell 6, and cell 6 has frequencies Y remaining
Cells 8 and 9 also use frequencies Y and Z
For cell 1, Z frequencies used only in sector a, not sectors b or c
For cells 8 and 9, only frequencies Y used in sector a

Figure 4–8
Channel borrowing and cell sectoring.

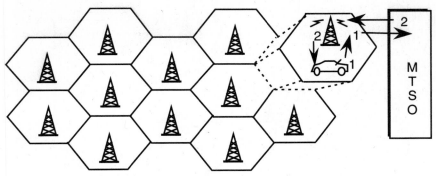

1. Power on, and registration
2. On-going monitoring of control channels

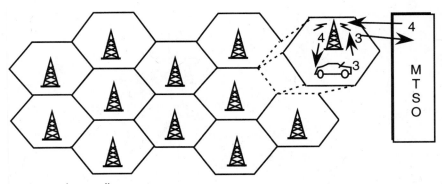

3. Request to make a call
4. Assignment of a channel

Figure 4–9
Example of a mobile cellular operation.

necting to the public telephone network, another cell at this MTSO, or to another cellular system.

Referring to Figure 4–10, a paging channel is used to handshake with a mobile station. When the unit receives a page, it responds. If the page is to notify the unit that it is receiving an incoming call, the MTSO will inform the unit of the specific channel that it is to use for the call. Since the mobile station is frequency-agile, it tunes itself to this channel, and accepts the call. Thereafter, the two parties communicate with each

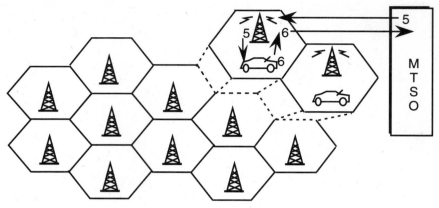

5. Page
6. Response to page

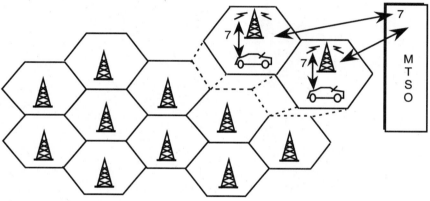

7. Ongoing communications

Figure 4–10
Paging and setting up the channel.

other across the air interface to and from the MTSO and the telephone network.

As seen in Figure 4–11, as the mobile station moves through a geographical region, it will likely move into another cell. Therefore, a hand-off takes place that allows the unit to be assigned a free channel in the new cell. As the signal strength between the unit and the base station

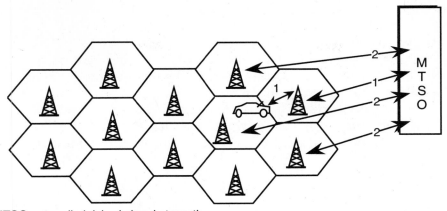

1. MTSO notes diminished signal strength
2. Other cells solicited to take over connection

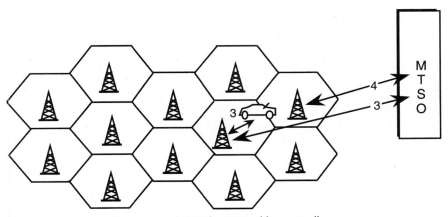

3. Communications established and channel set up with new cell
4. Channel in old cell is released for reuse

**Figure 4–11
Roaming and hand off.**

controller becomes weaker, the MTSO is informed. It then initiates procedures to pass the connection to a cell that has a strong reception of the mobile station's frequency. Once the unit has been given a new channel in the new cell, the old channel in the old cell is released and made available for another user in that cell.

SUMMARY

The signals in wireless mobile systems are quite different from conventional fixed, wire-based systems, due to multipath propagation. Both systems are demand-driven and thus they can be modeled with Erlang B.

Cell size is a critical component in the design of cellular systems. Equally important is the cell reuse pattern. Even with judicious matching of cell size and reuse, the network provider often must resort to cell splitting or sectoring to obtain more bandwidth to accommodate more users.

5

Channel Utilization Schemes

INTRODUCTION

This chapter examines multiplexing and compression techniques and how they are employed in mobile systems. Frequency division multiplexing (FDM) and time division multiplexing (TDM) systems are explained as well as specific implementations of frequency division multiple access (FDMA) and time division multiple access (TDMA). A refinement to TDMA, called extended/TDMA (E-TDMA), is also described. The subjects of frequency hopping and time division duplexing (TDD) are explained as well. The chapter concludes with an examination of spread spectrum techniques and code division multiple access (CDMA) systems.

It is assumed the reader understands the process of analog-to-digital conversion and pulse code modulation. If these topics are unfamiliar to you, the appendix at the end of this chapter should be read.

COMPRESSION AND MULTIPLEXING

The dual subjects of compression and multiplexing are included in this chapter because they both attempt to make better use of a valuable and expensive resource: the communications channel. Interestingly, to perform multiplexing, one is faced with the exact opposite problem than with compression. Multiplexing attempts to make better use of a poten-

Table 5–1   Compression and Multiplexing

Both techniques are designed to better utilize the communications channel

Compression:
- Sharing the channel with multiple users (maybe)
- Designed to use an overutilized channel more effectively

Multiplexing:
- Sharing the channel with multiple users (definitely)
- Designed to use a underutilized channel more effectively

tially underused resource. Compression attempts to make better use of a potentially overused resource. Thus, they have the same goal: make better use of the communications channel. But they achieve the goal with different methods. Table 5–1 provides a summary of the goals of compression and multiplexing.

MULTIPLEXING

Many of the technologies discussed in this book use some form of multiplexing. Multiplexing operations accept voice, video, or data signals from terminals, telephones, and user applications and combine them into one stream for transmission onto a link. A receiving multiplexer demultiplexes and converts the combined communications stream into the original multiple signals. Since several separate transmissions are sent over the same line, the efficiency ratio of the path is improved. Figure 5–1 shows three forms of multiplexing.

Frequency Division Multiplexing (FDM)

In the previous decade, the most widely used multiplexing technique was FDM (see Figure 5–1(a)). While it has largely disappeared from end-user equipment, it is still widely used in telephone, microwave, and satellite carrier systems. FDM divides the transmission frequency range (the bandwidth) into narrower bands (called subchannels). The subchannels are lower-frequency bands, and each band is capable of carrying a separate voice or data signal. Consequently, FDM is used in a variety of applications such as telephone systems, radio systems, and the familiar cable television (CATV) that many people have installed in their homes. CATV provides a separate FDM band for each TV channel.

The first generation cellular systems, such as AMPS, use FDM techniques to allow multiple callers to share the frequency spectrum. The

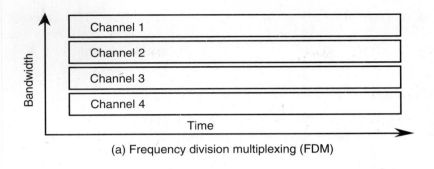

(a) Frequency division multiplexing (FDM)

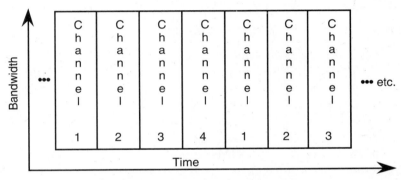

(b) Time division multiplexing (TDM)

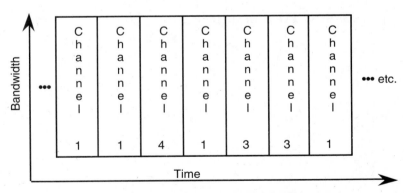

(c) Statistical time division multiplexing (STDM)

**Figure 5–1
Multiplexing.**

technique is called frequency division multiple access (FDMA). Each user is assigned a different frequency for the call. In some systems, two channels are used, one in each direction, between the mobile and land stations.

FDMA and TDD

In other systems, time division duplex (TDD) is used. With this approach, one frequency is used for both directions between two stations and each station takes turns using the channel. TDD is also known by two other names: flip-flop and ping-pong. Essentially, it is a half-duplex system that gives the illusion of full-duplex operations.

Time Division Multiplexing (TDM)

Time division multiplexing (TDM) provides a user the full channel capacity but divides the channel usage into time slots (see Figure 5–1(b)). Each user is given a slot and the slots are rotated among the users. A pure TDM (such as a T1 mux) cyclically scans the input signals (incoming traffic) from the multiple incoming points. Bits, bytes, or blocks of data are separated and interleaved together into frames on a single high-speed communications line. TDMs are discrete signal (digital) devices and will not accept analog data.

The conventional TDM wastes the bandwidth of the communications line for certain applications because the time slots are often unused. Vacant slots occur when an idle terminal has nothing to transmit in its slot. Statistical TDM multiplexers (STDMs) dynamically allocate the time slots among active terminals (see Figure 5–1(c)). Dedicated time slots (TDMs) are not provided for each port on a STDM. Consequently, idle terminal time does not waste the line's capacity. It is not unusual for two to five times as much traffic to be accommodated on lines using STDMs in comparison to a TDM.

In cellular systems the shared use of a TDM channel is called time TDMA, which is similar to STDM, the subject of the next section of this chapter.

MULTIPLE ACCESS WITH FDM AND TDM

As just stated, TDMA is used extensively in newer mobile and wireless systems. It is a combination of FDM and TDM operations. Like FDMA, the frequency spectrum is divided into channels, and signals are im-

Burst 1	Burst 2	Burst 3	Burst 4	Burst 5	Burst 6	Burst 7	Burst 8	Burst n
0.577 ms	0.577 ms	0.577 ms	0.577 ms	0.577 ms	0.577 ms	0.577 ms	0.577 ms	0.577 ms
0.577 ms	0.577 ms	0.577 ms	0.577 ms	0.577 ms	0.577 ms	0.577 ms	0.577 ms	0.577 ms
0.577 ms	0.577 ms	0.577 ms	0.577 ms	0.577 ms	0.577 ms	0.577 ms	0.577 ms	0.577 ms
0.577 ms	0.577 ms	0.577 ms	0.577 ms	0.577 ms	0.577 ms	0.577 ms	0.577 ms	0.577 ms

etc. / 200 kHz / 200 kHz / 200 kHz

Each 200 kHz channel occupies part of the full bandwidth.

Figure 5–2
Multiple access with FDM and TDM.

pressed onto a carrier frequency in each channel. However, unlike FDMA, TDMA impresses digital signals onto the carrier. As shown in Figure 5–2, traffic is burst onto the channel at specific periods, in this example from the Global System for Mobile Communications (GSM) technology, each burst lasts 0.577 ms. Up to eight mobile stations are assigned to a communications channel of 200 kHz bandwidth. Thereafter, their bursts are controlled such that each station knows when to send its burst onto the channel. In this manner, the eight users do not interfere with each other. The bursts shown in Figure 5–2 are also called time slots.

In order to prevent a TDM burst from interfering with the burst from another slot, the cellular specifications define the amplitude and time requirements for the signal. Figure 5–3 shows the requirements for a burst as defined in the GSM specifications. The transmitter in this example must switch its signal on in 28 µs, and then send its information for 542.76 µs, which permits the sending of 147 bits during this burst. It then has 28 µs to turn off its transmitter. A guard time (guardband) on each side of the 542.76 µs burst requires the signal must be below –70 dB. The GSM specification requires the signal increase and decrease in the 10 and 8 µs intervals that are shown in the bottom part of this figure. The idea is to concentrate the 147 bits in the middle of the burst, where it is the most robust.

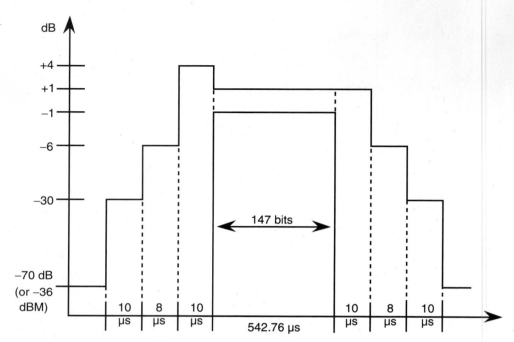

Figure 5–3
Burst with the power and time compared.

TIME DIVISION MULTIPLE ACCESS (TDMA)

We learned earlier that TDMA is a version of TDM. Indeed, many of the concepts of TDMA were derived from TDM systems such as T1, which uses the TDM techniques shown in Figure 5–1(b), but modified as in Figure 5–1(c). Like T1 systems, users are assigned predefined slots in which to send and receive digitized voice traffic. Each slot carries voice traffic pertaining to an individual voice circuit (see Figure 5–4).

TDMA takes advantage of the fact that conversations between people have frequent periods of silence (at least with some people) and the TDMA system will interleave the digitized talkspurts of multiple users across one channel.

The bottom part of Figure 5–4 depicts how the analog signal is converted to digital code through the analog-to-digital converter (A/D). The digitized code is buffered (in a buffer or register) at the mobile station, and released onto the channel to fill a predefined time slot. Thus, while

(a) Based on TDM technology of assigned slots:

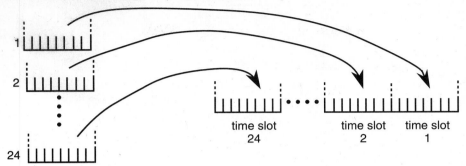

(b) TDMA approach—each subscriber has assigned time slot, buffer released at a specific time:

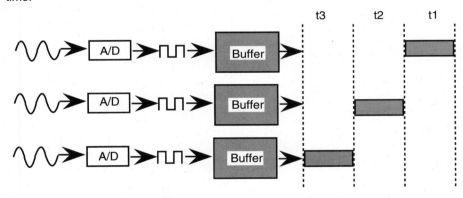

Figure 5–4
Time division multiple access (TDMA).

each user (up to eight) is occupying the same frequency domain, their signals do not interfere because they are occupying a different time domain.

The user's traffic is divided into fixed-length TDMA slots and then multiplexed into a TDMA frame. The frame is then sent across the channel by modulating the radio frequency (RF) carrier. As shown in Figure 5–5, each slot contains synchronization and control fields, which include an error correction field (to repair damaged bits). Due to the variable delay that can accrue in a wireless system, extra bits are contained in the slot to compensate for these delays. These bits comprise the temporal guardband fields. They are also called tail bits in some systems and guard time and/or ramp time bits in other systems. They are placed at the beginning and ending of the burst to serve as guard time during the

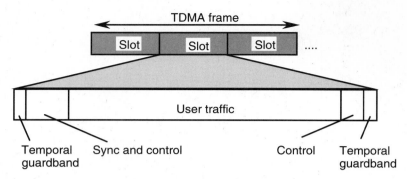

Figure 5–5
The TDMA frame and slot.

ramping up and down of the signal. The synchronization bits are a fixed sequence of bits that are known by the receiver, and are used by the receiver to train itself onto the signal. Some systems place these bits in the middle of the burst, which is called a "mid-amble."

Silent periods in a voice conversation occupy more time than nonsilent periods. Most studies reveal that the ratio is about 60/40. This value is derived from a typical conversation where a talkspurt lasts 1.5 seconds, and the silent period lasts 2.25 seconds [CALH92]. Thus, the ratio is 1.5/1.5 + 2.25 = .40, which means that an unaltered voice channel is not utilized very well. Figure 5–6 depicts this idea.

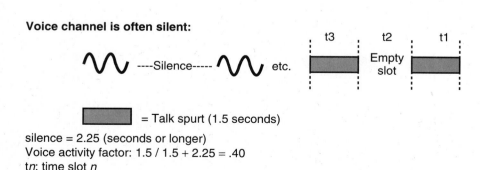

Figure 5–6
Talkspurts and silent periods. [CALH92]

For many years, selected analog speech signals have been processed through time-assigned speech interpolation (TASI). This technology places other speech or data signals into the silent periods of a conversation, which provides additional capacity on multichannel links. Today, the concepts of TASI are applied to digital signals and tagged with new names—one example is TDMA.

Vendors vary on how they allocate TDMA slots and frames. One approach allocates one voice channel per frame to accommodate a 32 kbit/s digitized voice. The speech stream is coded into a packet in 16 ms time slots. Each packet contains 128 4-bit samples. This coding convention results in a 32 kbit/s transmission stream, based on the following calculations:

$$1 \text{ second} / 8000 \text{ samples per second} = a \text{ .000125 sample interval}$$
$$.000125 * .128 = .016 \text{ packet interval}$$

The packet is 64 octets in length (512 bits). Therefore, the 32 kbit/s transmission stream is derived by:

$$1 \text{ second} / .016 = 62.5$$
$$62.5 * 512 \text{ bits} = 32,000$$

With this approach, the voice port uses a 32 kbit/s companded delta modulation scheme (also called logarithmic companded delta modulation [LCDM]). LCDM provides good tolerance to noise, a low data rate, and acceptable performance over a wide range of input signals.

Some systems perform voice activity compression (VAC). Only speaking persons require channel slots, so VAC makes it possible to share channels among multiple voice transmissions.

Figure 5–7 depicts the interactions of the mobile station (MS) and the base station controller (BSC) in the reservation of a TDMA slot. First, the voice signal is detected and converted to digital images. During this process, a voice activity detector (VAD) discerns that a voice signal is active. It sends to the BSC a request for the allocation of bandwidth. Since this request and its subsequent assignment take only a few milliseconds, this handshake does not interfere with the voice analog-to-digital translation process and the ongoing quantizing and coding operations. That is, the BSC returns an "assign slot" signal to the MS before the MS is ready to send its signal onto the channel. In this example, the talkspurt is ready for transmission after it has filled a buffer, which takes about 40 ms.

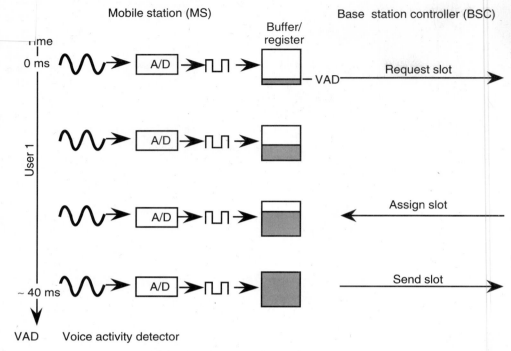

Figure 5–7
Request and assignment procedure.

E-TDMA

Figure 5–8 shows one approach in increasing the capacity on TDMA systems [CALH92]. It is called extended TDMA (E-TDMA). Using digital speech interpolation (DSI) to eliminate silent periods, the spectrum is divided into 12 frequencies, with 6 time slots assigned to each frequency. A total of 72 channels are available, of which 9 are set aside for control signaling. As we learned in previous discussions in this chapter, a 40 ms delay at the mobile station gives the system sufficient time to request and allocate a time slot for the transmission.

Figure 5–8 shows the frequency and time slot allocations. The twelve frequencies are shown as F1-F12. The six slots are shown as columns across the frequency bands. While 63 slots are available for user traffic, an E-TDMA can actually support more than 63 users simultaneously (with DSI), due to the bursty nature of talkspurts, and enhanced

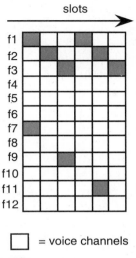

Figure 5–8
Extended TDMA capacity.
[CALH92]

☐ = voice channels

■ = control channels

compression schemes. One proposal uses a half-rate voice coding scheme (4.5 kbit/s) and DSI, which supports 6 connections per carrier.

EIA/TIA IS-54

The EIA/TIA IS-54 standard provides specifications for a cellular system to operate in a dual mode. During the handshake between the mobile station and the base station, the mobile station sends a message to the mobile station indicating if it is configured to support conventional FDMA AMPS operations, or if it can operate as a dual mode station to support TDMA operations. For the latter operations, six slots are sent in the frame. Each frame consists of 1944 bits and is 40 ms in duration. Twenty-five frames are sent per second. This technology permits mobile stations to operate at full-rate or half-rate. Full-rate channels utilize two slots in the frame, and half-rate channels use one slot.

CODE DIVISION MULTIPLE ACCESS (CDMA)

Code division multiple access (CDMA) is quite different from TDMA. First, CDMA uses a single spectrum of bandwidth (not slices of band-width) for all users in the cell. It transmits all the users' signals onto the channel at the same time, which allows the users' signals to "interfere" with each other.

Like TDMA, the analog speech is coded into digital signals, but unlike TDMA, each conversation is assigned a unique code (a "signature" for each individual transmission). The coded signal is extractable at the receiver, by the use of a complementary code. The codes of different users on the channel are designed to be as different from each other as possible, which means they are as random as possible (that is to say, the codes are *orthogonal* to each other).

Each speech signal is modulated ("spread") across an entire band (e.g., a 1.25-MHz band). The respective receiver demodulates and interprets the signal using the relevant code that is embedded in the signal. The final signal contains only the relevant conversation. Any other signals (other users' coded signals) are picked up as noise.

Many people describe CDMA with a language analogy. For example, imagine sitting in a room where several people are speaking different languages to each other. You, acting as the receiver, can discern the language or languages you know from the others. Even though all sounds (signals) are being received by your ear, your ability to "filter" out the superfluous conversations is analogous to a CDMA receiver examining the relevant codes in the signals and filtering out those that are not pertinent.

Other aspects of CDMA are noteworthy (although TDMA can provide some of these features as well, and these examples illustrate some commercial implementations). Multipath receptions of signals are coherently combined at the receiver, which enhances the quality of the signal. The power control system adjusts transmit power to enhance the quality of the signal. As a general practice, handoff is soft in that two cells share the call during handoff.

Coding and Decoding the Signal

This section provides an example of how a signal is coded and decoded, and how a wrong key at the receiver fails to decode the signal. For purposes of simplicity and brevity, I have created a simple model. The example accurately reflects the theory and practice of CDMA and spread spectrum systems. For a detailed explanation of my example, I refer the reader to [VITE95].

Successful operations. Figure 5–9 shows an uncoded binary signal of 1010 that party A is to send to party B. Before sending this signal, party A encodes the bits with a pseudo-random code (also called a key by

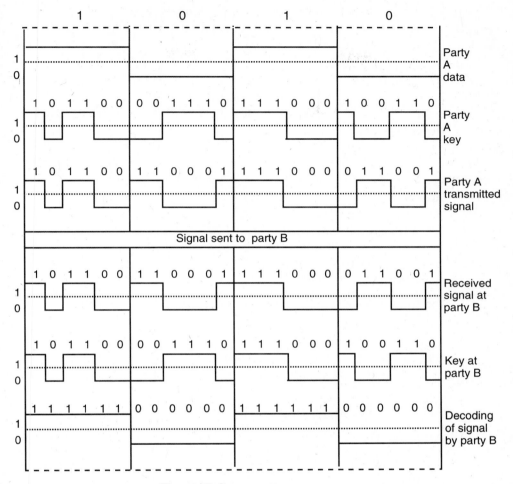

Figure 5–9
Coding and decoding a signal.

some vendors) that has been generated by a Bernoulli sequence. That is, the relative frequencies of 0 and 1 are 1/2, and run lengths of 0s and 1s follow the coin-flipping experiment:

1. 1/2 of 1 or 0 run lengths are unity
2. 1/4 of the run lengths are of length 2
3. 1/8 of the run lengths are of length 3
4. A fraction 1/2 of all runs are of length n for all finite n

The code shown in Figure 5–9 is 6 bits in length for each binary number. This small code is necessary for this example, but common systems use run lengths of over 100 bits.

In Figure 5–9, the code is labeled "Party A key." The sending machine matches the data stream with the code. The result is labeled "Party A transmitted signal." The rules for the coding are straightforward. For each user bit of 1, the pseudo-random code (PC) is left unaltered, and sent to the receiver. For each user bit of 0, the bits (actually + or − signals) are inverted and sent to the receiver. This approach has the characteristics of a bitwise function. The result is based on a bitwise NOT XOR. A conventional bitwise XOR inverts bits. That is, an operand that has a 1 bit will cause the resultant bit to be inverted, and an operand that has a 0 bit will cause the resultant bit to remain unchanged. The NOT XOR operation has the exact opposite result.

The reader may conclude that this discussion is a convoluted explanation of other bitwise operations, such as AND or OR. Such is not the case. Table 5–2 shows the differences. In Figure 5–9, the user signal represents the first operand in this table and Party A key represents the second operand.

The "Party A transmitted signal" is modulated onto the carrier and sent to the receiver, party B in Figure 5–9. The random signals become a waveform that has the characteristics of noise, except to the receiver that has stored the proper code to interpret the signal.

It also can be seen in Figure 5–9 that multiple bits are sent onto the channel as a code for each bit in the user bit stream. The original signal is spread into pseudo-noise through the pseudo-random sequences. The clock period for the sequence is called the chip duration or chip rate. This term describes how many bits are encoded per user bit, and is described in chips per second. Of course, CDMA requires more bandwidth because it is sending more bits onto the channel than what is in the original user bit stream. For a chip rate of n, then n times more bandwidth is required than that in the original user bit stream.

Table 5–2   Bitwise Operations

First Operand	Second Operand	AND	OR	XOR	NOT XOR
0	0	0	0	0	1
0	1	0	1	1	0
1	0	0	1	1	0
1	1	1	1	0	1

While CDMA and spread spectrum use a lot of bandwidth, the need for a channel of more capacity is offset by this fact that the approach provides better signal-to-noise performance than a conventional TDMA or FDMA system. It is also more effective in measuring and rejecting noise (or the other user signals embedded in the signal).

Referring to Figure 5–9 again, at the receiver, Party B must first synchronize itself onto the incoming signal. This operation is performed by the receiver matching the received signal with the stored PC (the pseudo-random code). A proper bit mapping and matching sequence occurs when Party B has correlated the code to the incoming stream and decoded something other than noise. This ongoing synchronization results in about the same number of 1 and 0 (+ and – signals) bits being decoded (which is perceived as noise) until the decoding process finds the exact bit alignment of the incoming stream to the PC, and decodes to non-noise signals. This process is shown in the bottom part of Figure 5–9.

Note that the decoding process follows the rules for NOT XOR functions, which means that if the received bit is a 1, the PC bit remains the same. If the received bit is a 0, the PC bit is inverted.

Unsuccessful operations. Figure 5–10 shows what happens at a receiver that does not have the correct code sequence to decode the incoming signal. Party B is using the wrong code (perhaps trying to hack the signal). The result is a signal that looks like noise because there are almost the same number of 1s and 0s (+ and – signals) in the decoded signal. The next section explains this concept in more detail.

As we learned from Figure 5–9, the opposite situation holds true when Party B decodes the proper part of the signal (the signal from Party A for Party B). The resultant output results in non-noise bit sequences. In effect, within a chip period, for each original user 1 bit, more 1 bits than 0 bits are derived from the process; for each original user 0 bit, more 0 bits than 1 bits are derived.

Examples of output. The decoding process separates combined signals by accumulating the + and – signals through integrator and comparator functions. In an ideal operation, the output resembles the accumulated (staircase) signals in Figure 5–11. Each bit in the chip set contributes to the resultant signal. A 1 contributes to a + ascension up the staircase, and a 0 contributes to a – descension down the staircase. This figure is an ideal operation, since the decoding process has produced all 1s for each user 1 and all 0s for each user 0.

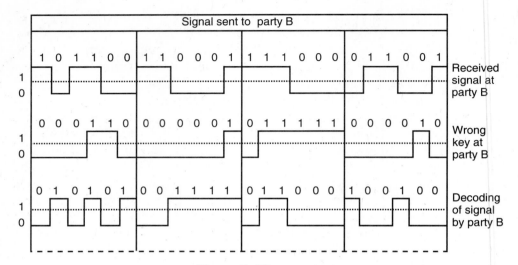

Figure 5–10
Incorrect decoding.

Spread Spectrum and Frequency Hopping

In some systems, spread spectrum is used also with frequency hopping, as shown in Figure 5–12. After all, even with spread spectrum, the signal is spread across a defined spectrum. Therefore, if a cellular system has 12.5 MHz of bandwidth, it can be split into ten channels, each operating at 1.25 MHz.

As discussed earlier, TDMA divides the frequency spectrum into smaller bands. In contrast, CDMA uses the full bandwidth of the channel. All users' traffic is placed onto the channel at the same time. However, the receiver is able to recognize and separate each user's traffic because the transmitter places unique codes into each user's traffic.

The frequency changes rapidly based on a wide range of selectable frequencies (which are selected in a pseudo-random manner). The decoding at the receiver can take place correctly if the receiver knows the sequence of frequency selections.

One of the attractive features of frequency hopping is its support of multiple users on a limited bandwidth channel. Figure 5–13 shows an example of how some systems provide this feature (based on the original concept of frequency hopping to avoid jamming, a subject of

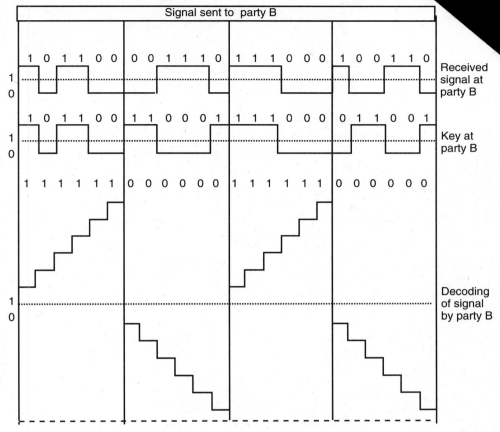

Figure 5–11
Decoding the signal (ideal situation).

Chapter 13). Each user is allowed to frequency hop; that is, the user transmitter changes its carrier frequency often. In this figure, three users burst onto the channel during different time periods while alternating their carrier frequencies. Since the alteration of the frequencies may not be coordinated, users may use the same frequency at the same time, which leads to interference and the distortion of the signals. However, a well-designed system should not experience many of these "collisions." A few of them will not affect the quality of the signal, if the slots are small—resulting in small losses of the voice signal.

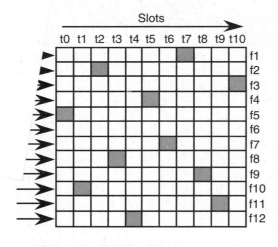

☐ = Time slots of coded traffic

**Figure 5–12
Frequency hopping.**

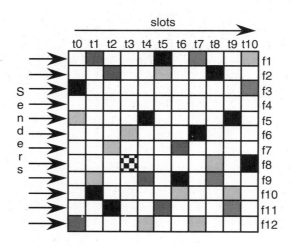

☒ = Mutual interference

Different shadings represent different users

**Figure 5–13
Frequency hopping and multiple users.**

TIA/EIA IS-95-A

The TIA/EIA-95-A standards provides the specifications for dual-mode operations across an air interface. The CDMA technology is employed by using 1.23 MHz of spectrum that is centered on one of the AMPS 30 kHz channels.

COMPARISONS OF AMPS, TDMA, AND CDMA

Table 5–3 compares AMPS, TDMA, and CDMA. The table was derived from [CRAW94]. If one views the TDMA/CDMA debate from afar, it is well to remember the saying, "Where one stands depends on where one sits." Those that have invested in TDMA support TDMA; those that have invested in CDMA support CDMA.

Most people recognize that FDM is inherently limited and its features have been exploited to their limit. The debate between TDMA and CDMA has been one of the main issues in the wireless industry for the past several years. The debate is starting to wane as CDMA matures and as products based on CDMA enter the marketplace.

Notwithstanding, there are still diehard TDMA proponents and diehard CDMA proponents. This writer sees attractive features of each technology and believes both technologies will continue to grow. It is unlikely that they will displace each other in the near future.

Table 5–3   AMPS, TDMA, and CDMA

Operation	AMPS	TDMA	CDMA
Bandwidth	12.5 MHz	12.5 MHz	12.5 MHz
Frequency reuse	k = 7	k = 7	k = 1
RF channel	0.03 MHz	0.03 MHz	1.25 MHz
Number of RF channels	12.5/0.03 = 416	12.5/0.03 = 416	12.5/1.25 = 10
Channels per cell	416/7 = 59	416/7 = 59	12.5/1.25 = 10
Usable channels per cell	57	57	10
Calls per RF channel	1	3	38
Voice channels per cell	$57 \times 1 = 57$	$57 \times 3 = 171$	$10 \times 38 = 380$
Sectors/cell	3	3	3
Voice calls/sector	57/3 = 19	171/3 = 57	380
Capacity vs. AMPS	—	3×	20×

COMPRESSION OPERATIONS

Most of the discussion in this chapter has centered on multiplexing techniques. We now turn our attention to compression operations. The first part of this section discusses voice compression; the second part discusses data compression.

Voice Compression Techniques

In addition to the waveform analysis techniques discussed in the appendix to this chapter (such as pulse code modulation [PCM] and delta modulation), the industry has devoted considerable research to a technique called parameter coding (also, vocoding). Vocoders are not used on the telephone network because they are designed to encode speech signals only and cannot accommodate other analog signals, such as modem transmissions. In contrast, PCM can convey data or voice.

Vocoders do not preserve the character of the waveform; rather, the input waveform is processed into parameters that measure vocal characteristics. The speech is analyzed to produce a varying model of the waveform. Parameter coding then computes a signal that most closely resembles the original speech. These parameters are transmitted through the channel (or stored on disk) for later reproduction of the speech signal. Vocoders are commonly used for recorded announcements (e.g., weather information), voice output, and electronic video games.

Channel vocoders were developed in the late 1920s. Today the channel vocoders operate from a range of 1 to 2 kbit/s. These systems analyze the signal spectrum as a function of time. A series of bandpass filters are used to separate the energy of speech into sub-bands. The bands are then filtered to determine the relative power levels to each other. The channel vocoders also determine the voiced and unvoiced nature of the pitched frequency of the input signal. The disadvantage of the channel vocoder is the difficulty of analyzing the pitch of the voice signal. Nonetheless, some of the vocoders today produce fairly high quality (if synthetic) sound at 2400 bit/s.

In the past few years, voice compression techniques have given us the ability to carry voice images at bit rates as low as 2.4 kbit/s. One system is a variation of the channel vocoder, and is called the formant vocoder. This system takes advantage of the fact that most of the energy of speech is concentrated within a bandwidth of approximately 2 kHz. The formant vocoder encodes only the most significant short-time components of a voice signal. This technique provides a fairly intelligible speech signal with a fewer number of bits.

Linear predictive coding (LPC) is an example of the vocoders. LPC is based on the fact that speech produces a vocal tract that is either voiced or voiceless. The vowel "e" in keep is a voiced sound; the "s" in sir is a voiceless sound. Both of these mechanisms sampled to produce a stream of impulses. The impulses can then be stored as digital images for later use.

Another related technique is called vector quantization. (Variations of this technique are called code-excited linear predictive coding [CELP] and vector-sum excited [see Figure 5–14].) The pattern of a speech signal is defined in 20 to 50 ms durations called speech segments or parcels. Next, the segments are stored in a register in 6 PCM word blocks. These blocks are compared against a table of values (a codebook). The entry in

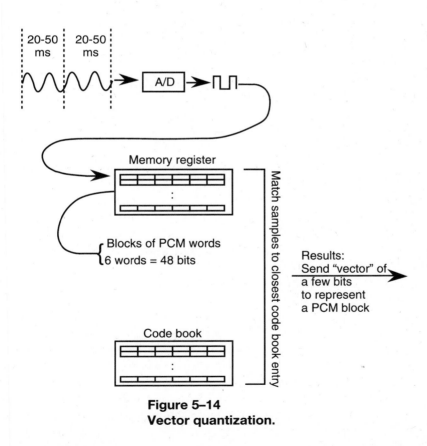

Figure 5–14
Vector quantization.

the table that is closest to the actual value is used as the transmitted value instead of the longer PCM block.

So, the library member whose value gives the best match to the signal is selected as the code word. The advantage of this approach is that each code word can be represented by a fewer number of bits. For example, if a library has 4000 members, only 10 to 12 bits are required to represent and/or transmit the information about the full speech segment.

This technique is attractive because the code book allows transmission at only 2.4 kbit/s. A high-quality 9.6 kbit/s telephone line supports four-time division multiplexed (TDM) 2.4 kbit/s LPC transmissions. This data rate is substantially lower than the waveform techniques of 64 kbit/s, 32 kbit/s, or 16 kbit/s. The main disadvantage of any type of compression is that the speech reproduction is not as high quality as PCM.

Since bandwidth is so precious in a wireless environment, all new systems employ some type of voice compression using LPC techniques.

Data Compression

Practically all symbols generated and used by computers are comprised of a fixed number of bits coded to represent a character. The codes (for example, ASCII) have been designed as fixed length because computers require a fixed number of bits in a code to efficiently process data. Most machines use octet (8-bit) alignment.

The fixed-length format requirement means all transmitted characters are of equal length, even though the characters are not transmitted with equal frequency. For example, characters such as vowels, blanks, and numbers are used and transmitted more often than consonants and characters such as a question mark. This practice can lead to considerable link inefficiency and is especially important in wireless and mobile systems that have limited channel capacity.

One widely used solution to code and channel utilization inefficiency is to adapt a variable-length value (code) to represent the fixed length characters. In this manner, the most frequently transmitted characters are compressed—represented by a unique bit set smaller than the conventional bit code. This data compression technique can result in substantial savings in communications costs.

To gain an understanding for the need for data compression capabilities, consider that a normal page of text contains 1920 characters.

Assuming an eight-bit code is used to represent a character, a total of 15,360 bits will be transferred across a communications link (this number is significantly understated because it does not include start/stop bits and other control functions). Therefore, the use of a conventional V.22bis 2400 bit/s modem can cause significant throughput and response time problems for certain types of transmissions.

With this background information in mind, we now examine some common data compression operations.

Bit mapping is used in a number of applications besides data communications (data storage for example). It is often used on data that exhibit a large number of specific character types such as zeros and blanks. A simple implementation of bit mapping uses one octet to describe the absence or presence of character types. This system only compresses one particular character. If a data stream contains a high incidence of more than one character, other variations of bit mapping can be employed that use more than one control octet, or other compression techniques can be used.

Run length encoding is a variation of character suppression, but requires three characters to convey the intelligence. Consequently, it should be used in data streams in which the characters occur frequently and continuously. It is counterproductive if used with recurring short strings of repeating characters. It has proved to be an effective approach for compressing graphic images.

The repeated characters are compressed as follows. The first character indicates the next two characters are compression codes. The second character is the code of the repeated character, and the third character is the count field indicating the number of consecutive, uninterrupted occurrences of the characters in the data stream.

A well known personal computer protocol, Kermit, uses this compression technique. The transmitting Kermit module precedes the repeating character with (1) a control character, (2) the repeat count, and (3) the character that is needed.

The IBM 3780 data communications system provides blank (space) compression as one of its features. If the 3780 is operating in nontransparent mode and the compression feature enabled, space characters will be automatically compressed when loading the data and expanded with input from the line. This is accomplished by sending an EBCDIC or ASCII character and a count character in place of the deleted spaces. The count character indicates that 2 to 63 spaces were removed.

Relative encoding is a widely used and simple technique. It is generally employed on a data stream that exhibits symbols or symbol strings that vary slightly relative to each other. Process control and telemetry data often exhibit this attribute. Relative encoding does not perform well if the fluctuations between successive values require numbers longer than the original values. It is quite effective for small fluctuations and on data with similar or redundant patterns within the stream.

V.42

V.42 has aroused considerable interest in the user community because it addresses two major problems that have developed with the increased use of asynchronous devices (and especially asynchronous personal computers): (1) an asynchronous-to-synchronous conversion protocol, and (2) a more sophisticated error-detection process for asynchronous systems than exists with simple echo checks and parity checks. V.42 is designed to perform code conversion as well as error detection and retransmission of damaged data. V.42bis is an optional feature of V.42, and is the culmination of several years of efforts by ITU-T, working in conjunction with users and vendors.

During the work on V.42, which was completed in 1988, an ITU-T study group decided that a data compression enhancement was needed to further the performance of error correcting modems. Consequently, a number of existing schemes were analyzed, notably British Telecom's BTLZ, Hayes' System, Microcom's MNP5 and MNP7, and the ACT Formula. The decision was made to use the BTLZ algorithm, which we examine shortly.

The V.42bis data compression recommendation has a compression ratio of 3:1 to 4:1 (based on the use of ASCII text).

The recommendation requires approximately 3K of memory, which makes it attractive for small machines such as portable unit. The dictionary size for the characters and strings can be as little as 512 bytes and up to 2048 bytes. The designer must analyze the tradeoffs between smaller and larger dictionaries and must consider the fact that the larger dictionaries provide better performance with higher compression ratios even though they consume more memory. Readers should keep in mind that V.42bis permits the same software to be used on different size dictionaries.

The V.42bis compression algorithm works on strings of characters. It does not work on character substitution, but encodes a string of characters with a fixed length code word. The system also uses a dictionary to store frequently occurring character strings along with a code to represent these character strings.

Fax Compression

One of the most useful applications for data compression is the transmission of documents or graphics, commonly known as facsimile transmission (fax). Documents lend themselves to compression because their contents have many recurring redundant patterns of space (white patterns) or print patterns (black patterns). The ITU-T publishes several recommended standards relating to facsimile transmission. These classes are described as Group 1, Group 2, Group 3, and Group 4 and are labeled as ITU-T Recommendations T.2, T.3, T.4, and T.5, respectively.

Fax compression treats each fax line as a series of white and black runs. A scanner examines a document left to right and top to bottom and creates an electronic image of the runs. The runs are coded based on their length, and the code is transmitted instead of the full "bit picture" of the document.

The facsimile scanner creates a bit map of the page image. The bit map describes the black or white regions of the document. Each bit map contains the blackness of each dot as the document is read. A typical document would require approximately 3.5 to 4 million dots to represent an 8 1/2″ × 11″ page, if one bit were represented per dot. It is easy to see that an excessively long transmission time would be required to process a one page letter. However, over 80 percent of copy consists of white picture elements. Consequently, it is possible through compression to reduce the number of bits needed to represent the document. Moreover, successive scan lines are often similar. This permits further compression by describing only how a succeeding row differs from the preceding row.

SUMMARY

Multiplexing and compression are vital techniques for bandwidth-limited wireless channels. Compression was used originally for data, but transmission is now used widely in voice systems, and is gaining in use in new mobile and wireless systems. The TDMA and CDMA techniques are highly effective methods for increasing channel capacity.

APPENDIX: BASICS OF DIGITIZED VOICE

Introduction

The process of voice digitization was developed to overcome some of the limitations of analog systems. Several problems arise regarding the analog signal and how it is transmitted across the channel (see Figure 5–15). First, the signal is relayed through amplifiers and other transducers. These devices are designed to perform the relaying function in a linear fashion; that is, the waveform representing the signal maintains its characteristics from one end of the channel to the other. A deviation from this linearity creates a distortion of the waveform. All analog signals exhibit some form of nonlinearity (therefore, a distortion). Unfortunately, the intervening components to strengthen the signal, such as amplifiers, also increase the nonlinearity of the signal.

Second, all signals (digital and analog) are weakened (or attenuated) during transmission through the medium. The decay can make the signal so weak that it is unintelligible at the receiver. A high-quality wire cable with a large diameter certainly mitigates decay, but it cannot be eliminated.

Digital systems overcome these problems by representing the transmitted data with digital and binary images. The analog signal is con-

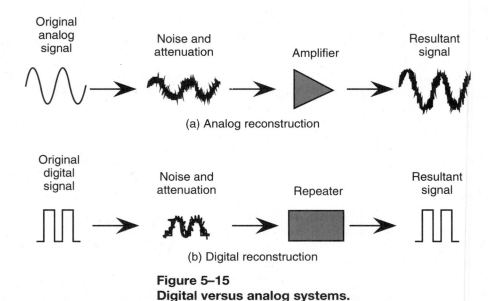

(a) Analog reconstruction

(b) Digital reconstruction

Figure 5–15
Digital versus analog systems.

verted to a series of digital numbers and transmitted through the communications channel as binary data.

Of course, digital signals are subject to the same kinds of imperfections and problems as the analog signal—decay and noise. However, the digital signal is discrete: The binary samples of the analog waveform are represented by specific levels of voltages, in contrast to the nondiscrete levels of an analog signal. Indeed, an analog signal has almost infinite variability. As the digital signal traverses the channel, it is only necessary to sample the absence or presence of a digital binary pulse—not its degree, as in the analog signal.

The mere absence or presence of a signal pulse can be more easily recognized than the magnitude or degree of an analog signal. If the digital signals are sampled at an acceptable rate and at an acceptable voltage level, the signals can then be completely reconstituted before they deteriorate below a minimum threshold. Consequently, noise and attenuation can be completely eliminated from the reconstructed signal.

The periodic sampling and regeneration process is performed by regenerative repeaters. The repeaters are placed on a channel at defined intervals. The spacing depends on the quality and size of the conductor, the amount of noise on the conductor, its bandwidth, and the bit rate of the transmission.

The Analog-to-Digital Conversion Process

Several methods are used to change an analog signal into a representative string of digital binary images (see Figure 5–16). Even though these methods entail many processes, they are generally described in three steps: *sampling*, *quantizing*, and *encoding*.

The devices performing the digitizing process are called channel banks or primary multiplexers. They have two basic functions: converting analog signals to digital signals (and vice versa at the other end); and combining (multiplexing) the digital signals into a single time division multiplexed (TDM) data stream (and demultiplexing them at the other end).

Analog-to-digital conversion is based on Nyquist sampling theory, which states that if a signal is sampled instantaneously at regular intervals and at a rate at least twice the highest frequency in the channel, the samples will contain sufficient information to allow an accurate reconstruction of the signal.

The accepted sampling rate in the industry is 8000 samples per second. Based on Nyquist sampling theory, this rate allows the accurate re-

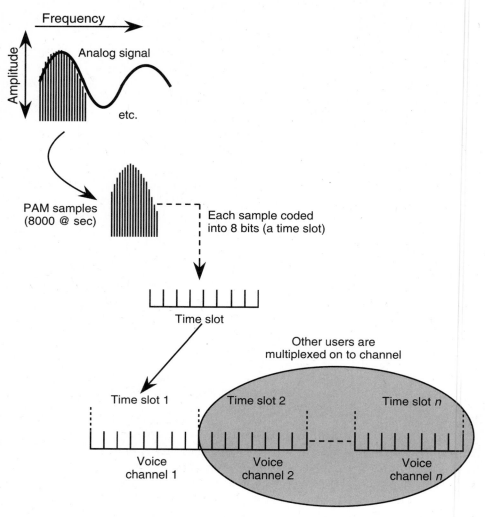

Figure 5–16
Analog-to-digital conversion.

production of a 4 kHz channel, which is used as the bandwidth for a voice-grade channel. The 8000 samples are more than sufficient to capture the signals in a telephone line if certain techniques (discussed shortly) are used.

With pulse amplitude modulation (PAM), the pulse carrier amplitude is varied with the value of the analog waveform. The pulses are

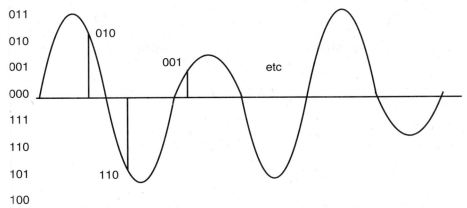

Actual sampling: 8000 times a second * 8 bits per sample = 64,000 kbit/s

Figure 5–17
Signal sampling. [FLAN90]

fixed with respect to duration and position. PAM is classified as a modulation technique because each instantaneous sample of the wave is used to modulate the amplitude of the sampling pulse.

As depicted in Figure 5–17, the 8 kHz sampling rate results in a sample pulse train of signals with a 125 µs time period between the pulses (1 second/8000 = .000125). Each pulse occupies 5.2 µs of this time period. Consequently, it is possible to interleave sampled pulses from other signals within the 125 µs period. The most common approach in North America utilizes 24 interleaved channels, which effectively fills the 125 µs time period (.0000052 * 24 = .000125). The samples are then multiplexed using TDM and put into a digital TDM frame.

The signal f(t) can be reconstructed from the samples by a low pass filter. Theoretically and ideally, the sampling provides an amplitude value at a specific time and the continuous signal is reconstructed by applying the samples to the low pass filter. Practically speaking, sampling is done over a finite time and the reconstruction filters are not ideal. Nonetheless, the process is sufficient to provide adequate reproduction at the receiver.

In 1933, Harry Nyquist defined the minimum sampling frequency needed to convey all information in an analog waveform:

$$f_s > 2BW$$

where f_s = sampling frequency; BW = bandwidth of the input signal.

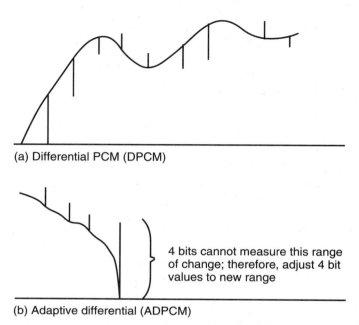

(a) Differential PCM (DPCM)

(b) Adaptive differential (ADPCM)

4 bits cannot measure this range of change; therefore, adjust 4 bit values to new range

Figure 5–18
Differential PCM (DPCM) and adaptive differential (ADPCM).

Other techniques. Today's systems have more sophisticated approaches than the conventional PCM technique. One widely used system is differential pulse code modulation (DPCM) (see Figure 5–18[a]). This technique encodes the differences between samples of the signal instead of the actual samples. Since an analog waveform's samples are closely correlated with each other (almost sample-to-sample redundant), the range of sample differences requires fewer bits to represent the signal. Studies reveal that the predictability between adjacent 8-kHz samples is 85 percent or higher. This redundancy in the PCM codes can be exploited to reduce the bit rate.

However, DPCM is subject to errors when an input signal changes significantly between samples. The DPCM equipment is not able to code the change accurately, which can result in large quantizing errors and signal distortion.

DPCM can be improved by assigning the 4-bit signals to represent different ranges of the signal. For example, the 4 bits can be coded to represent a change between samples. This technique is called adaptive

DPCM (ADPCM) because the systems increase or decrease the volume range covered by each 4-bit sample value.

ADPCM (also see Figure 5–18[b]) uses a differential quantizer to store the previous sample in a sample-and-hold circuit. The circuit measures the change between the two samples and encodes the change. ADPCM achieves a smaller voice digitization rate (VDR) than do the conventional PCM techniques (32 kbit/s, for example). These systems have seen extensive use in digital telephony.

Some DPCM systems use a feedback signal (based on previous samples) to estimate the input signal. These systems are called adaptive predictive DPCM (AP DPCM). The technique is quite useful if the feedback signal varies from the input (due to quantization problems) and the next encoding sample automatically adjusts for the drift. Thus, the quantization errors do not accumulate over a prolonged period.

Many systems store more than one past sample value, with the last three sample values commonly used. The previous samples are then used to produce a more accurate estimate of the next input sample.

Since DPCM and ADPCM do not send the signal but the representation of the change from the previous sample, the receiver must have some method to know where the current level is. Due to noise, the level may vary drastically, or during periods of speech silence (no talking), several samples may be zero. Periodically, the sender and receiver may be returned (referenced) to the same levels by adjusting them to zero.

Another widely used analog-to-digital (A/D), digital-to-analog (D/A) technique is delta modulation (DM). It uses only one bit for each sample, and follows the same concepts of DPCM by exploiting the sample-to-sample redundancy of the speech signal.

Delta modulation measures the polarity of difference of successive samples and uses a 1 bit to indicate if the polarity is rising and a 0 bit to indicate if the signal is decreasing. A pulse train supplies pulses to a modulator, which adjusts the polarity of the pulses to coincide with the amplitude changes of the analog signal.

The technique actually approximates the derivative of the analog signal and not its amplitude. The signal is encoded as a "staircase" of up and down sequences at each sampling time (see Figure 5–19[a]). The digital code can later be used to reconstruct the analog signal (A/D process) by "smoothing" the staircase back to the original signal.

DM is simple to implement. However, it requires a higher sampling rate than PCM or DPCM because each sample does not carry much information. Many systems use 32,000 samples a second to derive a 32 kbit/s digital signal.

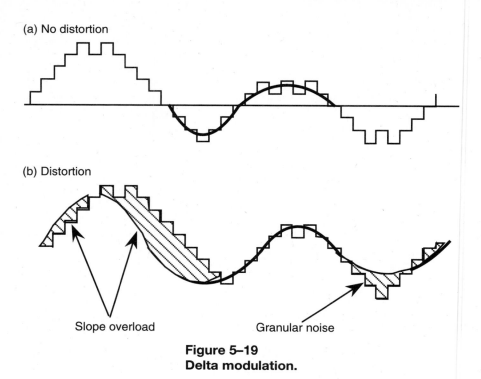

Figure 5–19
Delta modulation.

DM assumes the encoded waveform is no more than one step away from the sampled signal. However, a signal may change more rapidly than the staircase modulator can reflect, producing a problem called slope overload. In contrast, a slow-changing signal also creates distortions, called granular noise (see Figure 5–19[b]). The effect of inaccurate representation of the waveform is called quantization noise (it also occurs with PCM systems) and can be mitigated by measures that are explained next.

One widely used variation of DM is continuously variable slope delta modulation (CVSD) (see Figure 5–20). (Another term for this technique is adaptive delta modulation). CVSD transmits the difference between two successive samples and employs a quantizer to change the actual quantum steps based on a sudden increase or decrease of the signal. CVSD increases the staircase step size when it detects the waveform's slope increasing and decreases the step size when it detects a decrease in the slope.

CVSD does not send any information about the height of the curve (PCM) or the change in the height of the curve (ADPCM). It only sends information about the changes in the shape of the curve. A CVSD transmitter compares the input signal (its voltage) to a controlled reference

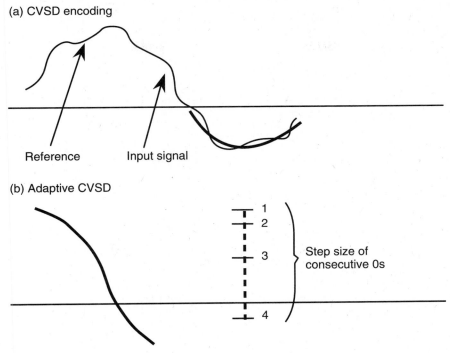

Figure 5–20
Continuously variable slope delta modulation (CVSD).

signal. It increases or decreases the reference (bends up or bends down) if the input is greater or smaller than the reference. In effect, CVSD steers the reference signal to follow the input.

A CVSD receiver reconstructs the original signal by increasing the slope of the curve when a 1 is received and decreasing the slope when a 0 is received. A filter is then used to smooth the curve (waveform). CVSD monitors the input signal for the occurrence of successive all ones (1111) or all zeros (0000). The former indicates the signal is rising too fast for the reference; the latter indicates the signal is falling too slow for the reference. In other words, slope overload is occurring. These signals are used to produce an increased step-size voltage.

While CVSD systems exhibit some fidelity problems at the beginning of words and very strong syllables (slope overload), the technique generally produces high-quality signals. Some CVSD systems operate at rates less than 32 kbit/s with adequate (but poor quality) fidelity and crispness.

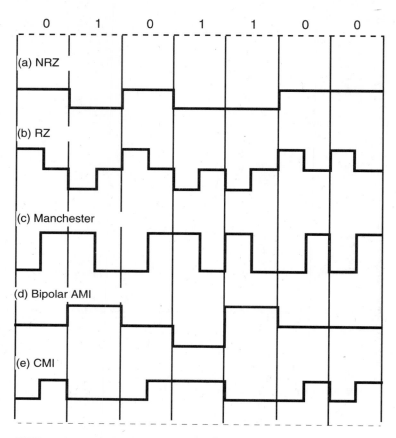

NRZ = nonreturn to zero
 RZ = return to zero
AMI = alternate mark inversion
CMI = coded mark inversion

Figure 5–21
Examples of digital codes.

Coding Schemes

Figure 5–21 provides an illustration of several common binary coding schemes used in the industry. We will discuss each of them and describe their advantages and disadvantages. These signals exhibit one or several of the following four characteristics:

- *Unipolar or unbalanced code.* No signal below zero voltage or no signal above (i.e., algebraic sign does not change: 0 volts for 1, 3 volts for 0).
- *Polar or balanced code.* Signal is above and below zero voltage (opposite algebraic signs identify logic states: +3 volts and −3 volts).
- *Bipolar code.* The signal varies between three levels.
- *Alternate mark inversion (AMI) code.* Uses alternate polarity pulses to encode binary 1s.

6

The Advanced Mobile
Phone System (AMPS)

INTRODUCTION

This chapter examines the widely used cellular mobile system called the Advanced Mobile Phone System (AMPS) and describes EIA/TIA-533, which is the formal specification for AMPS. The procedures for registration between the cellular provider and a mobile station are described, and how a wide variety of messages are exchanged between these two entities. Examples are provided of these messages, and their contents are explained at the end of the chapter.

The AMPS specifications are somewhat terse and are not meant as tutorials. Also, they were written before state diagrams and time-transition diagrams became popular. I have attempted to clarify the specifications with the use of text, figures and tables.

AMPS is the current mobile cellular system being used in the United States and many other countries. This system replaced most of the Improved Mobile Telephone Service (IMTS), which is described in earlier chapters.

AMPS was conceived by Bell Labs to overcome some of the deficiencies of IMTS, principally to use the spectrum space more effectively. Consequently, AMPS was designed around the concepts of cells to allow the reuse of radio frequencies. Also, through the adaptation of cell splitting, frequencies can continue to be reused. The AMPS air interface (radio interface) is published as EIA/TIA-533 by the Electronic

Industries Association and the Telecommunications Industry Association.

EARLY MILESTONES

In the late 1970s, the FCC allocated spectrum space for AMPS in the 800 MHz spectrum, and issued licenses for test systems in Chicago and Washington, D.C. The tests were followed shortly thereafter by the construction of commercial systems, the first system was brought on line in 1983. In a few short years, AMPS was available in all the major cities in the United States. These events were the fruition of extensive research and development conducted by the Bell System in the 1960s and 1970s.

The 800 MHz spectrum was chosen because of the limited spectrum space available at the lower frequencies. TV and FM systems operate at the lower frequencies, with FM operating around 100 MHz and TV systems operating from the range of 41 to 960 MHz. Other systems, such as air-to-ground systems and maritime services, also operate in the lower frequency ranges. In addition, the choice of the 800 MHz band was dictated by the fact that the using of higher frequencies (for example, in the 10 GHz range) at that time were subject to severe information loss due to weather conditions (such as rain), multipath fading, and unacceptable propagation path loss.

With some exceptions, the 800 MHz band was not being utilized. Even though parts of this spectrum space were originally assigned to educational TV stations, some of the load that would have probably been assigned to these stations was assumed to be allocated to cable TV services. Nonetheless, 800 MHz was certainly a compromise because technology had improved by the late 1970s and early 1980s. At that time, it was possible to provide high-quality services well beyond this limited bandwidth. We shall have more to say about these subjects in later discussions on broadband PCS.

THE AMPS SPECTRUM AND CHANNELS

AMPS is a narrowband channel structure supporting 3 kHz analog channels that are modulated onto 30 kHz channels (30 kHz channel spacing). AMPS occupies parts of the spectrum ranging from 824 MHz to 894 MHz. The frequency spectrum is split into two categories (or groups),

Table 6–1   AMPS Frequency Allocations

- *Band A:*
  Transmit: 824–835 MHz and 845–846.5 MHz
  Receive: 869–880 MHz and 890–891.5 MHz
- *Band B:*
  Transmit: 835–845 MHz and 846.5–849 MHz
  Receive: 880–890 MHz and 891.5–894 MHz
- 312 usable RF pairs divided by 7 (the reuse factor) = roughly 45 channel pairs per cell

---

also called bands. The A band is set up for independent carriers. The B band is set up for the traditional wireline carriers, such as the Regional Bell Operating Companies (RBOCs). The intent of this structure is to ensure that competition exists in all markets, yet restrict the (potential) proliferation of many companies that would complicate spectrum allocation/management, and degrade trunking efficiency.[1] Each of these two operators is allocated one-half of the available bandwidth in their respective marketing areas.

Table 6–1 shows how the AMPS frequency spectrum is allocated to the A and B bands, and Table 6–2 shows the resultant channel numbers and frequencies. Each base station transmit and receive channel is separated by 45 MHz. A total of 416 channels are allocated for the customer's traffic channels and control channels. The traffic channels (TCH) are used for the calls. Band A has channels 1 to 312 and band B has channels 355 to 666. So, each carrier has 312 voice channels at its disposal.

The control channels are used by the mobile and base stations to set up and clear calls, and exchange other network management and provisioning messages. Both bands contain 21 control channels for a total of 42 channels. Band A has channels 313 to 333, and band B has channels 334 to 354.

---

[1]The FCC conducted studies to determine if the licensing of more than one carrier was justified. From the technical standpoint, one carrier is more efficient than two or more carriers. The FCC made the decision that the decreased efficiency of frequency usage would be offset by the introduction of another service provider, which would "encourage" the traditional wireline, B band carrier to keep its rates competitive with A band carrier.

Table 6–2 Channel Numbers and Frequencies

System	MHZ	Number of channels	Boundary channel number	Transmitter Center Frequency, Mhz	
				Mobile	*Land*
Not used		1	(990)	(824.010)	(869.010)
A"[1]	1	33	991	824.040	869.040
			1023	825.000	870.000
A[2]	10	333	1	825.030	870.030
			333	834.990	879.990
B[2]	10	333	334	835.020	880.020
			666	844.980	889.980
A'[1,3]	1.5	50	667	845.010	890.010
			717	846.480	891.480
B'[1,3]	2.5	83	717	846.510	889.510
			799	848.970	883.970

[1]Added later. Sometimes referred to as extended AMPS (EAMPS)
[2]Channel 1-666 have a 20 MHz range
[3]May use optional 5 MHz

The provider is free to use the control channels in any manner deemed appropriate. A logical way to approach the allocation of the control channels is to group them to control the voice channels (remember if the total channels available equal 333, it means that 312 voice channels and 21 control channels are available). Therefore, each control channel can be associated with a group of voice channels. In this scenario, each set of voice channels can be grouped into about 16 channels with each group associated with a control channel.

IDENTIFICATION NUMBERS

Three identification numbers are used in AMPS. They are (1) the mobile station's serial number (SN), (2) the mobile system's system identification (SID) number, and (3) the mobile station's mobile identification number (MIN).

The FCC requires a serial number (SN) (also called an electronic serial number, or ESN) to be used for each mobile station in service in the

**Figure 6–1
The serial number.**

cellular system. The SN is a 32-bit binary number that uniquely identi-fies a cellular unit. The ESN for a mobile station is established by the manufacturer at the factory and is not supposed to be easily altered. It is burned into ROM so that circuitry providing the number is secure and any attempt to change the serial number is supposed to make the mobile station unusable.

The format of the serial number is shown in Figure 6–1. (High-order bit first is the convention used in EIA/TIA-533.) The manufacturer's code (MFR) is an 8-bit field that is assigned by the FCC to each manufacturer of mobile equipment. Bits 23 to 18 are reserved for later use and are set to all zeros. Bits 17 to 0 are assigned by the manufacturer. The idea is that when a manufacturer uses all its serial number space, it can obtain another number from the FCC, which allocates the next sequential num-ber within the reserved block.

System identification numbers (SIDs) are 15-bit binary numbers that are assigned to cellular systems. Each cellular system is identified by a unique SID number. The mobile station in the cell must transmit the SID to a base station so the cellular receiver can determine the sys-tem through which they are communicating. An additional purpose of the SID is to determine if the two stations (mobile and fixed) are work-ing within the same system or if they are in a roaming situation. The FCC assigns one SID to each cellular system and these systems may transmit only their assigned SIDs (or another SID, if this other group so permits).

The mobile identification number (MIN) is a 34-bit number that is derived from the mobile station's 10-digit telephone number. The specifi-cation refers to MIN1 (24 bits that correspond to the 7-digit directory number) and MIN2 (10 bits that correspond to the 3-digit area code). EIA/TIA-533 provides several simple conversion algorithms that describe the conversion process. Table 6–3 provides a summary of the major as-pects of the three identification numbers.

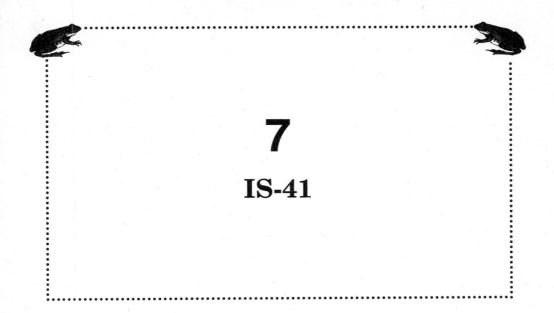

7

IS-41

INTRODUCTION

This chapter is devoted to an examination of EIA/TIA IS-41. We shall see that it is a companion standard to AMPS. The IS-41 network operations are explained; that is to say, the operations on the network (not user) side of the MSC. We also examine the operations between MSCs, VLRs, and HLRs.

THE IS-41 MODEL

IS-41 exhibits a topology and model that is quite similar to other mobile systems discussed in this book, such as PCS and GSM. Figure 7–1 depicts the functional entities of IS-41 and the associated interfaces (reference points) between the functional entities.

Parts of the specification are written in a somewhat abstract manner. The intent of this approach is to allow implementors some leeway in their specific implementations of the messages and protocols. In addition, Figure 7–1 is a conceptual model only and a piece of physical equipment may have several functional entities and reference points internal to the equipment. That being the case, these components are not required to adhere to the IS-41 standard.

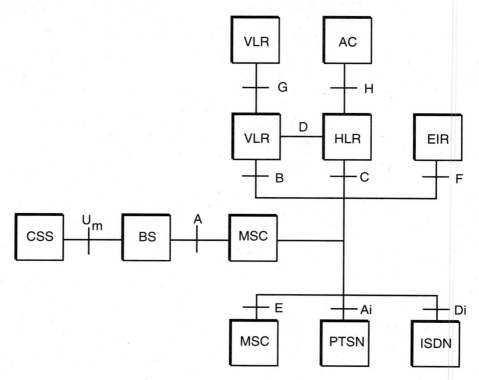

AC   Access control
BS   Base station
CSS   Cellular subscriber station
EIR   Equipment identity register
HLR   Home location register
ISDN   Integrated services digital network
MSC   Mobile switching center
PTSN   Public telephone switched network
VLR   Visitor location register

Figure 7–1
IS-41 entities and reference points.

    The terms in Figure 7–1 are listed at the bottom of the figure; most of these have been explained in earlier parts of this book. The term cellular subscriber station (CSS) is a generic term that describes the mobile station. I will continue to use the term mobile station in order to remain consistent throughout the book. The reference points in the figure labeled U_m, A, B, etc. are used to describe the interfaces and procedures (protocols) between the IS-41 entities, such as MSCs, BSs, and the CSS.

This chapter concentrates on the A, E, C, G, and B interfaces. IS-41 has not defined the F and H interfaces. The A_i and D_i interfaces are beyond the scope of this book. The U_m interface is covered in the previous chapter on AMPS pertaining to the operations between the mobile station and the land station.

KEY TERMS AND CONCEPTS

In order to explain the operations of IS-41, we need to define a few terms and concepts. First, the term *anchor MSC* identifies the MSC which is designated as the initial contact point when an originating call is initiated by the mobile station or when a terminating call (to the mobile station) is received from the fixed telephone network. For the duration of a call, this MSC remains the anchor point even though the mobile station might be handed off to other MSCs.

In contrast, a *candidate MSC* is a MSC that is being requested to provide the next service during a handoff operation. This procedure entails the candidate MSC exchanging various messages with the current serving MSC to indicate the signal quality and to exchange identifiers. The intention of the process is to find the appropriate MSC for the roaming mobile station.

The *homing MSC*, explained earlier in this book, identifies the MSC that is the "owner" of the mobile system in the sense that it is the owner of the directory number from which the mobile station's MIN is derived. This homing MSC broadcasts the SID that is recorded in the mobile station's security and identification memory.

Next, the *serving MSC* is the MSC that is currently serving the mobile station at a cell site within a coverage area controlled by the MSC. Finally, the *target MSC* is the MSC that was selected from a list of MSCs as having the cell site that can service the mobile station with the best signal quality. The target MSC was selected from a list of candidate MSCs during the location request function, which will be described later in this chapter.

Identification Numbers

IS-41 uses identifiers that are described in the AMPS chapter. For a review, refer to Table 6–3 in Chapter 6. In addition, IS-41 uses an identifier called the switch number (SWNO). It uniquely identifies a particular switch within a group of switches with which it is associated. The switch

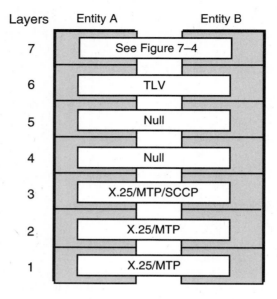

Figure 7–2
IS-41 and OSI.

identification (SWID) is the parameter derived from the concatenation of the SID and SWNO.

IS-41 AND OSI

IS-41 is organized around the Open Systems Interconnection (OSI) model. It does not make use of all of the layers in the model, which in Figure 7–2 are labeled null.[1]

Since the publication of IS-41 (1991), the OSI model has had changes made to the application and presentation layers. I will use the older IS-41 terminology, but correlate these terms to the current OSI terms.

---

[1]The term null is not completely accurate. A minimum core service is provided. A more recent term is "pass-through." Presentation, session, and transport layers are mostly pass-through layers.

The lower three layers of IS-41 can consist of the X.25 layers or the SS7 layers, known as the message transfer parts (MTPs) in SS7. These protocols are described in considerable detail in [BLAC91] and [BLAC89]. The SS7 signaling connection control part (SCCP) class 0 is also part of layer 3 (and some of layer 4, not a clean OSI fit).

Layer 6 uses the ISO/ITU-T transfer syntax (1984 = X.409; 1988 = X.209). This standard is covered in this chapter in the section titled "Formats of the Messages."

Layer 7 is shown in more detail in Figure 7–3. The IS-41 mobile application part (MAP) makes use of two OSI layer 7 protocols: the association control service element (ACSE) and the remote operations service element (ROSE). These two protocols are grouped together as applications service element (ASE) in Figure 7–3. ACSE is used to "bind" two applications together. For example, ACSE sets up an association between (for example) entity A and entity B. But that is about all it does. In essence, it is a housekeeping tool and is not invoked during ongoing transfer of

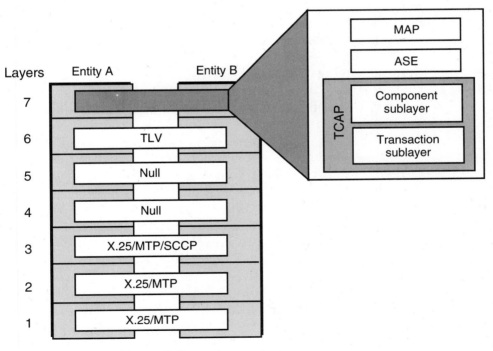

Figure 7–3
The Sublayers of the application layer.

IS-41 messages. ROSE is invoked for this purpose, which is explained next. Transaction capabilities application part (TCAP) is part of SS7.[2]

Use of the Remote Operation Service Element (ROSE)

IS-41 was published when the ROSE was part of the ITU-T X.410 Recommendation. ROSE is now published in the X.200 recommendations, and is used in this technology. This section provides a brief tutorial of ROSE and how ROSE is used in IS-41.

The OSI model supports a process for remote operations and remote procedure calls (RPCs). The remote procedure operation is based on a client server model, which is an asymmetric type of communications. Asymmetric means that a requester, such as a client, sends a request message to a process, identified as a server. It waits for an action to occur and receives a reply about the success or failure of the request. The client is not aware of the server's location (the server could be on a different machine in the network). This approach is in contrast to most of the OSI protocols and entities in which transfer is symmetric, in which traffic flows in both directions at the same time. The ROSE model is ideal for IS-41, since operations between MSCs, VLRs, and HLRs are asymmetric.

The OSI implementation of RPC is ROSE. It is based on two principal concepts: sending a request for an operation to a server (an INVOKE message) and conveying the results of that operation to the client (a RESULT message).

The results of the operation can report on various combinations of success or failure. ROSE also uses class numbers to describe the result of the operation, either for synchronous or asynchronous communications processes. Table 7–1 provides a summary of these aspects of ROSE.

Please refer to Figure 7–4 for this discussion. The term *req* means request and the term *ind* means indication. The ROSE operations are considered connectionless in that timers and retries are not invoked for this service, and no state diagrams are maintained to track the ongoing operations. Thus, primitives from the invoker (the user application that operates on top of ROSE) consist of the RO-INVOKE req, which is mapped to an INVOKE message, which is sent to the remote MSC, VLR, or HLR in the form of an RO-INVOKE ind. The reader should notice in Figure 7–4 that no response or confirm primitives are involved in this service.

---

[2]Although SS7 is beyond the scope of this book, I have provided a brief tutorial on this system in Appendix A of this book.

Table 7–1   ROSE Operations

Result of Operation	Expected Report from Server
Success or failure	If successful, return a result. If a failure, return an error reply.
Failure only	If successful, no reply. If a failure, return an error reply
Success only	If successful, return a result. If a failure, no reply
Success or failure	In either case, no reply

Class Number	Definition
1	Synchronous: Report success (result) or failure (error)
2	Asynchronous: Report success (result) or failure (error)
3	Asynchronous: Report failure (error) only
4	Asynchronous: Report success (result) only
5	Asynchronous: Report nothing

After the operation has been performed, the server returns the RO-RESULT req, which is eventually presented to the client as the RO-RESULT ind. The values in the INVOKE and RESULT messages must provide the invoke ID to correlate a request with a reply as well as an operation value that identifies a particular operation that is to be performed. The operation class defines synchronous or asynchronous operations and the type of reply that is to accompany it. Asynchronous operations are used in most IS-41 operations.

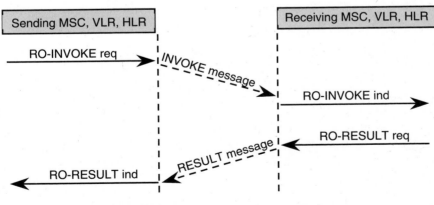

Figure 7–4
Use of INVOKE and RESULT messages.

Use of ROSE for Handing a Mobile Station from One MSC to Another

Figure 7–5 shows the ROSE messages that are exchanged when a mobile station moves from one MSC to another, in this case MSC A to MSC B. The initial ROSE invoke and result messages are used to initiate a handoff operation and perform tests (events 2 and 3). The next set of invoke and result messages in events 4 and 5 are used for administrative procedures to establish the circuit and verify that the connection is made. Finally, the last invoke in event 6 is sent from MSC B to MSC A to note that the handoff operation was successful.

The convention for this chapter will be to use the upper case letters to show a ROSE invoke and lower case letters to show a ROSE result.

We now have enough background information to examine IS-41 operations. It will be helpful during this discussion to keep AMPS in mind (Chapter 6), as it will be evident that the two standards are "partners."

OPERATIONS

This section shows several examples of IS-41 operations. The examples show the network side of a call, because IS-41 operates on the network side and not the on the side of the air interface. The serving MSC in

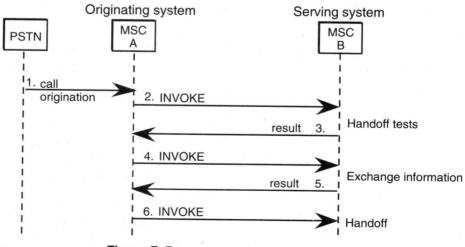

Figure 7–5
Example of ROSE and IS-41 operations.

these examples interwork the IS-41 messages with the AMPS messages (the air interface). These messages are described in Chapter 6 and it is assumed the reader has read Chapter 6 before continuing this chapter.

Registration in a New MSC

When a mobile station moves to a new location, IS-41 is invoked to coordinate the updates between the old serving MSC and VLR, the new serving MSC and VLR and the subscriber's HLR. Figure 7–6 shows the messages and operations for a mobile registration with a new MSC.

After the serving MSC has determined that the mobile station is in its area, it sends a registration notification message to its VLR (event 1, Figure 7–6). This message contains (at a minimum): (a) the 10-digit mobile identification number (MIN), (b) the 32-bit mobile serial number (MSN), (c) the qualification information code, (d) a system type code

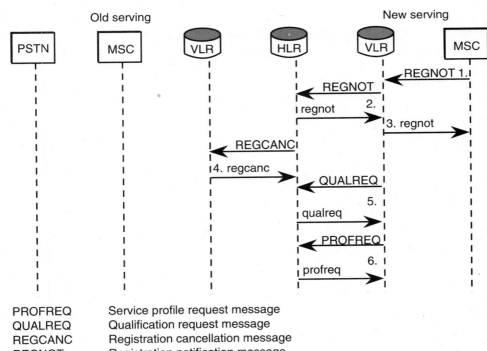

PROFREQ	Service profile request message
QUALREQ	Qualification request message
REGCANC	Registration cancellation message
REGNOT	Registration notification message

Upper case represents ROSE INVOKE messages
Lower case represents ROSE RETURN RESULTS messages

Figure 7–6
Registration with a new MSC.

(a code that identifies the vendor type of system (AT&T, Motorola, etc.), and (e) the 3-digit identifier of the specific system, which includes the registered SID.

If the mobile station had registered previously with an MSC that is within the domain of the VLR, no further action is taken by the VLR except to make certain that the MSC serving the mobile station is correctly recorded. In this example (event 2), the VLR sends a registration notification message to the subscriber's HLR. This message contains the MIN and the MSN. Upon receiving a response from the HLR, the new serving VLR sends a response back to the new serving MSC (shown in the figure as event 3).

In event 4, the HLR sends a registration cancellation message to the old serving VLR, if the station had been registered elsewhere. This message contains the same type of information that is in the registration notification message. This message can be sent by the HLR at any time after it receives the registration notification message from the new serving VLR.

Events 5 and 6 may or may not occur, depending on an actual implementation. In any event, the new serving VLR records the new mobile station. Event 5 is invoked by the VLR sending a qualification request message to the HLR. The purpose of this message is to authenticate the mobile station and determine the validation requirements. In event 6, the VLR may also send a service profile request to the HLR to find out more information about the new mobile station. The response to this request will contain information pertaining to the origination of the call, subscriber-restricted calls (i.e., sent-paid), and parameters dealing with ancillary services (i.e., call forwarding, and call waiting).

Calling an Idle Mobile Station in a Visited System

Figure 7–7 shows an example of a call made to a mobile station that is outside the serving area of the MSC that participates in the call origination. In this example, the mobile station is not busy (idle). The call is placed through the conventional PSTN (event 1), and is relayed to the originating system MSC through the identification of the mobile station's directory number. In event 2, the originating MSC sends a location request invoke message to the HLR that is associated with the mobile station. Once again, this association is made through the dialed mobile address digits. These digits may or may not be the MIN.

The HLR performs several validity checks to make sure the subscriber is legitimate and that call forwarding is allowed. If all goes well,

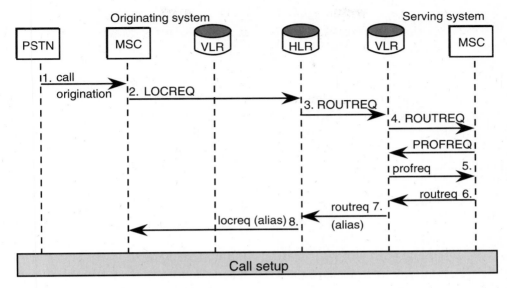

Figure 7–7
Calling an idle mobile station.

LOCREQ   Location request message
PROFREQ   Service profile request message
QUALREQ   Qualification request message
ROUTREQ   Routing request message
Upper case represents ROSE NVOKE messages
Lower case represents ROSE RETURN RESULTS messages

in event 3 the HLR sends a routing request invoke message to the VLR
that last provided information about the subscriber. This information
had been provided earlier from this VLR through a registration notification message. The VLR then forwards this routing request to the current
serving MSC (event 4). The VLR must know that the mobile station may
have roamed within the domain of the serving VLR and, if so, the station
has already reported its new location to that VLR through the serving
MSC.

If the MSC has not yet obtained information about this mobile station, it will obtain a service profile on the mobile station from its VLR.
The service profile may already be known by the MSC, in which case,
this information is not needed. This example shows the MSC sending a
profile request to the VLR with the VLR responding with result (event 5).
In event 6, the MSC responds to the VLR with its profile request result,
which was requested in event 4.

Next, in event 7 the serving MSC VLR allocates a routing alias and returns this information to the HLR in the routing request response message. Upon receiving this message, the HLR constructs a location request response to give to the originating MSC (event 8). This operation is performed by placing the MIN and ESN values of the mobile station into the location request response message. Upon the originating MSC receiving this information from the HLR, it establishes a voice path to the serving MSC, using an existing protocol such as SS7. The originating MSC performs this trunking through the routing alias that is specified in the location request response that came from the HLR.

Calling a Busy Mobile Station

If the mobile station is busy when a call is directed to it, the operations proceed as described in the previous section (events 1–4 of Figure 7–7), with the following alterations (shown in Figure 7–8) The serving MSC, upon checking its internal tables, determines that the mobile station is engaged in another call. This check results in the sending of the busy status message (of this mobile station) to the serving VLR (event 5),

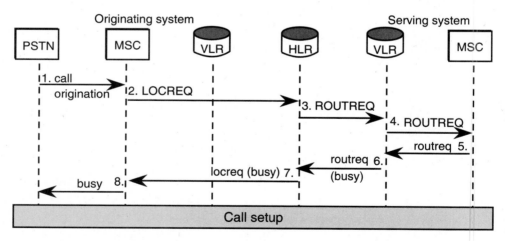

LOCREQ   Location request message
ROUTREQ   Routing request message
Upper case represents ROSE INVOKE messages
Lower case represents ROSE RETURN RESULTS messages

Figure 7–8
Calling a busy mobile station.

and then to the HLR in a routing request response message (event 6). The HLR looks at the profile of the mobile station and determines that (in this example) it does not have any special termination privileges (call interrupt, etc.) and returns a busy status signal to the originating MSC in the location request response (event 7), which means that the originating MSC must return a busy indication to the calling PSTN (event 8).

Call with No Answer

Figure 7–9 shows the actions when the mobile station does not send back the page response or does not answer to a control message. We pick up the activities in event 6. The serving MSC determines that the mobile

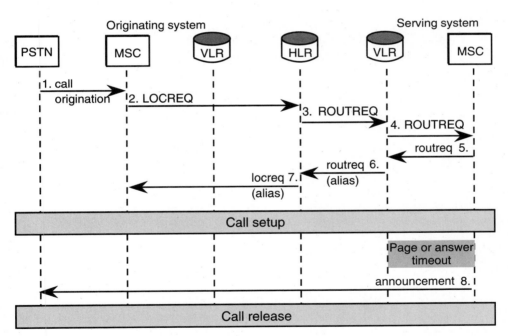

LOCREQ   Location request message
ROUTREQ   Routing request message
Upper case represents ROSE INVOKE messages
Lower case represents ROSE RETURN RESULTS messages

Figure 7–9
Call and mobile station does not answer.

station is idle and returns a routing alias to the HLR in the routreq response message. The HLR then adds the MIN and ESN to its routing information and returns a locreq with the alias to the originating MSC (event 7). After these registration procedures have been completed, the call is received at the serving MSC which is depicted in Figure 7–9 as the call set up operation. In this example, the mobile station does not respond to a page message nor to an alerting message. Therefore, the serving MSC, in event 8, routes the call to the originator with an appropriate signal (the actual contents of the signal depends on the nature of the system implemented). The call is disconnected with the operation depicted in Figure 7–9 as the call release.

Calling with Unconditional Call Forwarding

Figure 7–10 shows what happens when the called mobile system has subscribed to call forwarding. The term unconditional call forwarding refers to the mode in which the mobile station is never alerted or paged. It has designated the HLR to automatically (unconditionally) forward the call. Events 1 and 2 are the same as in previous examples. The location request message is sent to the mobile station's HLR. In event 3 the HLR

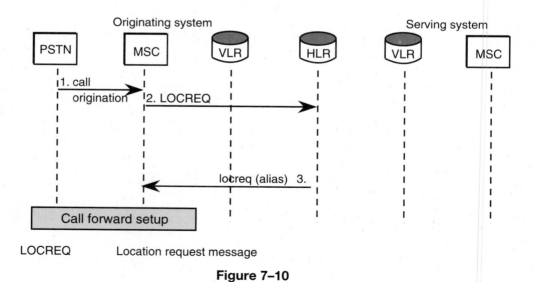

LOCREQ   Location request message

**Figure 7–10
Call forwarding.**

examines its structures and finds that an unconditional call forwarding mode is in effect. It then returns the location request response to the originating MSC. The call forwarding number is in this response, which is coded in the message as the destination directory number. It is then the responsibility of the originating MSC to establish the call forwarding setup operations with the PSTN.

Mobile Station Is Busy

We pick up the example of a mobile station is busy operation in Figure 7–11 and event 3, where the HLR sends the routing request invoke message to last known VLR. In turn, this message is forwarded to the current serving MSC, depicted in event 4. In events 5 and 6, the MSC determines that the mobile station is busy and does not have call waiting activated. Thus, in event 6, it returns a busy status in the route request response to the HLR. In turn the HLR examines its structures and discovers that the mobile station wishes call forwarding to be performed when the mobile station is busy. Therefore, in event 7 and the remaining part of this figure, call forwarding takes place in the same manner as in the call forwarding unconditional scenario.

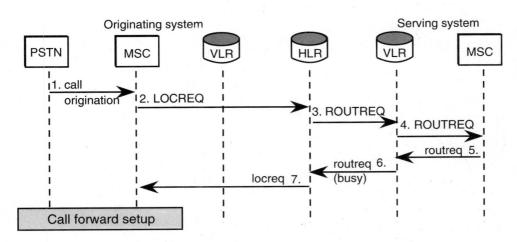

LOCREQ   Location request message

Figure 7–11
Mobile station is busy.

No Page Response or No Answer in Serving MSC

We pick up our examination of a no answer or no response in Figure 7–12 in event 5, in which the serving MSC determines that the mobile station is idle. As in previous scenarios, this information is forwarded to the HLR in event 6 where the HLR adds MIN and ESN information to its structures and in event 7 returns the location request response to the originating MSC. Thereafter, a voice path is established as depicted in this figure with the call setup. But, as depicted in the middle of the fig-

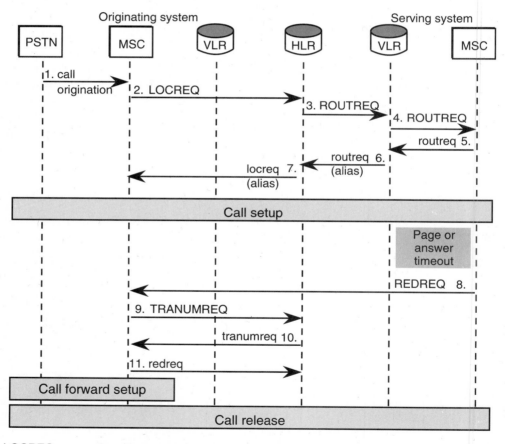

LOCREQ   Location request message
TRANUMBER   Transfer to number request message

Figure 7–12
No page response or no answer in serving MSC.

ure, the mobile station does not respond to a page or if a page is received it does not respond to a subsequent alert message. Therefore, in this example, the serving MSC determines from the service profile that the mobile station has call forwarding or no answer activated. Next, in event 8, the serving MSC sends a redirection request invoke message to the originating MSC. This message informs the originating MSC that the call is being redirected because the mobile station did not answer.

In this example, it is assumed that the MSC is able to redirect the call but before redirecting the call it sends a transfer to number request invoke message to the HLR (event 9). This message is required in order to obtain information from the HLR about the forward-to number that must be stored at the mobile station's home HLR. In event 10, the HLR sends this information to the originating MSC in the tranumreq response message. To satisfy the message delivered in event 8, the originating MSC in event 11 sends the redreq response message to the serving MSC. Thereafter, as depicted in the bottom part of the figure, call forwarding setup and call release operations are invoked.

Call Collision in the Serving MSC

Figure 7–13 shows the operations for a call collision. As we have learned in other examples, the serving MSC informs the HLR of the call setup by the return of the routreq message to the HLR (in event 5).

Since the call has not actually taken place from the perspective of these originating entities, it is possible that the mobile station can become engaged in another call. The most common event is for the user in the mobile station to make a new call by going off-hook. It could also occur because of the arrival of another call setup from a previous ROUTREQ. During the call setup operation depicted in Figure 7–13 with the call setup box, the serving MSC discovers the mobile station is busy. In this example, we assume that call waiting is not available. Also in this example, we assume that the mobile station has call forwarding on busy activated. Therefore, the serving MSC in event 8 returns to the originating MSC a redirection request message (REDREQ) noting that the station is indeed busy. The reader should note that this information flow is not passed through the HLR. In event 9, upon receiving this message, the originating MSC sends a transfer to number request message (TRANUMREQ) to the HLR indicating that the mobile station is busy and that it would like the HLR to return a call forwarding number (cf#). This request is honored in event 10. Finally, in event 11, the redirect request response is returned from the originating MSC to the serving MSC

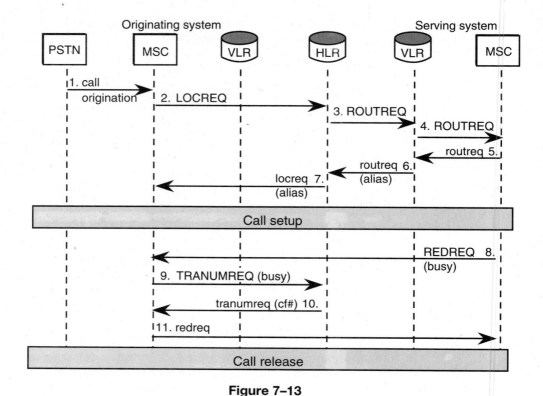

**Figure 7–13
Call collision.**

to complete the outstanding request message created in event 8. Thereafter, ongoing call forward and call release procedures are invoked as noted by a box in the bottom part of Figure 7–13.

Call Waiting

Call waiting procedures are invoked in accordance with the operations shown in Figure 7–14. We pick up these operations in events 5, 6, and 7. We learned earlier that the MSC can discover that a mobile station is busy. Furthermore, by examining the service profile of that station it can determine if the station has call waiting activated. In event 6, the serving MSC returns this information to the HLR route request in a response message. In event 7, the HLR performs its own ongoing operations discussed in previous examples. The call setup takes place with conventional operations described earlier. When this second call arrives

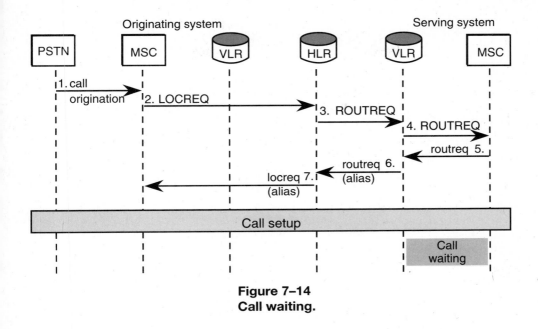

Figure 7–14
Call waiting.

at the serving MSC, the mobile service receives the call waiting treatment from the MSC, shown at the bottom of this figure.

Mobile Station Is Inactive

A mobile station is often powered down, for example, when the user is not in the vehicle. When the MSC sends page messages to the mobile station and receives no response, it notifies its VLR of this state through a CSS inactive message, as shown in event 1 of Figure 7–15. The VLR updates its records accordingly and responds to the MSC with a response. Next, in event 2, the same set of operations occurs between the serving VLR and the HLR.

In this example, we assume that the mobile station is powered up once again and the MSC detects the presence of the mobile station through the procedures described earlier in Chapter 6 (AMPS initialization procedures). In event 3, the MSC notifies its VLR of these events through the registration notification invoke message. Since the mobile system may have roamed while it was inactive, it is possible that the reporting MSC in event 1 is different from the reporting MSC in event 3.

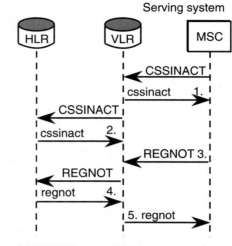

Figure 7–15
Mobile station is inactive.   CSSINACT   CSS inactive message

Whatever the case may be, the HLR will know about this roam because in event 4 the serving VLR sends the registration notification to the HLR. Thereafter, both the serving system and the HLR know that the mobile system is active and where it is located.

Recovery from Failure at the HLR

One hopes that the HLR suffers from few problems and even fewer failures. However, in the event of a failure at the HLR, Figure 7–16 shows the operations invoked to recover. In essence, the goals of these operations are to purge all information from all the associated VLRs that are correlated to the failed HLR, and at a later time, locate the mobile station and update the HLR and VLRs accordingly.

In events 1 and 2 of Figure 7–16, the HLR sends the unreliable roamer data directive invoke message to all its associated VLRs. Upon receiving this message, the VLRs remove the record of all the mobile stations belonging to the home HLR and return the unreldir response to the HLR. In event 3, and MSC discovers the presence of a mobile station in its area that belongs to the subject HLR. It first sends a registration notification message to its VLR. In turn and in event 4, the VLR sends this information to the HLR. Obviously, this information allows the HLR to

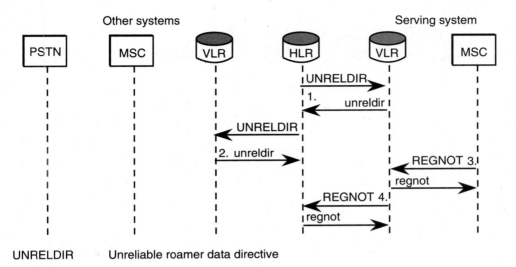

UNRELDIR   Unreliable roamer data directive

**Figure 7–16
Recovery from failure at the HLR.**

recover on a station-by-station basis as each station is found within the system.

Handoff Measurement Request

A serving MSC can query its adjacent MSCs to determine if the mobile system should be relocated to another serving system. This operation is achieved with the exchange of handoff measurement request messages, as depicted in Figure 7–17. In event 1, the serving MSC sends to its adjacent MSCs the request of a measurement level on a specific channel. The request message includes the station class mark (SCM) field of the subscriber station, the identifier of the serving cell site for the specific channel, the SAT color code, voice mobile attenuation code, and the channel number of the specific channel. These fields are described in the AMPS chapter.

In event 2, the adjacent MSCs respond with the handoffmeasurreq response, which contains the identifier of the responding cell site, and the quality of the signal (signal strength) that is being received on the specific channel.

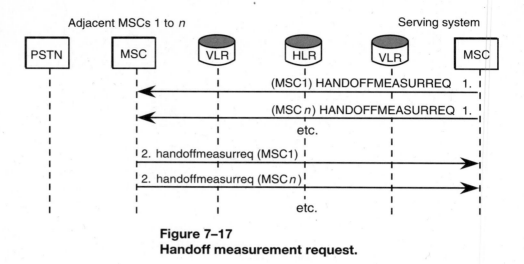

Figure 7–17
Handoff measurement request.

The serving MSC examines each response to determine if a handoff is or is not appropriate.

RELATIONSHIP OF IS-41 AND AMPS

Figure 7–18 illustrates how the IS-41 messages are used by the serving system to set up an AMPS convention with the mobile station. The events of 1 through 5 have been described in previous examples. Events 6 through 9 were described in Chapter 6, but warrant a few more comments here. I will correlate Figure 7–18 with Figure 6–5 in this explanation. The land station uses a control channel to page the mobile unit in event 6 (shown as event 2 in Figure 6–5). The mobile station accepts the page with the page response message in event 7 (shown as event 3 in Figure 6–5). Finally, the mobile station responds with the answer message in event 9 (shown as event 5 in Figure 6–5).

FORMATS OF THE MESSAGES

The previous examples are not all of the IS-41 operations. Our purpose is to understand the major aspects of IS-41, but it should do us no harm to delve a bit further. Therefore, Table 7–2 lists and describes all the IS-41 messages (transactions), the direction of the message, and its major functions.

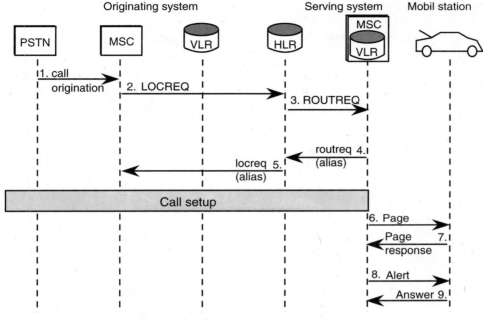

Figure 7–18
Interworking of IS-41 and AMPS.

Message Formats and Syntaxes

In previous chapters, the messages for AMPS, TDMA, and so on have been represented by figures. Remember that these messages are for control signaling operations, such as pages and route requests. For IS-41, this approach is not valid, since the standard uses the OSI presentation layer. This layer is designed to support syntax-transparent information exchange. That is, it allows machines with different data representations (syntaxes) to communicate with each other. For example, a machine that uses EBCDIC code can communicate with a machine that uses IA5/ASCII code.

This capability is furnished by the use of Abstract Syntax Notation One (or ASN.1), which is a language that describes data structures (structured information) that have been shown in the form of figures in previous chapters. The formats and syntaxes of the messages are established with ASN.1 code (which can then be compiled into C structures).

The IS-41 ASN.1 notations are coded into machine-independent messages (called a transfer syntax) at the sender. These messages are conveyed across the communications channel to the receiver in a

Table 7–2   IS-41 Transactions (Messages)

Transaction (message)	Operations		
	From	*To*	*Function*
HandoffMeasurementRequest	Serving MSC	Adjacent MSCs	Request measurement for a specific channel
FacilitiesDirective	Serving MSC	Target MSC	Request for channel data
MobileOnChannel	Target MSC	Anchor MSC	Status report: New MS has a successful handoff in the new cell
HandoffBack	Serving MSC	Previous MSC	Previous MSC sends channel data for target system
FacilitiesRelease	Either MSC	Either MSC	Release allocated resources
QualificationRequest[1]	MSC-V/VLR	VLR/HLR	Verify roamer's identify and account
QualificationDirective[1]	HLR	VLR	Notify of change in roamer's validation
Blocking[2]	MSC	MSC	Remove a circuit from service
Unblocking[2]	MSC	MSC	Restore a circuit to service
ResetCircuit[2]	MSC	MSC	Restore information about circuit conditions (lost due to problems)
TrunkTest[2]	Testing MSC	Looped MSC	Looped MSC is to setup loopback on designated trunks
TrunkTestDisconnect[2]	Testing MSC	Looped MSC	Discontinue loopback testing
RegistrationNotification[1]	VLR	HLR	Status report: Visitor has been registered and is active
RegistrationCancellation[1]	HLR	VLR	Visitor is no longer in VLR's service area
LocationRequest[1]	Switching system	HLR	Requests location of a called station and routing information
RoutingRequest[1]	HLR	MSC-V/VLR	Inquiry on best routing of pending call to called station
RemoteFeatureControlRequest[1]	MSC-V/VLR	HLR	Invoke remote feature control for MS
ServiceProfileRequest[1]	MSC-V/VLR	VLR/HLR	Verify visiting subscriber's service profile
ServiceProfileDirective[1]	HLR	VLR	Notify of change in roamer's service profile
UnreliableRoamerData Directive[2]	HLR	VLR	Status report: HLR has had a failure

Transaction (message)	Operations		
	From	*To*	*Function*
CallDataRequest[1]	Switching system	HLR	To obtain MIN, ESN, current serving MSC IDs
CSSInactive[1]	VLR	HLR	Status report: Station (CSS) is inactive
TransferToNumberRequest[1]	MSC	HLR	Request for visitor's "transfer to" number
RedirectionRequest[1]	Serving MSC	Originating MSC	Redirect the call to another number

[1]User with automatic roaming

[2]User OAM (operations, administration, and maintenance)

machine-independent format. At the receiver, this format is decoded into the receiver's machine-dependent format. These ideas are shown in Figure 7–19.

ASN.1 defines a number of "built-in" types. This term means that certain types are considered an essential part of the ASN.1 standard. They are, in a sense, predefined. They are called built-in because they are defined within the standard itself.

One might wonder what is a "non-built-in" type. This kind of type is not defined in the standard and is considered to be a type that is defined by an enterprise. For example, in the Internet Standards (as published by the Internet Activities Board [IAB]) a non-built-in type is a network address. This type is always identified as OCTET STRING Internet Protocol (IP) address, in which the type is usually coded as either network address.host address or network address.subnetwork address.host address.

The ASN.1 built-in types offer a wide array of types for the enterprise to use. Indeed, many organizations (in order to reduce the complexity of the presentation layer) choose to implement a subset of the built-in types.

IS-41 uses an OCTET STRING type for almost all the fields in its messages. This type identifies either text or data as a sequence of octets (bytes).

With this information in mind, the next section describes two of the message types that we used in the example on AMPS operations. They

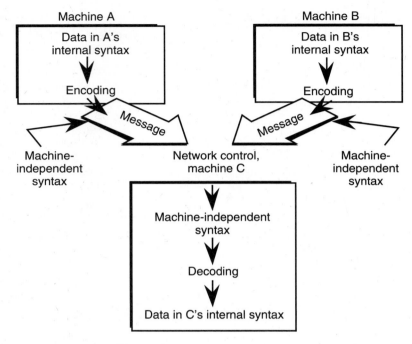

Figure 7–19
Machine-independent syntax.

are not exhaustive, but are included here to give you an idea of the contents of the messages. You may wish to refer back to some of the examples as you read this next section.

Registration Notification

The messages involved for mobile registration are the registration notification (REGNOT), the registration cancellation (REGCANC), the qualification request (QUALREQ), and the profile request (PROFREQ). These messages vary in how many fields (parameters) they carry, and the reader should study IS-41 5.A for more details. The message parameters for registration operations are:

- *Mobile identification number:* The 10-digit representation of the mobile station's MIN.
- *Mobile serial number:* The 32-bit ESN of the mobile station.

- *Qualification information code:* Indicates the type of qualification needed during the registration, such as validation and profile or validation only.
- *System my type code of VLR:* ID of vendor of mobile system.
- *MSC id of serving MSC:* Indicates the ID of a specified system. This 3-byte field contains a 2-byte SID and the 1-byte SWNO.
- *System my type code of HLR:* ID of vendor of mobile system.
- *Origination indicators:* Identifies the types of calls the mobile station is allowed to originate (local only, international, etc.).

Location Request

The location request message (LOCREQ) must contain four parameters. These parameters are described below; optional parameters are not described in this overview.

- *Dialed digits:* The number of a station that is called.
- *MSC identifier:* Indicates the ID of a specified system. This 3-byte field contains a 2-byte SID and the 1-byte SWNO.
- *System my type code:* An identifier registered for each mobile equipment vendor. For example, this could contain a value of 5 for GTE equipment, 6 for Motorola equipment, or 7 for NEC equipment.
- *Billing ID field:* Contains the ID of the anchor MSC system. It is initially assigned at the anchor system. Used principally for billing records but it can be used for identifiers as well. In addition to the anchor SID value, this field must also contain the anchor switch number as well as an ID number. The ID number is not required; but, the anchor SID and the anchor switch numbers are registered and are used in combination to form the SWID.

SUMMARY

IS-41 is designed to use the information at the AMPS interface to manage the network side of the cellular call. IS-41 is a relatively simple yet robust system. It relies on the well-founded principles of layered protocols, and uses the trusted workhorses X.25 and SS7 to support its lower layer operations.

8

Global System for Mobile Communications (GSM)

INTRODUCTION

This chapter introduces a second-generation mobile cellular system. The Group Speciale Mobile (GSM) forms the basis for the Digital Cellular System 1800 (DCS-1800). The GSM also is known as global system for mobile communications. The GSM protocols, interfaces, and functional entities are explained. The concepts of roaming, call establishment, and call disconnect are also covered. Many of the features in GSM are based on the first-generation mobile cellular systems, which are described in Chapters 6 and 7 on AMPS and IS-41. GSM combines the features of these two systems.

HISTORY OF GSM DEVELOPMENT

The GSM/DCS was initiated by the European Commission (EC) by adapting, in June 1987, a Recommendation and Directive for the Council of Ministers. The aim of this document was to end the incompatibility of systems in the mobile communications area and to create a European-wide communications system structure. The aim was also used to accelerate the efforts of individual countries to develop a European-wide digital cellular system.

GSM/DCS is targeted to include a wide variety of services including (naturally) speech transmissions between mobile units (or any portable unit), message handling services (such as X.400), facsimile transmission, emergency call, and variety of data transmission services.

Figure 8–1 illustrates the major components of GSM and a typical GSM topology. The interface with the mobile station (MS) is provided through the base transceiver station (BTS). These two components operate with a range of radio channels across an air interface. The BTS acts as the interface of the MS to the GSM network. Like other base stations described in this book, the BTS is usually located in the center of a cell.

The BTSs are controlled by the base station controllers (BSCs). They are responsible for handover operations of the calls as well as controlling the power signals and frequency administration between the BTSs and MSs. The BSC is quite intelligent, and much of the on-going housekeeping activities between the BTS and the MS are performed by the BTS. The BTS and BSC may be co-located, or the BSC may be located at the mobile services switching center (MSC), which is discussed next.

Although not shown in Figure 8–1, the term base station subsystem (BSS) is used to describe systems in which the BTS and BSC are part of

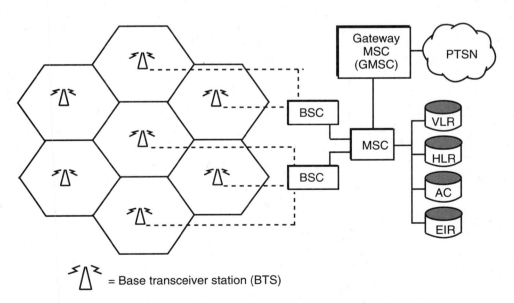

Figure 8–1
DCS 1800/GSM 900.

one entity. This approach is not uncommon, and will be used in this chapter in several examples of GSM operations.

The mobile services switching center (MSC) is the heart of GSM and is responsible for setting up, managing, and clearing connections as well as routing the calls to the proper cell. It provides the interface to the telephone system as well as provisions for charging and accounting services. An MSC with interfaces to the telephone network is called a gateway MSC (or GMSC). It is a complete telephone exchange, with capabilities of relaying calls between the fixed public switched telephone network (PTSN) and the cellular network.

GSM uses two databases called the home location register (HLR) and visitor location register (VLR). These databases store permanent and temporary information about each GSM subscriber that belongs to an area controlled by an MSC. Each HLR correlates a subscriber to its area. The HLR provides identifying information on the user (its IMSI, discussed shortly), its home subscription base, and any supplementary services provided to the user, such as call forwarding. The HLR also keeps information on the location of its "home" subscribers; that is, in which VLR a subscriber is registered.

The VLR stores information about subscribers in its particular area. It contains information on whether mobile stations are switched on or off, and if any of the supplementary services have been activated or deactivated. The VLR is used extensively during the call establishment and authentication procedures. The idea is to use the VLR for these operations in order to reduce traffic to and from the HLR.

The HLR is the primary entity used when a call originates from the public telephone network. The VLR is the primary entity used when the call originates from the mobile station. Even though a subscriber may be in its own home area, both the VLR and HLR are used in order to keep matters consistent.

In addition, two other major components are part of GSM. The authentication center (AC or AUC) is associated with the HLR, and is used to protect each subscriber from unauthorized access or from use of a subscription by unauthorized personnel. It also is used for authentication operations when a subscriber registers with the network.

Finally, the equipment identity register (EIR) is used for the registration of the type of equipment that exists at the mobile station. It can also provide for security features such as blocking calls that have been determined to emanate from stolen mobile stations, as well as preventing certain stations from using the network that have not been approved by the network vendor.

THE SUBSCRIBER IDENTITY MODULE (SIM) AND GSM ADDRESSES AND IDENTIFIERS

International Mobile Subscriber Identity (IMSI)

Each mobile unit is identified uniquely with a set of values. These values are used to identify the country in which the mobile system resides, the mobile network, and the mobile subscriber. These sets of values are known as the international mobile subscriber identification (IMSI) and are used as a fixed identifier within a network. The IMSI is also called the IMSN, for the international mobile subscriber number. The format for the IMSI is shown in Figure 8–2.

Up to fifteen digits can be used to form the contents of the IMSI. The first three digits are the mobile country code (MCC). The next two digits comprise the mobile network code (MNC), which is a unique identifier of a network provider, also called the public land mobile network (PLMN). As examples, an MCC of 05 identifies Australia; an MCC of 234 identifies the UK. An MNC of 01 identifies Telecom Australia, and an MNC of 234 identifies UK Vodafone.

The remainder of the IMSI is made up of the mobile subscriber identification code (MSIC), which is the customer identification number. The IMSI also is used for an MSC/VLR to find out the subscriber's home PLMN.

The Subscriber Identity Module (SIM)

The IMSI is stored on the subscriber identify module (SIM), which is located in the subscriber's mobile unit. In addition to containing the IMSI, the SIM contains subscriber-specific information such as phone numbers, a personal identification number (PIN), and security/authentication parameters (later sections will explain these items). It can also be used to store short messages that have been received through the network.

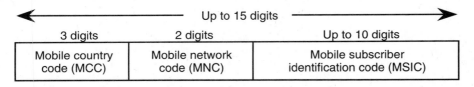

Figure 8–2
The IMSI.

The SIM can be a small plug-in module that is placed (somewhat permanently) in the mobile unit, or it can be a card (like a credit card) that is also inserted into the unit. In the latter option, it is used like a smart card. The mobile unit is personalized to the subscriber whenever the module or card is operating in the unit. The mobile unit is not usable (except for emergency calls) if the SIM is not inserted into the mobile unit terminal.

A modular portable SIM allows a user to use different terminal sets. For example, a traveler need not carry a mobile unit, but can rent one from say a car-rental agency, and "customize" the unit to the subscriber's needs, by inserting the smart card into the unit. As another example, if a terminal is out of order, a subscriber can obtain another unit while the repair takes place, and simply insert the smart card into the new unit to continue ongoing operations. Instead of the mobile station roaming, the smart card allows SIM roaming.

Mobile System ISDN (MSISDN)

For additional addressing outside a network, another address is required. It is called the mobile station ISDN (MSISDN) (see Figure 8–3). It is so named because it uses the same format as the ISDN address (based on ITU-T Recommendation E.164). Unlike a conventional telephone call, a GSM call to a mobile station does not identify the called party, but an HLR. The HLR uses this number to provide routing instructions to other components in order to reach the subscriber.

Location Area Identity (LAI)

Another identifier used in GSM is called the location area identifier (LAI). It is similar in content to the IMSI, except that it identifies a cell, more commonly in a group of cells. Figure 8–4 shows the format for the LAI. The mobile country code (MCC) and mobile network code were explained earlier (see Figure 8–2). The location area code (LAI) identifies a

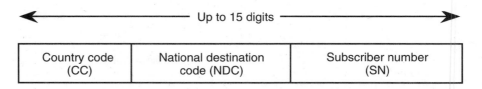

Figure 8–3
The MSISDN.

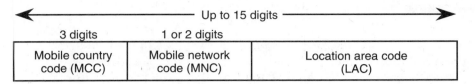

Figure 8–4
Location area identifiers (LAI).

cell or a group of cells. This latter field plays a role in handoff operations. When a mobile station roams into another cell, if it is in the same LAI, no information is exchanged with any external network.

International Mobile Station Equipment Identity (IMEI)

The international mobile station equipment identity (IMEI) is assigned to the GSM unit at the factory (see Figure 8–5). As of this writing, the full use and management of the IMEI is still under discussion. In concept, when a GSM component passes conformance and interoperability tests, it is given a type approval code (TAC). Additionally, a final assembly code (FAC) is added to identify the place of final manufacture and or assembly. The serial number (SNR) is assigned to each piece of equipment within each TAC/FAC. This number is assigned by the manufacturer. A spare digit is available for further assignment.

Temporary Mobile Subscriber Identity (TMSI)

The temporary mobile subscriber identify (TMSI) is an alias, used in place of the IMSI. This value is sent over the air interface in place of the IMSI for purposes of security. Chapter 13 explains the use of the IMSI in more detail.

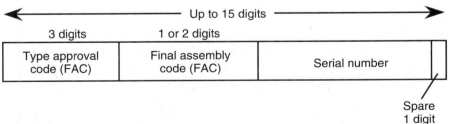

Figure 8–5
The international mobile station equipment identity (IMEI).

OVERVIEW OF GSM OPERATIONS

This section provides three examples of GSM operations: registration, call establishment (set up), and roaming. I have simplified the operations in order to give you a general idea of GSM operations. For a more detailed view of these three operations, refer to the section in this chapter titled "GSM Operations."

Registration

Figure 8–6 shows how a mobile unit registers itself with the network. After the unit is turned on, it scans the GSM frequency bands and locks onto a forward (base) channel. At this time the mobile unit knows if it is in a different area than it was when the unit was last used. If the area is different, a registration takes places with the exchange of the messages shown in Figure 8–6.

In events 1 and 2, the mobile unit requests and is granted a channel by the BSS. Although not shown in this figure, the BTS sends a signal to

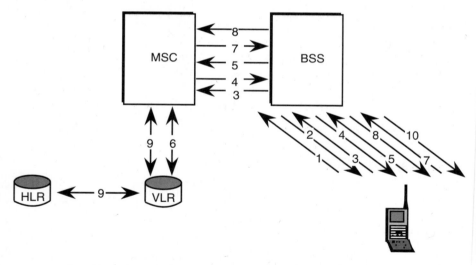

1 = channel request	6 = process authentication parameters
2 = channel assignment	7 = assignment of new area and TMSI
3 = location update request	8 = acknowledgment
4 = authentication request	9 = VLR and HLR updates
5 = authentication response	10 = channel release

Figure 8–6
Registration procedures.

the BSC as part of this process (I have these two systems combined into the BSS in these examples.). In event 3, the mobile unit requests a location update, which must be passed to the MSC. Before any other operations take place, the subscriber must be authenticated, which occurs in events 4, 5, and 6.

Assuming the authentication is verified, the mobile station is assigned to a new area and is given a temporary mobile subscriber identity (TMSI), which is used during the operation to identify the subscriber. These actions are shown in Figure 8–6 as events 7 and 8.

The MSC is responsible for coordinating the updating of the VLR and HLR (event 9), after which, the control channel is released.

Call Establishment

Figure 8–7 shows an example of a GSM call establishment, with the call coming from the public telephone network. The figure shows a telephone user placing a call through the public telephone network to the

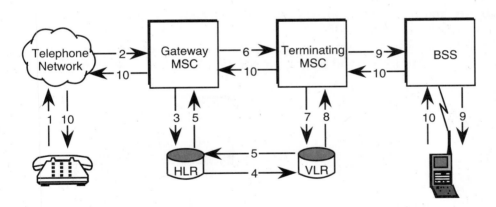

1 = call made to mobile unit
2 = telephone network recognizes number and gives to gateway MSC
3 = MSC can't route further, interrogates user's HLR
4 = interrogates VLR currently serving user (roaming number request)
5 = routing number returned to HLR and then to gateway MSC
6 = call routed to terminating MSC
7 = MSC asks VLR to correlate call to the subscriber
8 = VLR complies
9 = mobile unit is paged
10 = mobile unit responds; MSCs convey information back to telephone

Figure 8–7
GSM call establishment [BNR92a].

mobile unit by accessing the network in event 1. The call is routed to a gateway MSC (event 2), which examines the dialed digits and determines that it cannot route the call further. Therefore, in event 3, it interrogates the called user's HLR through the SS7 TCAP. The HLR interrogates the VLR that is currently serving the user (event 4). In event 5, the VLR returns a routing number to the HLR, which passes it back to the gateway MSC. Based on this routing number, the gateway MSC routes the call to the terminating MSC (event 6). The terminating MSC then queries the VLR to match the incoming call with the identity of the receiving subscriber (events 7 and 8). In event 9, the terminating MSC sends the BSS a paging request, which relays it to the subscriber and the call is completed (event 10).

Roaming

Figure 8–8 shows an example of how a cellular subscriber can roam from cell to cell and how the system keeps a record of the subscriber's location. Upon the mobile station crossing a boundary, it sends a location update request (event 1), which contains its identification, to the BSS. This message is then routed to the new VLR. If the new VLR has no information about the entry for this user (because the user has moved recently into its area), the new VLR sends a location update request mes-

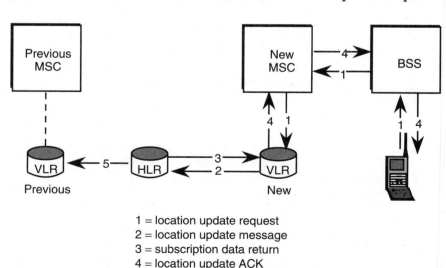

1 = location update request
2 = location update message
3 = subscription data return
4 = location update ACK
5 = location cancellation message

**Figure 8–8
Location updating.**

sage to the user's home location register (event 2). This message includes the identity of the user as well as the identity of the new VLR that sent the message. In event 3, the HLR stores the subscriber's new location as the new VLR and then downline loads the user's subscription database to the new VLR. Upon receiving this information, the new VLR sends the acknowledgment of the location update through the new MSC to the MSC, and back to the originating mobile user (event 4). Finally, in event 5, the HLR sends a location cancellation message to the old VLR to clear the subscriber's data from its database.

The mobile subscriber must be known only to one VLR at a time. In this example, when the subscriber has roamed to another area (another cell), the HLR has had to be updated. It can be seen that the HLR is the master of the subscriber databases and therefore coordinates changes to the VLRs and MSCs as the subscriber roams through the cells.

GSM INTERFACES

Four interfaces are defined in the GSM structure (see Figure 8–9). Two mandatory interfaces are the U_m interface and the A interface. The U_m interface is the air interface between the mobile station and the BTS. The A interface exists between the mobile services switching center (MSC) and the base station controller (BSC). A third interface, called A*bis*, defines operations between the BSC and the BTS. Finally, the mobile application part (MAP) defines the operations between the MSC and the telephone network as well as the MSC, the HLR, the VLR, and the EIR. MAP is an extension to ITU-T's SS7.

GSM is designed to permit functional partitioning. The major partitioning occurs at the A interface. One side of the interface deals with the MSC, HLR, and VLR operations, and the other side of the interface deals with the BSS and air operations.

The Air Interface (U_m)

The air interface (the U_m interface) is usually of the most interest to individuals. This interface uses a combination of frequency division multiplexing (FDM) and time division multiple access (TDMA) techniques (see Figure 8–10). The original GSM system operated in the 900 MHz range with 890 to 915 MHz allocated for the mobile station-to-base station transmissions and 935 to 960 MHz allocated for the base station-to-mobile station transmissions. The DCS-1800 now uses channel spectrum

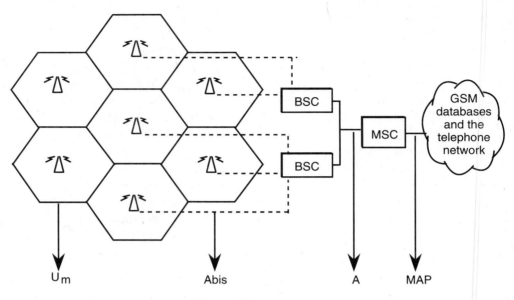

Figure 8–9
The GSM interfaces.

space from 1710 to 1785 MHz and 1805 to 1880 MHz, therefore increasing the capacity in bandwidth of DCS-1800 over that of GSM900.

One hundred-twenty-four channel pairs operate at full duplex (FDX) with the uplink and downlink allocated with different carrier frequencies. In this example, one channel is allocated to the 935.2 carrier and another channel is allocated to the 890.2 carrier. Thereafter, these FDM channels use TDMA. TDMA slots are allocated with 8 slots to a frame, and include information and control bits. Each individual slot comprises 156.25 bits with a bit time of .544 ms. However, the user only receives 114 bits from this slot. The remaining bits are used for synchronization and other control functions.

The instance of one particular time slot (such as slot number 3) in each frame makes up one physical channel and is shown in the bottom of Figure 8–10. This means that the physical channel uses one slot every 4.615 ms. Note from the figure that the same structure exists both on the uplink and downlink channels. In addition, the signals are separated into 124 channel pairs with a 200 kHz spacing to prevent channel interference.

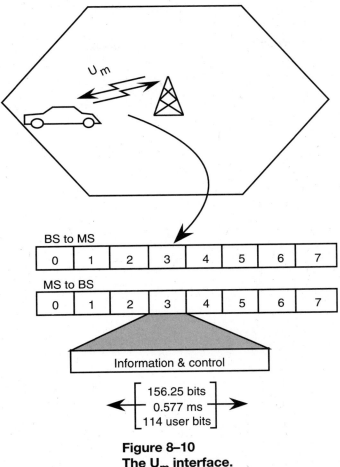

**Figure 8–10
The U$_m$ interface.**

GSM LAYERS AND PLANES

The GSM architecture is based on the Open Systems Interconnection (OSI) model. As such it uses layered protocols, service definitions, service access points (SAPs), and the concepts of encapsulation and decapsulation. Figure 8–11 shows the layers (consisting of protocols and physical connections) that exist at each interface. It is evident that GSM borrows heavily from ISDN and SS7, and that most of the GSM protocols owe their origin to these two standards.

Unfortunately, the GSM standards do not provide much information on GSM's overall architecture, and in some instances the standards do

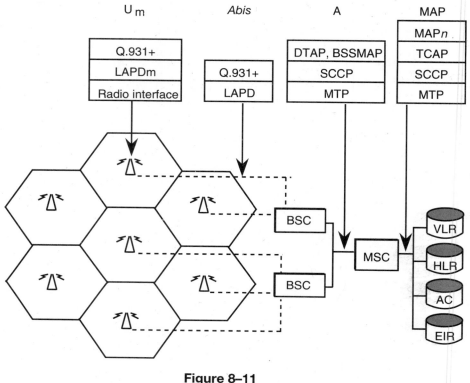

Figure 8–11
The GSM layers.

not provide a name for the protocol. In other instances, one name is used to describe a number of protocols operating at different interfaces. Figure 8–11 is an accurate representation of the GSM layers, but I have added the generic names to the description of GSM's architecture to aid in our dialogue. For example, the term Q.931+ is used to indicate the use of Q.931 with modifications.

Q.931 is an ISDN layer 3 protocol. In GSM, a modified version of Q.931 is used to set up, negotiate, and tear down a connection between the mobile station and the GSM machines. The link access procedure (LAP) has three versions, LAPDm (LAPD for a mobile link), LAPD (link access procedure for the D channel), and MTP level 2. Their function is to ensure the safe delivery of traffic across the physical channel.

The signaling connection control part (SCCP), message transfer part (MTP), transaction capabilities application part (TCAP), and are derived from the SS7 standard, and have been modified for GSM operations.

Comparisons of the Layer 2 Protocols

As illustrated in Figure 8–11, GSM uses more than one link layer protocol at its interfaces. The protocols LAPDm, LAPD, and MTP2 are quite similar in functions and are all derived from the high level data link control (HDLC) specification. One of the principal differences between these three protocols is the use of framing conventions. LAPD and MTP2 use the conventional HDLC flags to delineate the beginning and ending of a frame on the channel. For LAPDm, the use of flags is not necessary because of structure blocks existing at the underlying physical layer.

In addition, LAPD and MTP2 use the conventional HDLC operation for error checking with a frame check sequence (FCS) field. LAPDm does not need this mechanism because of the error detecting operation with the underlying physical layer.

The formats for these three data link protocols also vary. LAPm and LAPD use the conventional HDLC frame format whereas MTP2 (while similar to HDLC) uses a format specific to the layer 2 of SS7. Whatever the format, the purpose of these data link layers is to deliver the traffic safely across the interface between two machines.

If the reader wishes to see how these three protocols operate (with minor variations between them), see Chapter 11 under "The Data Link Layer."

Protocols at the A*bis* Interface

For the A*bis* interface and as shown in Figure 8–11, the conventional LAPD link layer protocol is used at layer 1, and a modified version of Q.931 (called Q.931+) is run of top of LAPD at layer 3. LAPD was described in the previous section, so we need not dwell on it further. Examples of Q.931 are provided in the last section of this chapter.

Figure 8–12 shows the general structure of the messages for Q.931+. The GSM Q.931+ messages use a similar format. The message must contain these parameters:

- *Protocol discriminator (4 bits):* Identifies who is to process the message once it has arrived at the destination. Since different entities reside in a GSM machine, the originator of the message codes this field to indicate the proper recipient.

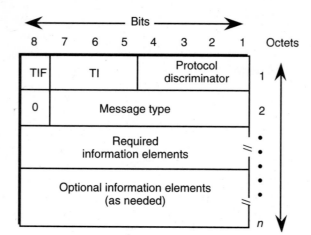

Figure 8–12
The Q.931+ message.

- *Transaction identifier flag (TIF) (1 bit):* Identifies the sender of the message. It is set to 0 by the originator and to 1 when the respondent returns a reply.
- *Transaction identifier (TI) (3 bits):* Similar to a Q.931 call reference number (which this field replaces in this message), it distinguishes between multiple connections and their association messages (transactions).
- *Message type (7 bits):* Identifies the message function, such as a setup or disconnect.

The *other information elements* field may consist of many entries, and its contents depend on the message type.

Protocols at the A Interface

The A interface makes use of many of the SS7 protocols. MTP level 1 (as shown in Figure 8–11) performs the functions of a traditional OSI physical layer. It generates and receives the signals on the physical channel. The notation "MTP" in Figure 8–11 refers to MTP1, MTP2, and MTP3.

MTP2 relates closely to the OSI layer 2. It is a conventional data link level, and is responsible for the delivery of traffic on each link between SS7 nodes. The traffic in the upper layers of SS7 are encapsulated into MTP2 "signal units" (this term is used instead of the conventional

HDLC "frame"), and sent onto the channel to the receiving node. This node checks for errors that may have occurred during transmission and takes remedial action (discussed later).

MTP 3 performs OSI layer 3 functions, notably, the routing of messages between machines and between components within a machine. It performs load-sharing operations across multiple links, and reconfiguration operations in the event of node or link failure. In GSM, MTP 3 is used to transfer messages between the entities on the A interface, and to perform its conventional functions in relation to managing "linksets" (multiple links between machines.)

SCCP corresponds to several of the operations associated with OSI layer 3 (and although not generally discussed in literature, OSI layer 4, as well). Some of its principal jobs are: (1) supporting the MTP layers with global addressing, (2) providing connectionless or connection-oriented services, and (3) providing sequencing and flow-control operations. It is quite rich in its functions, and not all of them are used in GSM. At the A interface, two classes of operation are used: class 0 for overall operations not pertaining to a specific mobile station, and class 2 for setting up a connection.

Finally, direct transfer application part (DTAP) and BSS management part (BSSMAP) messages are sent between the MS and the MSC as well as the BS and the MSC respectively. As seen in Figure 8–11, they run on top of SCCP. The destination of these messages is indicated by a header in the application running on top of SCCP, which is called a discrimination flag. The purpose of the flag is to indicate if the BSC is a transit node for the message or the final destination.

Protocols at the MAP Interface

Most of the protocols at the mobile application part (MAP) interface have been described earlier. Although Figure 8–11 denotes the interfaces between the MSC and several other components as MAP, different procedures are used between, say, the MSC and a VLR or the MSC and an HLR. Unfortunately, the GSM standards are not consistent in providing a name for each of these interfaces, so I have grouped them under the name MAP. Table 8–1 lists the specific MAPn protocols and where they operate. In order to be consistent with existing literature, I cross-checked this table with two authoritative texts on the subject [MOUL92] and [REDL95].

The transaction capabilities application part (TCAP) corresponds to several of the functions of the OSI layer 7. It is quite similar to the re-

Table 8–1   MAPn Interfaces

Interface Designation	Between
B	MSC-VLR
C	MSC-HLR
D	HLR-VLR
E	MSC-MSC
F	MSC-EIR
G	VLR-VLR

mote operations service element (ROSE). As such, it performs connectionless remote procedure calls on behalf of an "application" running on top of it.

FUNCTIONAL PLANES

Figure 8–13 shows one of the more important aspects of the GSM architecture, the functional planes. These planes are used to describe the detailed operations of the GSM communications at the physical sites, and across the interfaces. This section provides an introduction to the planes, and a later section in this chapter provides several detailed examples of their operations.

Five planes are present in GSM, as shown in this figure. The reader may wonder what happened to the OSI layers. They are still present. A good way to view the functional planes is that they include the functions of some of the protocols described earlier, and they also include functions that are not described in the those protocols. For example, Q.931 can be found in some of the operations of the communication management (CM) plane, yet other operations in this plane are not described on any Q.931 specification. Some writers place these planes at the OSI network layer (layer 3), but many of the operations deal with layers 1 and 2 of the OSI model. Parts of GSM machines are obviously concerned with transmission and reception of signals, which of course refers to the physical plane.

The radio resource management (RR) plane provides the link support, and is concerned with establishing and releasing connections between the mobile station and the MSC. Some of the major operations of

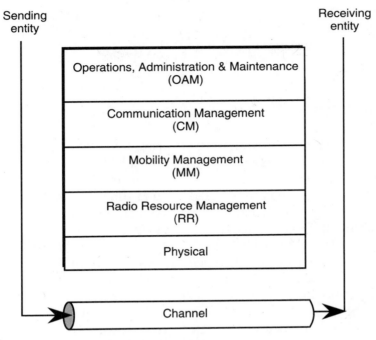

Figure 8–13
GSM functional planes.

RR include the assignment and release of channels, managing channel changes during handovers across cells, setting cipher mode operations, receiving status reports from the mobile station, changing frequencies, and managing frequency hopping.

The mobility management (MM) plane is responsible for the subscriber databases (such as subscriber location data). It operates on the HLR and MSC/VLR. Some of the major operations of MM include the registration of the mobile station, verifying the user with the EIR, checking which services the mobile station is allowed or not allowed to use, and most of operations pertaining to location management with the HLR and VLRs.

The communication management (CM) plane is responsible for setting up and tearing down calls. The operations are quite similar to ISDN layer 3 operations.

Finally, the operations, administration, and maintenance (OAM) plane deals with network management functions, such as monitoring activities and configuration operations.

GSM CHANNELS

GSM physical channels are managed through various multiplexing techniques. The resulting schemes create logical channels on the physical link. Logical channels are a well known concept used in many systems such as X.25, frame relay, and ATM. The reader should understand that a logical channel is not a dedicated physical channel but one that is shared by multiple users. GSM uses this approach not only to allow the multiplexing of a physical channel but to provide different formats for the traffic and also different types of logical channels as well. Figure 8–14 shows the general organization of GSM channels. Traffic channels carrying user payload are noted with the initials of TCH. GSM defines a full-rate TCH and half-rate TCH—these are shown in this figure as TCH/s and TCH/f, respectively. The TCH/s is designed for future use and will double the capacity of the TCH/f channel. The latter channel runs at 13 kbit/s to carry digitized speech transmissions. Both TCH/f and TCH/s can accommodate data traffic as well. The full rate operates at 13, 12, 6, and 3.6 kbit/s, which is adequate to support modem speeds of 9.6, 4.8, and 2.4 kbit/s. The half-rate supports only 4.8 and 2.4 kbit/s data transmissions. Once TCH channels are allocated to the user, the user has dedicated bandwidth on that channel.

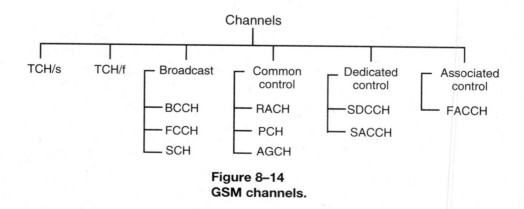

Figure 8–14
GSM channels.

Each traffic channel is associated with another channel used for signaling. This channel is also a dedicated channel, as its name implies, and it is a control channel (which is shown in Figure 8–14). It is called the slow associated control channel (SACCH) and uses the term associated because it is always associated with the user channel (as one option). It may also be associated with a stand-alone dedicated control channel (SDCCH) that is also used for the transfer of signaling information between the base station and the mobile station. These two dedicated control channels are used in a variety of ways that are explained further in this section.

The associated control channel, called the fast associated control channel (FACCH), is not a dedicated channel although it might carry the same information as the SDCCH. As we noted earlier, the SDCCH is a dedicated channel unto itself. In contrast, the FACCH is part of a traffic channel. Indeed, it may borrow some bandwidth from the traffic channel under certain conditions. As we shall see in the next section, there is a flag in the message that announces that FACCH is stealing some bursts from the traffic channel. Also, be aware that some literature substitutes the term FACCH with the term fast associated signaling (FAS).

Three broadcast channels are available in the GSM system. The broadcast control channel (BCCH) is used to send various system parameters to all mobile stations. These parameters include the operator identifiers, the location of the cell, the name of the cell, and frequency information. The frequency correction channel (FCCH), as its name implies, is used by the base station to give the mobile station information about frequency references. It is used for a frequency correction burst. The synchronization channel (SCH) is used by the base station to provide the mobile station synchronization training sequences. And, as we shall see in the next section, the SCH channel is actually mapped into the synchronization burst format.

Three channels are grouped under common control channels. These channels are used for the establishment of links between the mobile station and the base station as well as for ongoing call management, such as call setup and call disconnect. The random access channel (RACH) is used by the mobile station and not the base station. As we shall see later, RACH is mapped into a random burst format and it contains information used by the mobile station to the requested dedicated channel from GSM. It is the first message sent from the mobile unit to the base station.

The base station uses the paging channel (PCH) to communicate with individual mobile stations within its cell. And, finally, the mobile station receives information about the dedicated channel it is supposed to use on the access grant channel (AGCH). This information also contains data about timing and synchronization.

In effect, all these channels are considered logical channels in GSM. In practice, many of them are simply a different way of formatting messages and/or putting the messages in various time slots on the physical channel.

FORMATS OF MESSAGES (THE TIME DIVISION MULTIPLE ACCESS BURST)

Earlier we learned that the GSM burst was a duration of .577 millisecond (ms). Figure 8–15 shows the slot in relation to an 8-slot frame that yields a time period of 4.615 ms (rounded off). The figure also shows one option for sending traffic on the channel, and that is to multiplex 26 frames together for a 120 ms time period. We shall see shortly that other multiplexing schemes are available for combining traffic.

Figure 8–15 also shows the format and bit configuration for one of the bursts on the channel. This example is for a normal burst, which

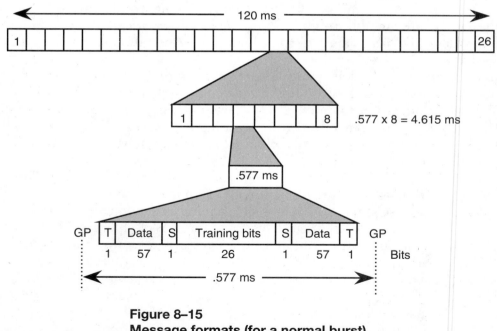

Figure 8–15
Message formats (for a normal burst).

would contain ongoing user traffic. As discussed earlier, each burst contains 114 bits of user data. For a normal burst, the data are divided into two subslots each consisting of 57 bits. The tail (T) bits consist of two bits, one at the beginning and one at the ending of a burst, that are used for ramping up and ramping down the signal during periods when the signal is in transition. The tail bits are always set to 0. In addition, 2 bits in this figure are labeled the S bits, which mean signaling flags, are used to indicate if the traffic contained in the burst is signaling traffic or user traffic.

In addition, this figure shows some guard period (GP) that is "wrapped around" the entire burst. No data are sent during the guard period. The guard period is approximately 8.25 bits and since each bit is 1.69 µs in duration, the guard period is 30.4 µs.

Finally, the training bits are placed in the middle of the burst to allow the receivers to synchronize themselves to the burst. It is especially useful in this technology because it helps compensate for multipath fading. GSM uses eight different training sequences because signals might be arriving at the receiver at approximately the same time. If the training sequences are the same, there is no easy way for the receiver to distinguish these signals. Thus, the training sequences in GSM are noted for their distinct bit structure in that they are not correlated to each other.

GSM OPERATIONS

The remainder of this chapter is devoted to a detailed discussion of how the GSM sets up a call between two users. Some of this material is based on a prototype developed by Bell Northern Research (BNR), United Kingdom [BAHI91]. The remainder of the material is based on the GSM specifications from the ETSI standards. The detailed aspects of this section should be of interest to designers and programmers. For this audience, note that the operations between the GSM functional planes are implemented with operating systems calls or program function calls.

It may prove helpful for you to review the GSM authentication procedure in Chapter 13.

Request for Connection Establishment

Figure 8–16 shows the request for the establishment of a link between the MS and the BSS. In event 1, a call is initiated by the call control sublayer (CC) of CM to the MM sublayer. The service request in-

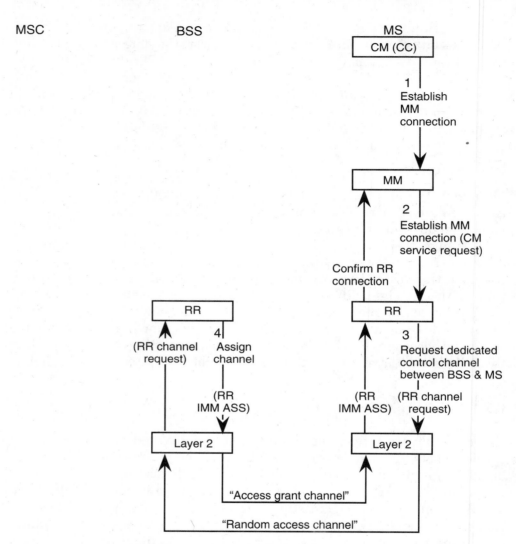

Figure 8–16
GSM operations example (request for establishment).

cludes a parameter indicating if the call is a normal or an emergency call.
Prior to event 1, the MS is in an idle state, listening to BCCH.

In event 2, MM requests the establishment of an RR connection,
which includes the information pertaining to immediate assignment procedures for a new physical channel. This CM service request contains the
MS identity and other information needed for the handshake.

In event 3, RR requests a dedicated control channel on a new physical channel. This message is sent on the random access channel (RACH) to the BSS.

At the BSS, when the RR receives this channel request, it allocates a physical channel by sending a message across the channel to the MS RR function. These actions are grouped as event 4.

Signaling Link Establishment

Figure 8–17 shows the operations to set up a link. In event 1, once the RR has been assigned a dedicated control channel, it then requests the establishment of a signaling link on that channel. The signaling link is a logical link that operates over the physical channel (the physical link). This results in the issuance of a set asynchronous balanced mode (SABM) frame in event 2 by the use of the LAPDm protocol. The I field in this message contains a CM service request (SERV REQ) layer 3 message which gives the identity of the mobile station (IMSI or TMSI) and the type of call being established.

In events 3 and 5, a confirmation is sent back to the mobile station indicating that the signaling link was established properly. The unnumbered acknowledgment (UI) frame accomplishes this task. The MS checks the information field in the SABM frame (which contains the original (M SERV REQ message) as an error-check. In event 4, layer 2 at the BSS sends to the RR of the BSS an indication that the signaling link has been established with the MS. The RR then passes the layer 3 CM SERV REQ message to the BSSMAP.

In event 6, BSSMAP generates a layer 3 message containing information about the identity of the MS, a cell number, and the location area code (LAC).

The result of this operation allows the connection-oriented SCCP, in event 7, to send a connection request message to the MSC. This message is passed from the MSC SCCP (CO) through the BSSMAP and (in event 8) to the MM. This indicates to the MSC that an RR connection has been established between the MS and the BSS.

In event 9, the MSC generates the PROCESS ACCESS REQUEST MAP message to the VLR. This message contains the identity of the MS and is used by the VLR to determine whether to authenticate the MS and whether a cipher mode setting is required.

The result of the operations in Figure 8–17 is (1) a signaling link is established, (2) an RR connection is complete, and (3) the VLR has registered the MS.

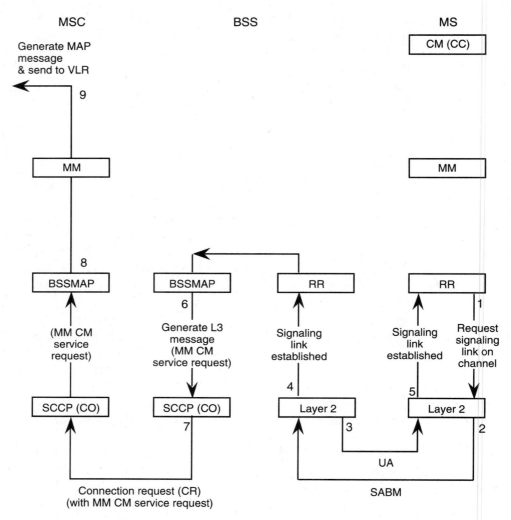

Figure 8–17
Signaling link establishment.

Authentication

As we mentioned earlier in this chapter, GSM supports user/network authentication with encryption techniques. Figure 8–18 shows the authentication procedures. In event 1, the VLR has processed the PROCESS ACCESS REQUEST message and returns an AUTHENTIFICATION REQUEST to the MSC. This message is only sent if the VLR

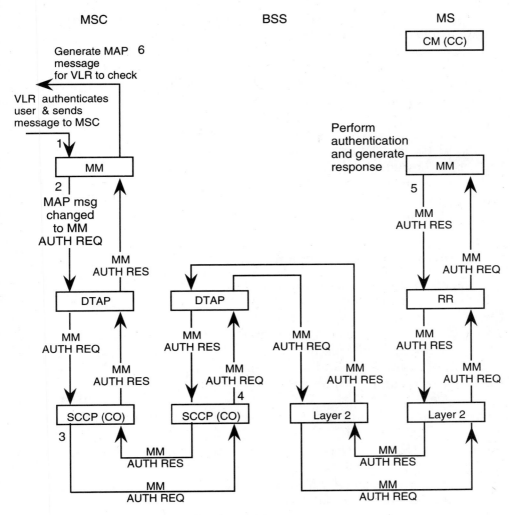

Figure 8–18
Authentication procedure.

recognizes the TMSI of the MS. Otherwise, the VLR requests the IMSI. The AUTHENTICATION REQUEST message contains a ciphering key sequence number (CKSN) and a random number (RAND). In event 2, the MM at the MSC converts this message into a layer 3 air interface authentication request message (AUTH REQ). This message is sent to the BSS through the direct transfer application part (DTAP) of BSSAP. In event 3, SSCP (CO) relays this request to the BSS.

In event 4, the DTAP at the BSS receives the request and bypasses the RR sublayer of the BSS because the message already contains the air interface header information (in event 5). The AUTH REQ is relayed finally to the MM of the MS, which uses the ciphering key sequence number and the random number to begin the authentication operation. The result of this process is sent to the MSC through another DTAP message.

Finally, in event 6, the MSC receives this message and converts it into a MAP AUTHENTICATION RESPONSE message and forwards it to the VLR. The VLR then authenticates and determines if the subscriber is allowed to use the system.

The result of the operations in Figure 8–18 are that the MS RR is still in the connected mode and that the MS is awaiting ciphering and MM establishment.

Ciphering and MM Establishment

Figure 8–19 continues the description of authentication and how an MM establishment occurs. In event 1, we assume the VLR authenticates the MS and so indicates by returning a MAP message to the MSC MM. The MM then generates a synchronization request with the RR sublayer and in event 2, BSSMAP generates the cipher mode command (CIPH MODE CMD) message and sends this message to the BSS. In event 3, the SCCP (CO) and BSSMAP pass this information to the RR sublayer.

In event 4, RR at the BSS generates the air interface CIPH MODE CMD message and will then begin deciphering all incoming air interface messages. The CIPH MODE CMD message is sent to the MS. In event 5, the CIPH MODE CMD is received by the RR sublayer of the MS and passes it to MM to indicate that ciphering has started. In turn, MS CM is notified of this situation by MM.

As a result of this handshake, in event 6, the RR sublayer of the MS can begin ciphering and deciphering all messages. It also sends a cipher mode complete (CIPH MODE COM) to the BSS.

In event 7, at the BSS, the receipt of this message means that stream-ciphering can begin at this machine. And, in event 8, the BSSMAP generates the CIPH MODE COM message for the MSC.

Finally, in event 9, the MSC MM sublayer of the MSC is notified of the completion of the synchronization at the air interface which means RR and MM protocols have finished their handshake.

These examples have shown the GSM initial handshakes. After all this activity, the MS CM can initiate an actual call by invoking the Q.931+ protocol.

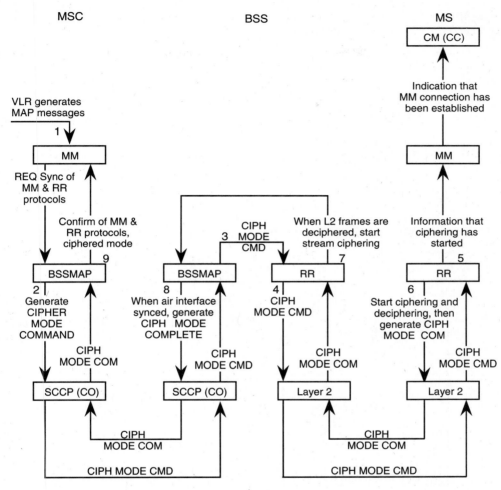

Figure 8–19
Ciphering and MM establishment.

Call Setup

Figure 8–20 shows how a Q.931+ message is generated by the MS to get the layer 3 connection setup. In event 1, the mobile station generates a setup message that is forwarded directly to the MSC MM. It is passed transparently through the BSS. This message contains the calling party number, the called party number, the identity of the mobile unit making

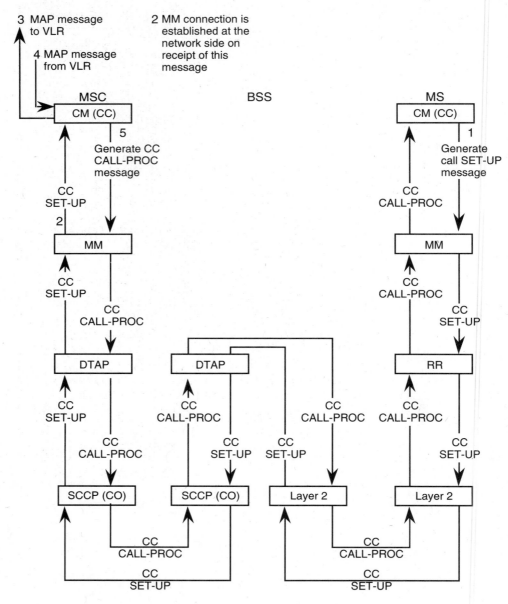

Figure 8–20
Call setup.

the call, any required error capability, and the high/low layer capability information needed for the call. In event 2, the setup message is received at the MSC CM and the result of this message means that an MM connection is established on the network side of the MSC. The process here is very straightforward. In event 3, the MSC processes the setup message and then generates a MAP message to send to the VLR. The VLR, in event 4, responds to this message by sending a complete call message back to the MSC CM if the call is successful. Finally, in event 5, the call proceeding message is sent back to the MS from the MSC. So, this operation is quite similar to an ongoing ISDN connection setup in that the call proceeding message informs the MS CM that the call is indeed being forwarded through the network to the end user.

The final result of these events is that the MMs have a connection and the call setup is proceeding.

Resource Assignment

Now the MSC call control sublayer can initiate resource assignment messages to the respective BSS and MS. This is shown in event 1 of Figure 8–21, by the generation of an resource assignment (RES ASS) message. Actually, BSSMAP (in event 2) generates this assignment request message. The message contains information about the type of channel to be allocated and what resources are needed to allocate the channel. This message is forwarded to the BSS as shown in event 3. Upon receipt of the message at the BSS, the BSS is required to begin the allocation of the resources for the affected MS. In event 4, the BSS generates an ASSIGNMENT COMMAND message across the air interface, which contains the information about the assigned channel, transmission power, and so on. This message is received at the MS RR; and, in event 5, the MS, makes the necessary housekeeping functions, switches to the proper channel, and generates an ASSIGNMENT COMPLETE message back to the BSS over the newly assigned channel. In event 6, the receipt of the ASSIGNMENT COMPLETE message back at the BSS is used to indicate that the MS and BSS have successfully established a channel and are properly synchronized. The results of these actions, means that in event 7, the BSSMAP can generate an ASSIGNMENT COMPLETE message and send it back to the MSC. This message is received (in event 8) at the MSC. The MSC then uses this message and (in event 9) sends an INITIAL ADDRESS message to the relevant exchange handling the call.

(text continues on page 209)

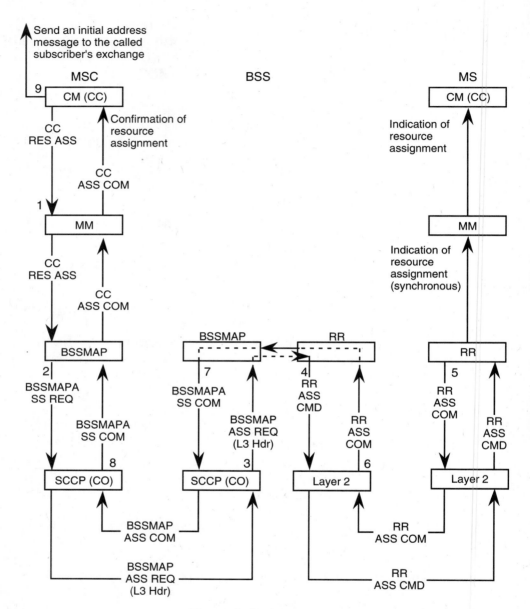

Figure 8–21
Resource assignment.

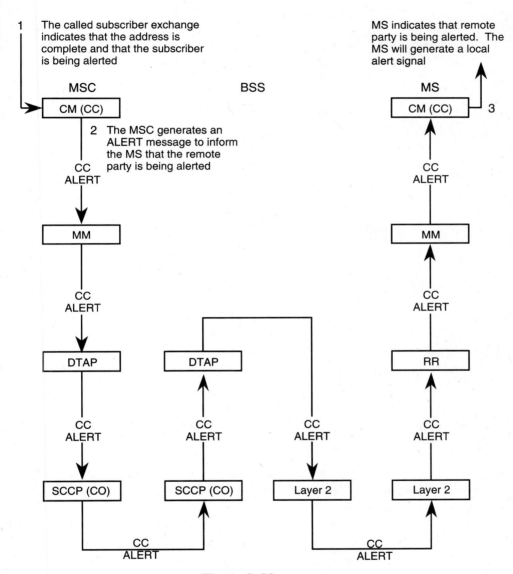

1   The called subscriber exchange indicates that the address is complete and that the subscriber is being alerted

MS indicates that remote party is being alerted. The MS will generate a local alert signal

MSC   BSS   MS

CM (CC)

CM (CC)   3

2   The MSC generates an ALERT message to inform the MS that the remote party is being alerted

CC ALERT

CC ALERT

MM

MM

CC ALERT

CC ALERT

DTAP

DTAP

RR

CC ALERT

CC ALERT

CC ALERT

CC ALERT

SCCP (CO)

SCCP (CO)

Layer 2

Layer 2

CC ALERT

CC ALERT

Figure 8–22
Call confirmation.

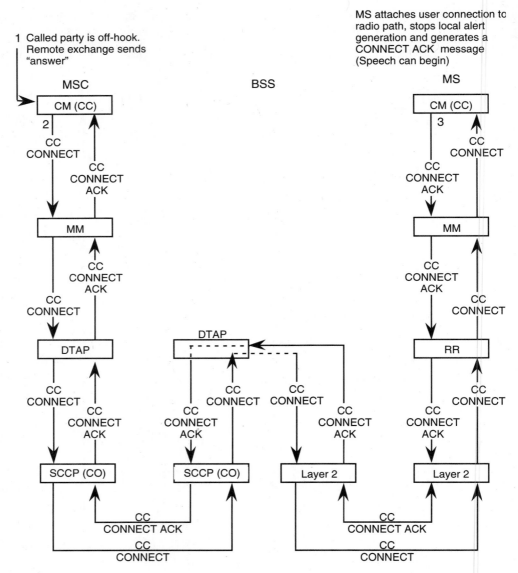

**Figure 8–23
Call connection.**

Consequently, after all these operations, the connection is still being established through the MSCs and other telephone exchanges, but the resources are assigned and ready to operate on the air interface.

Call Confirmation

The next series of operations, shown in Figure 8–22, are initiated from the called subscriber exchange. In event 1, the MSC receives information that all is well, that the address is understandable and complete, and that the subscriber is being alerted to the call. Upon receiving this message, the MSC generates an alert message to forward back to the MS to let the MS know that the remote party has been alerted. In event 3, this message arrives at the MS CM, which allows the MS to generate a local alert signal.

Call Connection

Finally in Figure 8–23, the called party goes off-hook and this operation is reflected in an answer signal coming from the remote exchange to the serving MSC, shown in event 1. The receipt of this message allows the MSC CM to generate a connect message in event 2 and forward this directly to the MS CM. As the figure shows, this signal is sent transparently through the BSS. Upon receipt of this signal, in event 3, the MS attaches the user connection to the radio path, stops its local alert generation signals, and then generates a connect acknowledgment message to be sent back to the MSC CM. Once again, these signals are sent transparently through the BSS, where the message arrives in event 4 at the MSC. We have now completed the full call setup and ongoing speech can take place.

SUMMARY

GSM is one example of a second-generation mobile cellular system. It uses TDMA technology and uses of the SS7 and ISDN layers, interfaces, and protocols. It is rich in function and quite complex. Several PCS vendors and service providers have selected GSM for their PCS protocol.

9

Personal Communications
Services (PCSs)

INTRODUCTION

This chapter is devoted to the examination of personal communications service (PCS), also known as personal communications networks (PCNs) in Europe. We begin the analysis of PCS by explaining what it is (defining it). We then examine several so-called first generation systems. Next, second-generation systems (being implemented today) are explained. The PCS auctions are revisited and comparisons are made between different several systems for the protocols and interfaces that have been proposed for PCS in the United States and other countries.

Please note that I will be using two terms in this chapter to describe the network provider's access node to the user station: PCS base station and radio port (RP). Both terms are used in the industry.

WHAT IS PCS?

The term "personal communications service (PCS)" has crept into the vocabulary of the telecommunications industry over the past few years. It has been used to describe a variety of services and technologies. Yet, no one agrees on an exact definition. The situation is made more complex by the fact that "personal" communications services on wireless media have been in existence since the advent of the technology. After all, what could be more personal than a conventional telephone call? The term is a part of our lives and we shall have to deal with it, even though it is somewhat meaningless in regard to the services rendered.

However, PCS is called "personal" for a good reason. It is a technology that is targeted for the personal consumer industry, and it has features that are quite different from conventional cellular systems (such as AMPS). Therefore, PCS is viewed as a technology for mass consumption, unlike the first-generation AMPS-type systems that are relatively expensive and used mainly by business (organizations that write off the use of the technology as an expense).

To place the discussion in the context of the FCC's view of PCS, Figure 9–1 shows that a PCS user employs an inexpensive, lightweight portable handset to communicate with a PCS base station. Connection to a wide variety of networks is provided by PCS switches that interface to the public telephone network through a local exchange carrier. Networks that are connected include the conventional telephone network, the AMPS cellular system, specialized mobile networks, and cable TV systems (CATV).

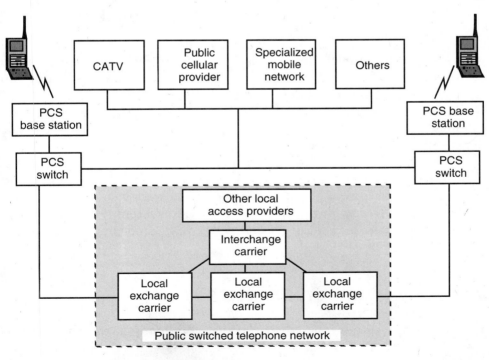

Figure 9–1
The FCC view of PCS.

It will prove helpful in this analysis to distinguish between high-tier and low-tier mobile systems. *High-tier* systems include the AMPS systems, paging systems, and satellite-based systems—the current systems we are using today. They are designed for high-mobility units and large cells (with cells that have large power requirements, e.g., running from a 12-volt battery in a car). High-mobility means that the mobile station can move about at a fast speed, such as an automobile moving at many miles an hour.

Low-tier PCS systems exhibit low mobility through the cells. The mobile station is carried by a person who is walking or standing, but is not in an automobile. Therefore, low-tier PCS consists of pedestrian traffic on a street, inside a building, and so on. It is anticipated that low-tier traffic will be much higher than conventional high-tier cellular systems and much of the traffic will be indoors.

In essence, low-tier PCSs are envisioned as a high-quality portable communication service that is available over a very wide area. It may include both a originate-only one-way service or two-way service. The handset is small with low power requirements. This attribute of PCS is quite important. The cells must be small in order to accommodate low-power transmitters with small, long-life batteries, which permits the handset manufacturer to build a small, lightweight handset. However, this attribute also has its limitations. The placement of the base station outside a building for occupants inside the building must be considered carefully. A building adds about 20 dB attenuation (a factor of about 100) to a signal, which is quite significant for the low-power PCS signal.

It should be emphasized that the quality of PCS service and the amount of traffic generated places a significant burden on the infrastructure used to support this technology. For example, a cellular phone housed in a car receives limited usage. But, a handset that is carried with a person is more likely to be used. While estimates vary, some studies reveal that a PCS phone will be used like a wire-based phone with a use factor of at least fourfold over a high-tier system. Bellcore studies also reveal that the market potential by the year 2005 could be 46 million subscribers.

DISTRIBUTION PLANT WITH WIRELESS ACCESS

Wireless PCS does not mean that the system has no wires. The interface between the subscriber unit (SU, the telephone handset) and the wireless provider's access node (a PCS base station, as seen in Figure 9–1) is wire-

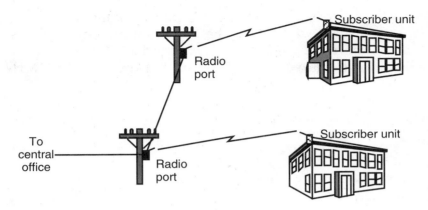

Figure 9–2
Wireless access to wired system.

less. But other interfaces may be wire-based. Figure 9–2 shows one arrangement in which the PCS air interface is supported from a central office through a radio port. The subscriber unit (SU) is mounted at the customer premises, and the network's radio port is mounted to a current distribution plant, and then through the outside copper plant or the fiber distribution system to the central office.

The telephone companies clearly have a vested interest and a big stake in the scenario depicted in Figure 9–2. It is recognized that the costs to maintain the outside copper plant are rising steadily and rapidly. Limited access to block cables, limited rights of way, and tree trimming problems are contributing factors. Thus, the telephone companies see PCS as an effective technology to reduce their costs.

EARLY PCS ACTIVITY

The concept of PCS is new to the general public, but it has been around since the late 1980s when the regulatory bodies of several countries established the framework for PCS. One of these early initiatives was launched in the United Kingdom (UK) in 1989 when the government announced its plans for accepting applications for PCN (European term) licenses.

Like most countries that were entering into the PCS arena, the UK decided the present first-generation AMPS-based system (TACS) was too restrictive to growth based on limited bandwidth, and too expensive for the average consumer. Therefore, the UK approach opened up the spectrum space in the 1.7–2.3 GHz band and awarded licenses in 1989 and in 1991 mandating the use of DCS 1800 (based on the GSM 900 MHz technology).

Other countries followed similar paths toward the road to PCS. I will have more to say about these countries later in this chapter.

"FIRST-GENERATION" PCS TECHNOLOGY

During this period (late 1980s and early 1900s), other systems are being installed, with the service providers choosing not to wait for formal PCS standards to take effect. For lack of a better term, some vendors and regulatory bodies call these systems "cordless telephony." They should not be confused with the cordless telephones used in homes, which are called "cordless residential telephony." Three systems are discussed next: CT2, DECT, and CT2 Plus.

CT2

The CT2 technology (cordless telephone or cordless communications) is a continuation of work that was done in the mid-1980s on cordless standards. While CT2 was not envisioned to be a long-running standard, it has been widely supported because it is an evolution of ongoing technology.

In the UK, the government granted four licenses for public systems in 1989 with the requirement that the operators had to support the interworking between systems. Initially, the CT2 systems were not compatible, but later these operators developed a common air interface (CAI) between their systems that was accepted later as a standard by the ETSI in April 1992. Several vendors participated in the development of CT2: AT&T, BT, GPT, Kenwood (owns Libera), Nortel (owns STC), and Orbitel.

The CT2 technology operates on frequency division multiple access (FDMA) concepts that support a speech rate of 32 kbit/s using ADPCM for speech coding over forty channels. Operating frequencies at this time range from 8.461 to 868.1 MHz. Carrier spacing is 100 kHz. The transmitter data rate is 72 kbit/s. CT2 uses time division duplex (TDD), which allows the land and mobile station to share one channel. As shown in Figure 9–3, the TDD frame is 1 ms in length, with the channel "ping-ponged" on 2 ms intervals. Each slot contains 64 bits of information

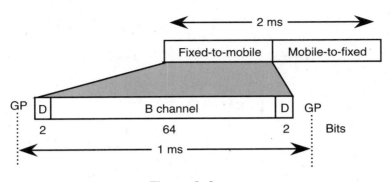

Figure 9–3
CT 2 TDD slots.

(B channel), and 4 bits of control (D channel). Eight bits of guardband surround each slot. Since each station is given 500 1-ms slots per second, each TDD B channel supports 32 kbit/s (500 ∗ 64 = 32,000). The D channel rate is 2000 bit/s (500 ∗ 4 = 2000). The channel is selected by the call originator, either the land or mobile station. This approach is called dynamic channel assignment (DCA).

During the past few years, the CT2 CAI standards have been accepted in the industry (after being reviewed and approved by a number of industry organizations and several European PTTs). As a consequence of this acceptance, several manufacturers decided to abandon their proprietary plans and migrate forthwith to the standard (by using the standard in their products). Some vendors such as Ferranti's ZonePhone and Hayes Communications Forum Phone chose to stay with proprietary standards for the time being.

Support of data applications. CT2 is capable of supporting voice and data traffic. The work that enhanced CT2 to support data was largely through the efforts of the Canadian vendors in their research and trials.

For CT2 data capabilities, four types of services have been defined. These services operate on ISDN B channels at 32 kbit/s in a circuit-mode environment. These services are:

1. Asynchronous services: Supported for full duplex operations with speeds ranging from 300 to 19,100 bit/s. Flow control operations are provided with this service as well as automatic request for repeat (ARQ) and forward error control (FEC) provisions.

2. Transparent synchronous services: Provided for full duplex channels. These services operate on the 32 kbit/s B channel, although lower rates can be supported as well. With these implementations, FEC is provided but ARQ is not.

3. Conventional X.25 service

4. Conventional ITU-T group 3 FAX service.

CT2 CAI now exists as a organized European standard along with DECT. It has received support throughout the world but is limited in its capacity due to its use of FDMA, a 32 kbit/s coding rate and its ongoing problems with shadowing and multipath fading.

DECT

The Digital European Cordless Telecommunications (DECT) standard was initiated by the CEPT in the mid-1980s as a method to move to a second-generation cordless telephone system. Several alternatives were evaluated by the CEPT in 1987 and eventually a technology known as Digital European Cordless Telephony was chosen. Later the name was retitled to the Digital European Cordless Telecommunications standard to reflect that it supported not only voice traffic, but also data traffic. With the formation of ETSI in 1988, the responsibility for DECT standardization was passed to this organization. In 1992, DECT became a formal European common air interface standard known as the European Telecommunications Standard, ETS 300-175. The approval test standard is published in I-ETS 300176. It is now "enforced" as a standard by the European Commission Directive 91/287.

DECT operates on frequencies ranging from 1880 to 1900 MHz. Like CT2, it uses ADPCM 32 kbit/s for speech coding, in accordance with ITU-T G.721. Unlike CT2, it uses TDMA as an access method. Twelve slots share each physical channel, as illustrated in Figure 9–4. Each slot contains 320 information bits. DECT uses TDD with 10 ms periods for two frames (fixed-to-mobile and mobile-to-fixed). Since each user has 320 bits per slot, and 100 10 ms slots per second, the channel capacity is 32 kbit/s (100 * 320 bits = 32,000). The control channel (C channel) operates at a rate of 4 kbit/s (100 * 40 bits = 4000).

Similar to other systems previously described, the DECT frame contains various control fields, sync fields and guardband time.

Like CT2, DECT uses DCA, but the handset selects the preferred channel during the connection setup.

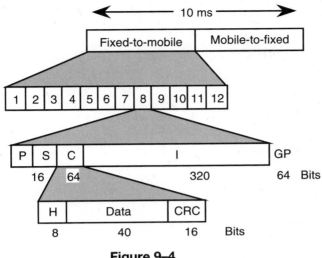

Figure 9–4
DECT TDD slots.

Support of data applications. DECT does not restrict itself to voice transmission only. It is also designed to support data applications (see Figure 9–5). For data transmission, DECT uses the layered protocol stack based on the OSI model and the IEEE 802 standards. The conventional physical medium access control (MAC) and logical link control (LLC) layers are employed. A gateway examines the addresses contained in packets and routes the packets accordingly. This routing entails the relaying of the traffic to attached LANs, other gateways, or attached cordless devices (such as workstations, printers, fax machines, and servers).

It is envisioned that most traffic will be carried with a connection-oriented procedure based on the DECT standard, although (technically) traffic can be sent in a connectionless mode. In addition, the gateway provides connections for voice traffic between workstations, telephones, and the telephone network.

One of the more widely known implementations of DECT with data is Olivetti's cordless LAN. This product was demonstrated in 1991 at the ITU-T Telecom Exhibition in Geneva, Switzerland. The Olivetti products were rolled out in 1992.

Table 9–1 lists some of the major attributes of CT2 and DECT [BNR95]. In most aspects, they are different, although both standards

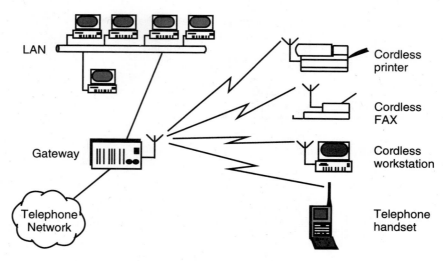

Figure 9–5
DECT support for data.

Table 9–1   Comparison of CT2 and DECT

	CT2	DECT
Forward band (MHz)	864–868	1880–1900
Reverse band (MHz)	864–868	1880–1900
Multiple access	FDMA	TDMA
Duplex	TDD	TDD
Carrier spacing (kHz)	100	1728
Channels per carrier	1	12
Bandwidth/two-way channel (kHz)	100	144
Channel rate (kbit/s)	72	1152
Modulation	FSK	GMSK
Modulation efficiency (bit/s/Hz)	0.72	0.67
Voice rate (kbit/s)	32	32
Control channel name	D	C
Control channel rate (bit/s)	2000	6400
Control channel message (bits)	64	64
Control channel delay (ms)	32	5

use the ITU-T 32 kbit/s coding scheme and neither provides error correcting operations. An important aspect of both CT2 and DECT is the fact that they (like AMPS) define the operations at the air interface only and not the network side of the hand station. A MAP-type system is needed to support these air interfaces on the network side.

CT2 PLUS

CT2 Plus was developed by Canada to improve the CT2 technology. The efforts have been coordinated by Industry Canada (formerly the Department of Communications [DCI]). It is now called (in Canada) CT2 Canada, and published as RSS-130.

CT2 Plus adds TDMA supervisory channels and operates in the 944 and 952 MHz band. It provides more features and improves roaming and handoff times (shorter times for the base and mobile station to locate each other). In addition, it automatically registers the station when it enters a new zone.

We will examine CT2 Plus in more detail later in this chapter when the PCS progress in several countries is discussed.

PCS AS VIEWED BY BELLCORE

The Bellcore view of PCS is based on five access services provided between the Bellcore client company (BCC) network and the PCS wireless provider (PWP) network (see Figure 9–6). Bellcore uses the term Wireless Access Communications Systems (WACS) as a generic description of PCS operations.

- PCS Access Service for Networks (PASN): A connection service for the provision of transport and signaling services to and from the PCS service provider (PSP). The PASN provides translation functions of a universal personal telecommunication number (UPT#) to a routing number (RN). PASN also ensures that calls are delivered to the appropriate PCS as well as PWP.
- PCS Access Service for Controllers (PASC): Designed for use with the PWP across radio channels and some type of automatic link transfer (ALT) capability. (ALT refers to the processing of signaling information during an active call without disrupting the call—in other words, an out-of-band signaling function.) The PASC per-

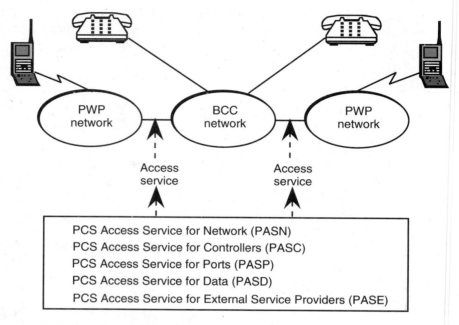

PWP = PCS wireless providers
BCC = Bellcore client company

Figure 9–6
Bellcore view of PCS.

forms all the functions of PASN in addition to dial-tone functions and call delivery operations.

- PCS Access Service for Ports (PASP): Designed to interface into a PWP that has very little functionality. In this situation, the service provider would own the license and the radio ports, but the BCC would handle most of the functions. In this type of service, the PCS provides the functions in PASN and PASC.

- PCS Service for Data (PASD): For services for transport of database information. It is an important component in PCS because it contains the information needed to establish and manage connections.

- PCS Access Service for External Service Providers (PASE): Used to accommodate other PCS support services such as specialized voice mail, paging, and alerting for other service providers.

The Bellcore vision for the PCS entails the use of the *universal personal telecommunication (UPT)* identification based on work done by the ITU-IS. UPT includes the ability of a caller to reach another subscriber at any location by simply dialing a single *UPT number (UPT#)*. This number is also used to identify unambiguously any user to the network. Presently, it is envisioned that UPT#s will be implemented with the E.164 numbering plan. In addition to the UPT, there will also be in place a *terminal identifier (TID)*, which is a code actually stored in the *user terminal (UT)*. The TID allows BCC networks and PWP networks to identify a specific piece of equipment. The format for the TID includes a country code, the provider of the terminal, and the terminal id itself.

One other identifier, which is important to the Bellcore PCS, is the *routing number (RN)*. This is used to deliver calls through the networks to specific locations. It is used in conjunction with the UPT# to provide a complete service to the user. The RN is also an E.164 number.

Bellcore PCS Architecture

Figure 9–7 shows the Bellcore PCS architecture. The air (A) interface connects the subscriber unit (SU) with the radio port (RP). The RPs do not have much functionality and will most likely be implemented with simple radio modems. One of their jobs is to convert the air interface to or from a wire or fiber signal.

The RPs are attached through the port (P) interface to the radio port control unit (RPCU), which supports PASP. Unlike the RP, the RPCU is complex. It operates with the SU signals on its P and A side and on the control (C) side, it operates with ISDN signals. It provides ISDN features to the SU but does not require the SU to implement ISDN.

The access manager (AM), visitor location manager (VLM), and home location manager (HLR) support mobility management by allowing calls to be sent and received to and from SUs in a group of cells called a registration area. These components interwork with the RPCU to support handoffs, which Bellcore calls automatic link transfer. They also support call authentication and security. The AM may be located at the switch or it may be part of an service control point (SCP).

Currently, Bellcore defines three physical layers for the P interface between the RP and the RPCU: the digital subscriber line (DSL), the high-bit-rate DSL (HDSL), or a T1 carrier.

The C interface supports ISDN, and is based on National ISDN-1 specifications. B channels are used to transport voice calls between the

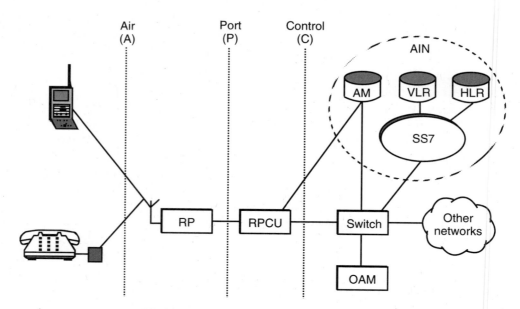

Figure 9–7
Bellcore PCS reference architecture.

RPCU and the switch. Standard ISDN layer 3 messages are employed at this interface.

The Advanced Intelligent Network (AIN).   Figure 9–7 shows another aspect of the PCS architecture. The Advanced Intelligent Network (AIN) is a collection of SS7, VLR, AM, and HLR that are tailored for PCS. This figure shows the Bellcore proposal (Bellcore documents GR-1129-CORE, GR-1298-CORE, and GR-1299-CORE), which is supported by some Regional Bell Operating Companies (RBOCs). However, other alternatives are being considered. An extension to IS-41 is also supported by a number of (RBOCs), cellular providers, and cable TV companies. Yet another alternative is the MAP of GSM, which is supported by MCI and a large number of equipment manufacturers.

For consistency, in this chapter, I shall continue to use the Bellcore model. In addition, the subject of AIN warrants an entire book in this series; nonetheless, I provide an example later in this chapter on how PCS and AIN interwork with each other.

Figure 9–8 shows another view of PCS interfaces and components in relation to the OSI bearer services layers (the lower 3 layers of the OSI

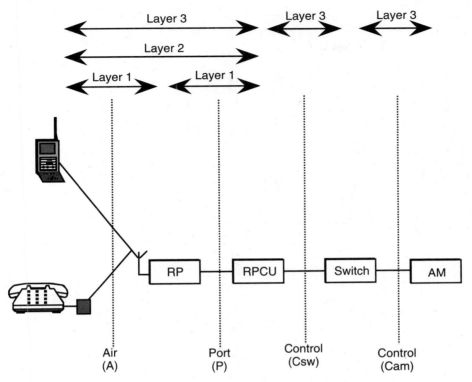

Figure 9–8
Another view of the interfaces.

model). As stated earlier, the operations between the SU and the RP are relatively simple, because the RP does not process any layer 2 or 3 messages. I have separated the switch and the access manager (AM) as separate entities in this figure. As stated earlier, they may be co-located in the same machine (the switch). This separation will allow us to examine the layer 3 operations in more detail later in this chapter.

The TDM/TDMA-Based Air Interface

As we have done in previous parts of this book, it is fruitful to examine the air interface frame format. Figure 9–9 shows the uplink and downlink frame formats. The downlink channel uses TDM operations. Its direction is from the RP to the SU. The uplink uses TDMA operations and its direction is from the SU to the RP.

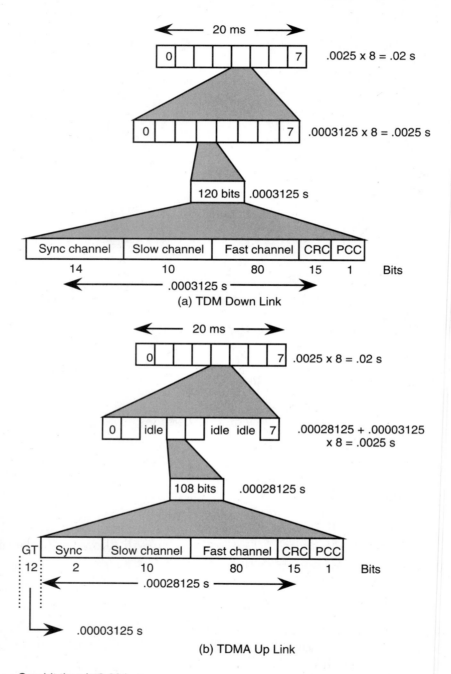

(a) TDM Down Link

(b) TDMA Up Link

One bit time is 2.604 μs

Figure 9–9
The TDM and TDMA frames.

The frame structure is 2.5 ms in duration. This short frame is compensated by the fact that the technology allows the use of low-delay speech coders and operates in a conventional 2-wire loop environment without the use of echo cancellers. Eight frames are multiplexed together to create a superframe 20 ms in duration.

The actual burst (slots) of the uplink and downlink differ slightly. As the figure illustrates, the downlink slot consists of 120 bits whereas the uplink frame consists of 108 bits. Therefore, the downlink slot duration is 312.5 μs and the uplink slot duration is 281.25 μs. It makes sense to have the uplink and downlink slots with consistent frame structures. However, the difference in the bit rate is to provide the uplink with a 12-bit guard time to compensate for variations in propagation delay as well as the turning on and off period of the SU's transmitter. When the guard time is added to the uplink slot time, it equals the full slot time of the downlink slot. The calculations to the right of this figure will illustrate these points.

This figure does not show that there is a time offset between the receipt of the downlink burst and the beginning of the transmission of the uplink burst, as measured by the SU antenna. This offset is 375 μs ± 4 μs.

The structure of each individual time slot in a downlink frame is as follows. The 14-bit synchronization channel (sync channel) is used for synchronization purposes and time slot numbering. The 10-bit slow channel field is used for signaling and control. For example, it is used to indicate if an errored frame has been detected on the uplink transmission and for other administrative operations. The fast channel contains user traffic. Since it operates at 80 bits for each slot with 400 frames per second, the nominal rate of the fast channel is 32 kbit/s. The 15-bit cyclic redundancy check (CRC) field is calculated from the slow channel and the fast channel for each burst. Finally, the 1-bit power control channel (PCC) is set in accordance with individual systems.

The basic structure for the uplink frame is as follows. The 2-bit sync byte is not defined in the standard. It can be used to serve as a phase reference to decode subsequent bits but it may also be used for other purposes.

The slow channel consists of 10 bits and it follows the same procedures as the slow channel on the downlink frame. The fast channel also contains 80 bits of information for signaling control, therefore its nominal rate is 32 kbit/s. The CRC field of 15 bits is used to perform an error check on the slow channel and the fast channel on each burst. Finally, the last bit is reserved (R) and currently it is to be set to zero.

EXAMPLES OF PCS CALL MANAGEMENT OPERATIONS

This section provides some examples of how PCS calls (as viewed by Bellcore) are managed across the A, P, Csw, and Cam interfaces. In keeping with my approach from chapter to chapter, I have reversed the components in Figures 9–7 and 9–8 in order to keep the mobile stations on the right side of the page.

The example for this call entails the sending of twenty-nine separate messages between various machines. Several years ago, this setup overhead was unthinkable, due to (at that time) slow processors. Certainly, protocol overhead is still a concern, but the fast microprocessor speeds of today's computers have masked much of this overhead from the end user. Figure 9–10, separated into Figure 9–10(a) and (b), illustrates that the RP does not participate in any of the layer 3 activities. Exchange of these

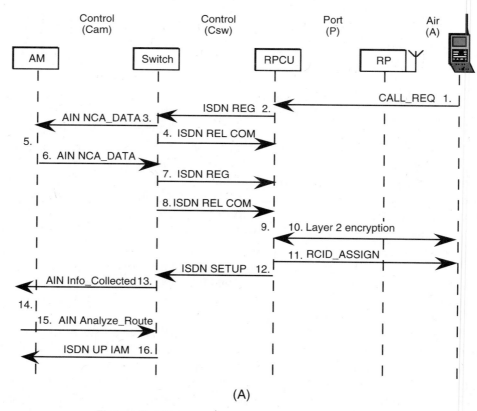

(A)

Figure 9–10
Example of PCS call management operations.

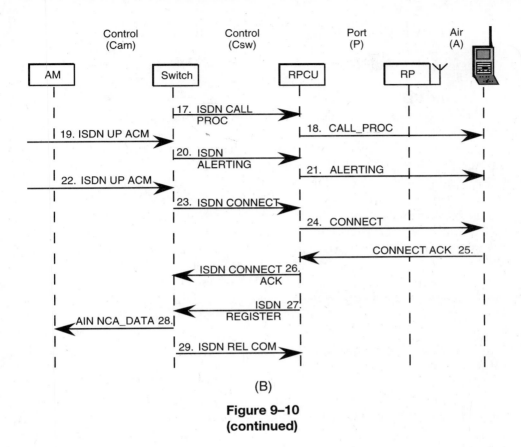

(B)

Figure 9–10
(continued)

messages occurs between the SU, the RPCU, the switch, and the AM. The reader will also note that the messages exchanged at the control interface are ISDN messages or AIN messages.

In event 1, the SU sends a call request message to the RPCU. This message must contain a called party identifier and bearer capability field. This latter field is used to identify any layer 1, layer 2, or upper layer protocol procedures that need to be invoked during this connection. Other fields are coded as options such as calling party or transit network selection.

In event 2, the RPCU sends an ISDN register message to the switch, which contains the call request message. It contains the same fields as the call request message in addition to administrative values that are used between the RPCU and the switch.

Next, in event 3, the switch receives the message, examines the call request message, and passes the message to the access manager inside a AIN NCA_DATA envelope. The switch then clears the reference for the

NCA signaling on the BRI (in event 4) by sending a release complete message back to the RPCU. When the access manager receives this information (in event 5), it authenticates this SU and notes that a call origination is requested; it then assigns a radio call identifier (RCID) and stores a record of the RCID in relation to the call. Next (in event 6), it sends a AIN NCA_DATA message (which has the RCID_ASSIGN message) to the switch. This traffic contains the RCID called party number, bearer capability, and other administrative fields. Upon the switch receiving this message, it retrieves the envelope and then sends the RCID assign message to the RPCU in the ISDN register message. This is shown as event 7 in the figure. Afterwards (in event 8), the switch clears the call reference for the NCA signaling on this BRI with the release complete message.

In event 9, when the RPCU receives this message and correlates the call origination with appropriate information it had stored earlier, the RPCU selects an appropriate physical interface and a B channel to serve the call. Then (in event 10), the RPCU and SU undergo the link encryption process. After this process is completed (in event 11), the RPCU sends to the SU the RCID_ASSIGN message. This message must contain the RCID and the alternate DN for the call. Next (in event 12), the RPCU sends to the switch a conventional ISDN setup message that contains the call party number and perhaps the calling party number. With this information, (in event 13) the switch sends an AIN info_collected message to the network. This contains the call party number and the calling party number as well as other administrative information. The arrow in event 13, which goes beyond AM, is used to signify that the call is sent into the network. Event 14 is used to indicate that the message from event 13 is stored by the access manager. The access manager also records the DM that is serving the call and changes the calling party number.

In event 15, the network sends back an AIN Analyze_Route message to the switch. This message contains the call party number, calling party number (if it passed screening), the IC and AMA information. Then (in event 16), the switch sends an ISDN, UP IAM message. Once again, this message contains the call party number, the calling party number, and the interface destination number.

We now move to Figure 9–10(b) to complete this examination. In event 17, the switch sends an ISDN call proceeding message to the RPCU, which in turn relays this message to the SU (depicted in event 18). Eventually, in event 19, the switch receives an ISDN UP address complete message from the network. After receiving this information, in event 20, the switch sends an ISDN alerting message to the RPCU and the network then provides audible ringing. In event 21, the RPCU sends the alerting message to the SU. In event 22, the network sends to the switch an ISDN UP answer message. This allows the switch (in event 23) to send and ISDN connect message to the RPCU. The network then terminates audible ringing after this event occurs. Then in event 24, the RPCU can now send a connect message to the SU, which is returned with the connect acknowledgment message in event 25. This message triggers event 26 at the RPCU, where it sends the ISDN connect acknowledge message to the switch. Then in event 27, the RPCU sends a connect message to the switch which is enveloped inside an ISDN register message. In event 28, the switch receives the message, retrieves the envelope, and sends the connect message to the AM in an AIN NCA_DATA envelope. Finally, the switch can clear the call reference for the NCA signaling on this basic rate interface with an ISDN release complete message shown in event 29.

This example is one of many operations that occur with PCS services. Obviously, call clears, loop back testing, and other administrative messages are part of the specification. It is beyond the scope here to go further with these examples. I hope that this discussion gives the reader an idea of the interworking of SS7/AIN, ISDN, and the air interface messages.

EXAMPLES OF PCS REGISTRATION, CALL MANAGEMENT, AND ROAMING OPERATIONS

This section provides some examples of PCS registration and roaming operations. I discuss the authentication part of these processes in more detail in Chapter 13 (security and privacy). These examples are not tied to a specific standard, since several proposals are under consideration in the industry. For consistency, the examples will use Bellcore's definition (TIDs, UPT#s, and RNS discussed earlier) and one of Bellcore's generic views [BELL92].

Mobility management (MM) is a Bellcore generic term. It encompasses the collective operations of the AM, VLR, and HLR. For this discussion, these components are grouped together.

Registration

When the subscriber unit's (SU) terminal is activated and a channel acquired, mobility management (MM) receives the SU UPT# sent by the SU in event 1 in Figure 9–11. MM then sets up entries in three tables in databases. In Table 1, the UPT# is associated with the TID and accessed by the UPT#.

An entry in Table 2 is also created. It correlates the RN to the TID and is accessed by the TID. The last entry in Table 3 is a local record of

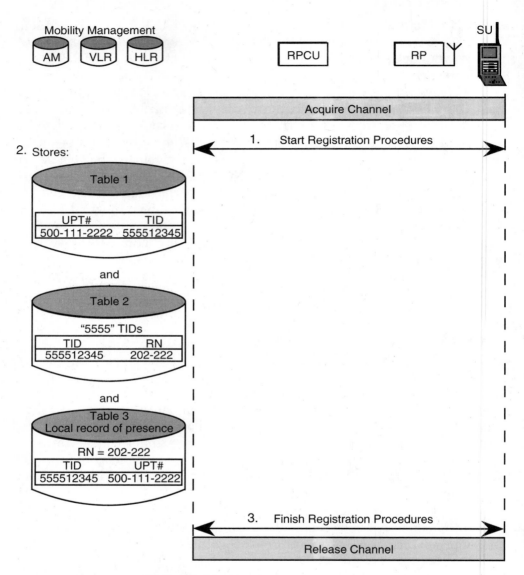

Figure 9–11
Creating records during registration.

presence that associates the TID with the UPT and a routing number (RN). So, the association is: UPT# = 500–111–2222 is associated with RN = 202–222. The RN is also associated with a registration area (a group of cells).

The association of the UPT and TID to the RN is quite important, because the RN is used to actually route and relay a call to its proper destination. This approach keeps the UPT and TID independent of any specific location since it is only the RN that is tied to a topology-specific location.

Establishing the Call to Home Subscriber

Figure 9–12 shows how a call is managed through the use of the MM tables. In event 1, the originating call is routed from the public switched telephone network (PSTN) to the routing switch such as a gateway mobile switching center (MSC). In event 2, this switch processes the call with its MM function or interworks with another MSC's MM. In either case, in event 3, a search of Table 1 reveals that UPT# 500–111–2222 can be reached at TID 555512345. This information is revealed by using 500–111–2222 as an access into Table 1 and retrieving 555512345 (event 4).

The MM queries Table 2 (in event 5) using the TID number. In event 6, the RN 202–222 is retrieved, and this identifier (and other routing information) is sent to the routing switch (in event 7). Next, in event 8, the call is directed to the local RPCU (not shown in the figure). Finally, the RPTU, in event 9, sets up the call with the subscriber unit (SU).

Registration in Another System

In order to expand this example we need to bring in another system and another SU. Figure 9–13 depicts the tables at system B for this unit. The SU in system B has UPT# 500–333–4444 and TID 666656789. The tables at system A reflect the information of the ongoing subscriber in our previous examples.

Let us assume the SU in system B turns off the mobile station terminal and moves to system A. The system B subscriber is going to use the terminal of the subscriber in system A (i.e., by placing a smart card into the terminal). The results of the registration are shown in Figure 9–14. The tables at system B show that UPT# 500–333–4444 is now associated with TID 555512345. The RN is irrelevant in Table 2 and this subscriber no longer has a record of the presence at system B (Table 3). At system A, another entry is made to table 3, that indicates 500–333–4444 is associated with TID 555512345.

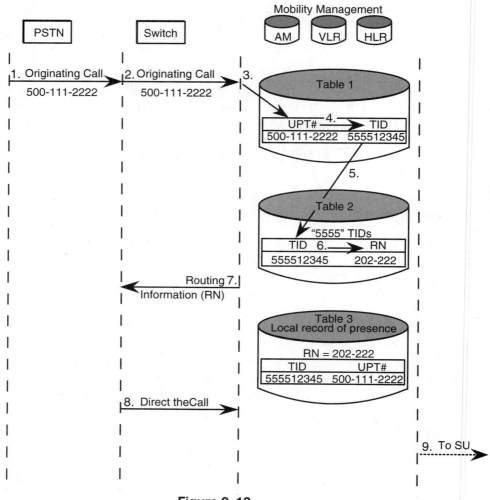

Figure 9–12
Establishing the call.

Establishing a Call to a Visiting Subscriber

Figure 9–15 shows the operations for establishing a call to UPT# 500–333–4444. The switch (in event 1) sends an originating call message to system B with the called number 500–333–4444 in the message.

In event 2, system B determines that this number is associated with TID 555512345. In events 3, 4 and 5, system A is queried to make certain that TID 555512345 is still correct and to obtain the RN for this TID. The response to the query occurs in event 6.

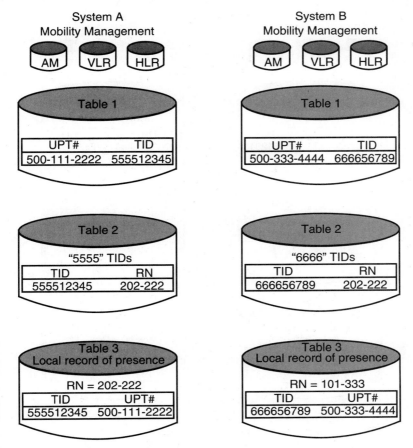

Figure 9–13
Registration of a person in another system.

These events then allow system B to inform the switch about the correct RN (event 7) and the switch routes the call to the correct system (event 8).

USING MAN AS A BACKBONE FOR PCS

The Metropolitan Area Network (MAN) standards are sponsored by the IEEE, ANSI, and the Regional Bell Operating Companies (RBOCs). Although 802.6 was designed initially for a LAN-to-MAN support service, the telephone companies see it as a technology to provide for interconnecting LANs to its central office and even the interconnection of tele-

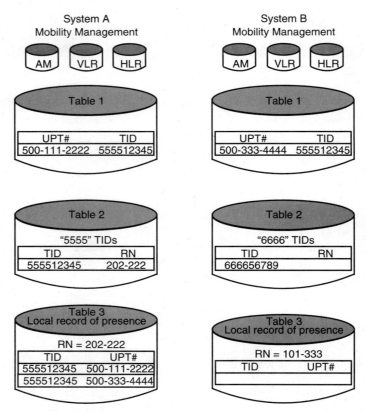

Figure 9–14
A person roams and is reregistered.

phone switching facilities. Several research studies also examine how the MAN can be used as a high-speed backbone for the PCS.

The DQDB Architecture

The MAN standard is organized around a topology and technique called distributed queue dual bus (DQDB). This term means that the network uses two buses. Each of these buses transmits traffic in one direction only. Current implementations of MANs provide for transfer rates from 34 to 150 Mbit/s, although nothing limits the MAN to these speeds.

The DQDB provides for two types of access. One access is called prearbitrated services, which guarantees a certain amount of bandwidth.

tered a climate that encouraged vendors to mass-produce their products. Due to economies of scale, this mass production led to decreased costs to consumers.

Moreover, a user has the ability to change providers and keep the same equipment. In turn, the vendor is not worried about committing to standardized technology, which has some resistance to obsolesce. This same benefit accrues to the user, who is not worried about having to buy new equipment based on standardized technology, for the reason just cited above.

On the other hand, there are also reasons for not imposing standards. For one thing, it locks the industry (both users and vendors) into one technology, which may not be best technology at that time. (The best technology is not always the one chosen, due to turf battles, politics, and so on. Just look at Microsoft Windows vs. the Macintosh Finder. There is no comparison.) Second, in some instances the establishment of standards has discouraged innovation, and slowed down the introduction of new technology. As examples, it is interesting to speculate where the industry would be (from the standpoint of technical progress) if T1 (for voice systems) and X.25 (for data systems) had not become standards. These technologies have endured for well over two decades, due to their widespread acceptance and use.

The TIA and ANSI formed joint study groups to review potential standards. Figure 9–18 summarizes their earlier activities. In addition, the FCC under Docket 90-314 stated its intentions to monitor these standards-setting bodies to ensure that systems are interoperable and roam seamlessly. The FCC view is to keep the competitive avenues open

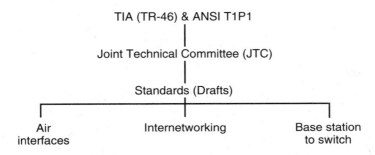

Figure 9–18
Initial organization of the PCS standards activities.

with the understanding that the industry will adopt PCS standards. Therefore, private industry will spearhead standards, and FCC will not (vendors may win, at the expense of a standard).

Table 9–2 lists the seven technologies that are under consideration for PCS interfaces. (Yes, seven different air interfaces. In the beginning of these deliberations, there were sixteen proposals). The technical ad hoc groups (TAGS) were formed in March, 1994 to analyze and establish or refine the specifications for each technology. Each technology is classified as a high-tier or a low-tier system. A brief description of each proposal follows.

TAG 1 • A composite CDMA/TDMA/FDMA technology
         • Proposed by Omnipoint
         • 5 MHz channels (licensed), 1.25 MHz (unlicensed)
         • Uses time division duplex (TDD) operations
         • Sponsors/users include Omnipoint, Cox Enterprises, Bell Atlantic, Ameritech
TAG 2 • An IS-95-based technology
         • Proposed by Qualcomm
         • 125 MHz channels with variable rate speech codes (8 to 13.8 kbit/s)
         • Uses CDMA technology
         • Sponsors/users include Qualcomm, AT&T, Motorola

Table 9–2   Candidates for PCS Standards

Technical Ad hoc Groups (TAGs)	Name	Technology
TAG 1	PCS 2000	Derived from Omnipoint system of a composite CDMA/TDMA/CDMA interface
TAG 2	IS-95	Qualcomm proposal for 1.25 MHz interface
TAG 3	PACS & PACS-U	Hybrid of Bellcore TR-1313 (TDMA/FDD) and Japanese PHS (Personal Handy Phone System) (TDMA-TDD)
TAG 4	IS-136	Based on frequency adaptation of TIA IS-136 (TDMA/FDD)
TAG 5	PCS 1900	Based on GSM 1800 with TDMA/FDD)
TAG 6	DECT	Based on DECT (TDMA/TDD)
TAG7	Wideband CDMA	5 MHz WCDMA from OKI and Interdigital

TAG 3 • A TDMA/FDD technology
        • Proposals from Bellcore and Japan's PHS system
        • 8 slot TDMA with FDD (licensed) and 8 slot TDM with TDD (unlicensed)
        • Sponsors/users include Hughes, NEC, Motorola, Panasonic

TAG 4 • An IS-136 technology
        • Interoperates between 800 MHz and PCS bands
        • 3 time slot TDMA-based system with half- or full-rate coders
        • Sponsors/users include AT&T, Ericsson, Hughes

TAG 5 • A GSM technology with frequency changes
        • Proposed for several vendors
        • Uses TDMA/FDD technology
        • Sponsors/users include many organizations

TAG 6 • A DECT-based technology
        • Uses 12 time slot TDMA/TDD
        • Uses CDMA technology
        • Sponsors/users include European DECT standards groups and vendors

TAG 7 • A wideband CDMA technology
        • Uses CDMA/FDD
        • Uses CDMA technology
        • Sponsors/users include OKI, AT&T, Interdigital

The North American PCS 1900 Action Group (NPAG)

During 1994 and 1995, the various working groups and standards organizations had many debates about the methods to be used in selecting an air interface (or interfaces), as well as the procedures for simulating and testing the protocols. Eventually these conflicts led the TIA to cease its participation in the JTC [YOUN95].

The end result of all these activities was the recognition of the North American PCS 1900 Action Group (NPAG). This group has been quite effective in getting many decisions made about a PCS air interface for North America. The group has made rather amazing progress in resolving issues pertaining to a vocoder, and the modification of the GSM standards for North American PC 1900.

As of this writing, draft standards have been published on a North American vesion of GSM. The air interface, called PCS 1900, is over 2400 pages. Other draft standards are being reviewed by the industry, such as mobile management, a network interface, and so on. The air interface is published as document J-STD-007, and is available from several reader services.

Personal Access Communications System (PACS) Forum

In the fall of 1995, several PCS vendors, service providers, and Bellcore founded the PACS Forum. This forum is developing specifications (and its members are implementing systems) based on the Bellcore architecture described in this chapter.

Companies such as Hughes, now provide radio parts and RPCUs based on the Bellcore standard. PACS will likely be a major contender in the PCS industry.

SUMMARY

The services of PCS are not defined in any formal manner. Nevertheless, the underlying technology of PCS is different from the present cellular systems. With the conclusion of the PCS auctions, we can expect the PCS offerings to grow very rapidly.

10

Satellite-Based Systems

INTRODUCTION

This chapter examines satellite systems with emphasis on satellite-based PCS. The topic of geosynchronous systems was introduced in Chapter 2, so this chapter picks up with an explanation of low earth orbit (LEO) systems. Next, satellite communications protocols are discussed with the ALOHA system and a satellite-based TDMA scheme used as examples. The chapter concludes with a discussion of satellite-based PCS.

LOW EARTH ORBIT (LEO) SATELLITES

In Chapter 2, we examined geosynchronous satellites, which are also called geostationary earth orbit (GEO) systems. The reader may recall that GEO satellites rotate around the earth and that, in relation to the earth's rotation, they appear to be stationary.

In contrast to GEO systems, LEO satellites rotate around the earth at a low orbit of a few hundred miles (the distance varies, depending on the system). They are not stationary relative to the earth's rotation, but are moving at a relative speed of over 10,000 miles per hour. Another notable feature for the upcoming LEO PCS satellite is their ability to relay calls from satellite-to-satellite.

The low orbit has its advantages and disadvantages. Its principal advantage is its low power requirements, due to the short distance between the sender and the receiver. This arrangement permits the use of handheld terminals. Additionally, the short distance translates into a small propagation delay between the terminal and the satellite. The major disadvantage of LEO technology is that the low orbit means that a satellite has a small coverage in relation to the earth's surface. Consequently, many satellites are required to provide for worldwide coverage. This arrangement means that a LEO system is expensive (many satellites are required, which means many expensive launches). One attribute that has its advantages and disadvantages is the relaying of calls between satellites, without the need to send calls up and down intermediate earth nodes. This process is efficient, but it is expensive and requires that considerable intelligence be built into the satellite. LEOs are explained in more detail later in this chapter.

THE ALOHA SYSTEM

While ALOHA is an old concept, it is included in this chapter because it was the forerunner to TDMA. In the early 1970s, Norman Abramson, at the University of Hawaii, devised a technique for uncoordinated users to effectively compete for a common channel. The approach is called the ALOHA system; it is so named because the word ALOHA is a Hawaiian greeting without regard to whether a person is arriving or departing.

The premise of ALOHA is that users are acting on a peer-to-peer basis in that they all have equal access to the channel. As shown in Figure 10–1, a user station transmits whenever it has traffic to send. Simultaneous transmission results in the signals interfering and distorting each other as the separate signals propagate up to the satellite transponder. These "collisions" necessitate the retransmission of the damaged frames for data (and ignored for voice/video). Since the users of the satellite link know exactly what was transmitted onto the uplink channel and when it was transmitted, they only need listen to the downlink channel at a prescribed time to determine if the broadcast packet arrived without damage.

If a data packet is damaged due to a collision, the stations are required to retransmit the damaged packet. In essence, the idea is to listen to the downlink channel one up-and-down delay time after the packet was sent. If the packet is destroyed, the transmitting site is required to wait a short random period and then retransmit. The randomized wait

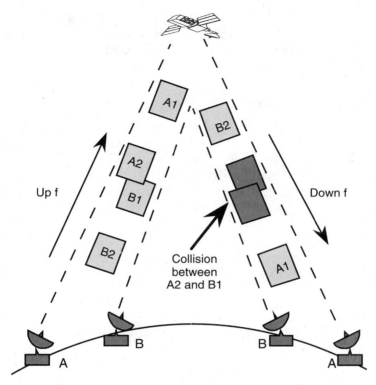

**Figure 10–1
The ALOHA scheme.**

period diminishes the chances of the competing stations colliding again, since the waiting times will likely differ and result in retransmissions at different times. When traffic increases, the randomized waits can be increased to diminish the collisions.

Figure 10–1 depicts a typical ALOHA system using satellite communications. Stations A and B are transmitting packets on a shared channel. The downlink channel shows that packet 1 from station A is transmitted up and down safely; packet 2 from station B is also transmitted without error. However, the second packet from A and the first packet from B are transmitted at approximately the same time. As the transmissions of the two stations are narrowcasted up to the satellite station, the signals interfere with each other, resulting in a collision.

The satellite station is not responsible for error detection or error correction; it transmits what it receives from the uplink. On the downlink, stations A and B note the packets have collided and, upon waiting a random period of time (usually a few milliseconds), attempt to retransmit. This approach is quite effective when the users are uncoordinated and are sending traffic in bursts, such as data from keyboard terminals.

Delay and Throughput Considerations

We assume a packet is initially transmitted, which takes t seconds, and is received after Nt seconds of transmission delay (see Figure 10–2). If interference occurs, the sender waits a random period (between O and K packet times) before retransmitting. On the average, a wait of $(1 + K)$ t/2 seconds takes place before another retransmission.

Let us assume further that s represents channel throughput; that is, the amount of traffic successfully delivered. The value g represents total traffic, including successful and unsuccessful deliveries. Therefore, the ratio g/s represents the number of times each packet has to be retransmitted before a successful delivery occurs.

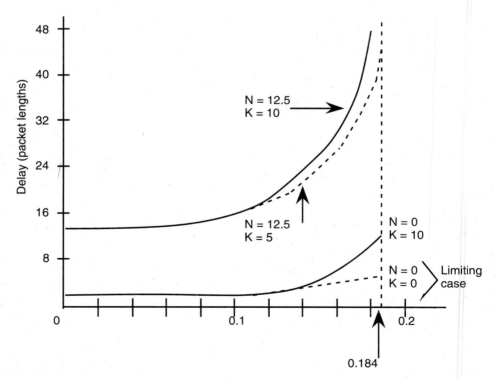

Figure 10–2
Delay and throughput considerations.

Given these assumptions, the total average delay (TAD) through an ALOHA channel is computed as:

$$\text{TAD} = t/2 \, [1 + e^{2g} \, (1 + 2N) + K \, (e^{2g} - 1)]$$

where t = packet length in seconds; g = total traffic (bits per second); N = propagation delay in packet lengths; K = retransmission protocol delay in packet lengths; e = 2.718 (base of natural logarithms).

This figure plots several ALOHA channel delay scenarios, with a channel rate of 50 kbit/s and a packet length of 1000 bits. The value t is 20 ms (1000/50000 = .02). The figure shows that little delay is encountered with a light load on the channel. As traffic increases, more collisions occur and the delay increases. The curves show the packet retransmission delay (K) increases as throughput (s) increases.

Random ALOHA experiences considerable degradation of throughput when the channel is heavily utilized. However, it should be kept in mind that what is transmitted across the channel is all end-user traffic. ALOHA uses no polls, selects, or negative responses to polls. Only end-user information is transmitted. Nonetheless, the pure random scheme can be improved by adapting a more efficient strategy for using the uncoordinated channel, called slotted ALOHA.

Slotted ALOHA

Slotted ALOHA requires that common clocks be established at the earth stations and at the satellite. The clocks are synchronized to send traffic at specific periods. For example, the clocks may require that packets are transmitted only on 20 ms increments. In this example, the 20 ms increment is derived from a 50,000-bit/s channel and 1,000-bit packets (1,000/50,000 = .020 second).

The 20 ms increment is referred to as the packet duration, which is the time in which the packet is transmitted on the channel. All stations are required to transmit at the beginning of a slot period. A packet cannot be transmitted if it overlaps more than one slot.

The slotted ALOHA approach increases throughput substantially on the channel, because if packets overlap or collide, they do so completely; at most, only one slot is damaged. However, like pure random ALOHA, the slotted ALOHA does offer opportunities for collisions. For example, if two stations transmit in the same clock period, their packets collide. As in the pure random ALOHA approach, the stations are required to wait a random period of time before attempting to seize a slot for retransmission.

Another refinement to slotted ALOHA is slotted ALOHA with nonowner. The channel slots are combined into an ALOHA frame. The ALOHA frame must equal or exceed the up-and-down propagation delay. This relationship is defined as:

$$AFL \geq PD$$
$$\text{or}$$
$$NSL * SLT \geq PD$$

where AFL = ALOHA frame length; PD = the up-and-down propagation delay; NSL = number of slots in an ALOHA frame; and SLT = time interval of a slot.

Consequently, a 1,000-bit packet lasting 20 ms would require a minimum of 12 slots to make up the ALOHA frame: 12 slots × 20 ms = 240 ms. The 240 ms period represents the minimum up-and-down propagation delay (120 ms [up] × 120 ms [down] = 240 ms).

Slotted ALOHA with nonowner requires that a station select an empty slot in the frame (see Figure 10–3). Once the user has seized the slot, it is reserved for the user for successive frames until the user relinquishes the slot. The relinquishment occurs by the station sending a code, such as EOT (end of transmission). Upon receiving an EOT, the next frame transmitted is empty for that particular slot. A user station then is allowed to contend for the slot with the next subsequent frame.

Another variation of slotted ALOHA is slotted ALOHA with owner (see Figure 10–4). The slots of each frame are now owned by users. The user has exclusive use of its slot within the frame as long as it has data to transmit. In the event that the user relinquishes the slot, it so indicates with an established code. The slot becomes empty and is available for any other user to seize it. Once another user has seized the slot, it has exclusive rights to the use of the slot, until the original owner seizes the slot. The rightful owner can claim the slot at any time by beginning transmissions within its designated slot in the frame. The relinquishment is required when the rightful owner transmits. Obviously, the first time the owner transmits in its slot a collision may occur. On the subsequent frame, the rightful owner retransmits. The relinquishing station then must look for another free slot or use its own slots if it has them. This refined approach of ALOHA is classified as a peer-to-peer priority structure, since some stations can be given priority ownership over other stations.

These operations should look familiar, since they form the basis for many of the TDMA operations that are now in existence in wireless systems.

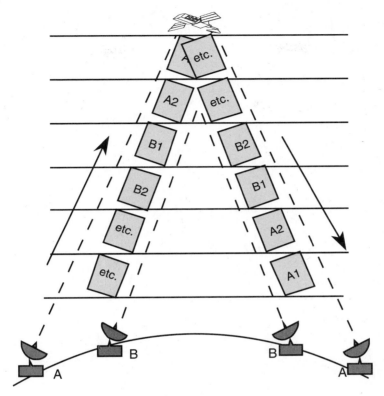

Figure 10–3
Slotted ALOHA.

SATELLITE-BASED TDMA

COMSAT initiated work on TDMA in the mid-1960s. Since then, scores of TDMA systems have been implemented worldwide. Chapter 3 explained their use in earthbound wireless systems. TDMA shares a satellite transponder by dividing access into time slots. Each earth terminal is designated a time and its transmission burst is precisely timed into the slot. This example of TDMA is chosen to allow the reader to compare this "old" system with the new systems covered in Chapter 3. They have many similarities.

This version of TDMA assigns slots as needed. However, unlike the ALOHA system, the slots are assigned by a primary station called the reference (REF) (see Figure 10–5). The reference station accepts requests from the other stations, and based on the nature of the traffic and available channel capacity, the REF assigns these requests to specific frames

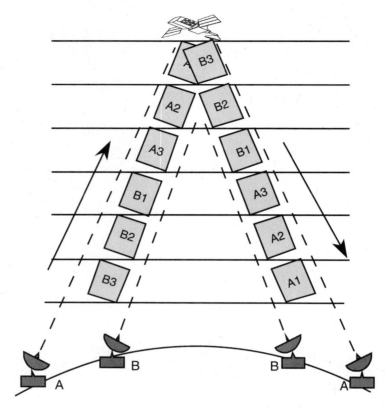

Figure 10–4
Slotted ALOHA with owner.

for subsequent transmission. Every 20 frames, the reference station is assigned to each transponder of the system. The REF is like the base station controller in a wireless land-based system.

Figure 10–5 shows the earth station components. The major components consist of the port adapter, the satellite communications controller (SCC), a burst modem, the transmit/receive device, and an antenna.

The port adapter is responsible for interfacing the user lines into the earth station. The adapter accepts voice images at a rate of 32 kbit/s, and data at rates varying from 2.4 kbit/s to 1.544 Mbit/s.

All digital images are passed to the satellite communications controller, which is a software-oriented unit that consolidates the functions of timing, station assignment, switching, and processing of voice and data calls. It calculates channel requirements based on the number of

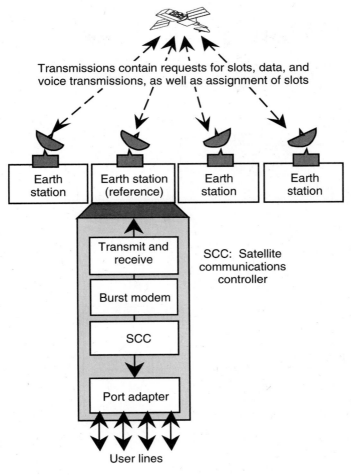

Transmissions contain requests for slots, data, and
voice transmissions, as well as assignment of slots

SCC: Satellite
communications
controller

Figure 10–5
TDMA on satellite.

voice connections, the number of data ports available, and the number of
queued data connection requests. It then assigns these requests to
TDMA frames.

The burst modem sends out a 48 Mbit/s signal with 15 ms frames
(.015 second) under the direction of the satellite controller (see Figure
10–6). Thus, each transponder has the capability of operating at 48
megabits per second.

On a 15 ms frame, the reference station (REF) transmits an assignment set for all SCCs using the transponder. As mentioned earlier, this

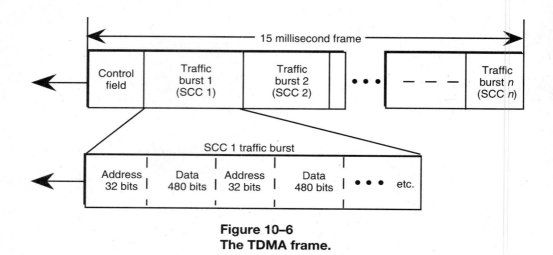

Figure 10–6
The TDMA frame.

transmission is sent every 20 frames. The assignment set specifies the capacity and position of each SCC's traffic burst to the transponder. Recall that assignments are made in response to the requests received in earlier frames. The control field of the frame contains the assignments and the requests from the competing stations. The remainder of the frame consists of the traffic, which contains the traffic bursts from each SCC that was assigned a position by the reference station.

The traffic is packed in 512-bit channels consisting of a 32-bit destination address and 480 bits of data. The 480-bit data frame was chosen to accommodate the requirement for a voice transmission rate of 32 kilobits per second (480 × [1 second/.015 slot] = 32,000).

The 32 kilobits per second rate uses only a small fraction of the total 48 megabit channel capacity. Consequently, many voice and data transmissions can be time division multiplexed (TDM) efficiently onto the high-speed 48 kbit/s channel.

LEO PCS PROPOSALS

In the early 1990s, Motorola created the Iridium project, a satellite-based technology for PCS (as it is now called). The idea is to have enough satellites in the sky to cover any spot on earth, with continuous line-of-sight coverage (see Figure 10–7). Furthermore, the satellites communicate directly with each other for control signaling and the passing-off of calls. Its "homing" capabilities (when implemented) will allow anyone to be

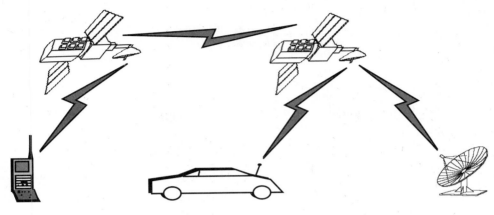

**Figure 10–7
Satellite-based PCS.**

tracked down—whether in a city or in a remote part of the world. It is expensive, but its potential is enormous. We shall have to wait to the end of this century to see if it will be successful.

Iridium is the first low orbit system for PCS-type technology. Originally, 77 satellites were considered, now reduced to 66, and it was named for the chemical element that has 77 electrons. It is now controlled by a consortium. The system has a 20 GHz range, with each satellite at a height of 413 nautical miles. As of 1995, the estimated cost is $3.37 billion to implement the system.

Iridium is not the only satellite-based PCS project. One of the more recent announcements came from Bill Gates and Craig McCaw, who intend to launch a service, called Teledesic, that will compete with Iridium. It will use many of the techniques of Iridium.

These endeavors are quite risky for the financial standpoint, yet they do fulfill a need or needs. One need is a readily available telephony service—no matter where a person is located. As an ancillary, second- and third-world countries have very poor communications facilities. In many instances, enterprises will pay the charges for a service, such as Iridium or Teledesic. Indeed, for many applications, a $3.00 per minute charge is not important. Additionally, some third-world countries charge this amount now.

The reader should also be aware that other satellite-based PCS systems are under development in Europe, and the Europeans have no intention of losing this potential market.

So, the issues are far from settled. These types of services can be useful, but no one knows if they can be economically feasible, and if all of them can successfully garner a profitable place in the market.

Example of a LEO and PCS System

Conventional satellites are passive microwave relay stations. Iridium takes a different approach, in that the satellites can process calls and switch/route them to a place on earth that is covered by the system. Figure 10–8 shows a general view of these operations.

This approach has several attractive features. First, the low-orbiting satellites allow the use of smaller antenna and the utilization of less power. Frequency spectrum can be reused, which gives this technology tremendous bandwidth capacity. Of course, the technology is expensive, and calls (the price is not yet determined) will be priced well above conventional land-line telephone calls.

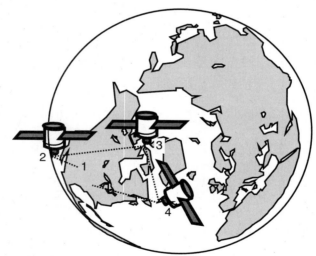

1. Call from portable handset sent to nearest overhead satellite
2. Call then routed to adjacent satellite to reach destination
3. Call routed to nearest satellite that can reach user
4. Call routed to user from this satellite

Figure 10–8
Iridium switching and routing calls.

OTHER VENDORS

There are other significant players in the satellite-based PCS market. While Iridium is the early entrant, Odyssey (from TRW, Inc.) and Globestar (from L.P. Qualcomm, Inc.) were approved by the FCC in January 1995. The three approved projects are estimate to $7.15 billion. As of this writing, the combined projects involve 126 satellites.

The FCC deferred the approval of Elipso (Mobile Communications Holdings Inc.) and Constellation Communications, Inc. The projects were directed to improve their financial positions.

Others are on hold (not reviewed formally), including the Teledesic project (sponsored by Gates and McCaw) and the Inmarsat-P (partially financed by COMSAT Corp.).

Tables 10–1 and 10–2 provide a summary of the LEO industry in the United States. The sponsoring companies, the number of satellites,

Table 10–1   Little LEO Satellite Systems in the U.S.

Name/Owner*	Number of Satellites	Weight	Launch Date
E-Sat/E-Sat Inc. Englewood, CO 80112	6	114 kg	1996–2000
FACS/Final Analysis Inc. Greenbelt, MD 20070	26	100 kg	1996–2000
GE Americom/ GE American Communications Princeton, NJ 08540	24	15 kg	1997–2001
Gemnet/CTA Inc. Rockville, MD 20852	38	45.2 kg	1997
Leo One USA/Leo One St. Louis, MO 63105	48	124 kg	1995–2000
Orbcomm/Orbital Sciences Corp. Fairfax, VA 22033	48	39.5 kg	1995
Starsys/Starsys Global Positioning Lanham, MD 20706	24	330 kg	1995–2000
Vitasat/Volunteers in Technical Assistance Arlington, VA 22209	3	136 kg	1995

*All the systems provide data services except Vitasat which provides disaster relief, medical and educational services.

Table 10–2   Big LEO Satellite Systems in the U.S.

Name/Owner	Services	Number of Satellites	Weigth (in kg)	Launch Date
Aries/Constellation Communications Inc. Herndon, VA 22070	Voice, paging	46	182	1996–2002
Ellipso/Mobile Communications Holdings Inc. Washington, D.C. 20036	Voice, data,	16	175	1996–2002
Iridium/Iridium Inc. Washington, D.C. 20005	Voice, data, paging, FAX	66	700	1996–1998
Odyssey/ TRW Odyssey Program Office Redondo Beach, CA 90278	Voice	12	2500	1996–2000
AMSC/ AMSC Subsidiary Corp. Reston, VA 22091	Voice data, FAX	12	2450	1995–1996
Globalstar/Loral-Qualcomm Satellite Services, Inc. Palo Alto, CA 94303	Voice, data paging, FAX	56	426	1995–1999
Teledesic/Teledesic Corp. Kirkland, WA 98033	Voice, data	840	795.5	2000–2001

their weights, and the projected launch dates are included in the tables. The low-earth orbiting (LEO) satellite is positioned around 500–1000 miles above earth. The medium-earth orbiting (MEO) satellite is positioned around 6200–9400 miles above earth.

Little LEOs are also identified with the applications they offer, which are typically non-voice products, two-way paging applications. Big LEOs and MEOs offer voice, data, messaging, fax, position locating— most everything a wireline system offers.

No one knows how many satellite systems for PCS can be implemented, given the limited customer base. The fees for use will likely be several orders of magnitude more expensive than the conventional wire-based or terrestrial-wireless counterparts. Each service provider is counting on being the preferred service. Only time will tell, but it is likely that some of these projects will merge. The issue of other governments granting licenses is still another area that must be addressed.

SUMMARY

Satellites are cost-effective systems for wireless applications. Early systems used ALOHA and slotted ALOHA schemes to manage traffic on the channel. The TDMA technology was used on satellite channels long before it appeared on land-based wireless systems. The Iridium project and others hold great promise for the implementation of PCS on satellites.

11

Data over the Mobile Link

INTRODUCTION

This chapter describes how data are transmitted across the air interface between mobile and land stations. We begin the chapter with a brief overview of modulation, followed by an explanation of the ITU-T V-Series Recommendations for modems. The chapter also examines several options for sending data over private and public mobile-based networks. In this part of the chapter, we compare several vendors and their offerings.

A LAYERED MODEL FOR THE WIRELESS LINK

It will prove fruitful to pause for a moment to describe the data communications layers that are used across the air interface between the mobile and land stations. The OSI model is used in this discussion because most commercial systems use its layered approach. It is beyond the scope of this book to describe the OSI model and the detailed operations surrounding the layers. The reader would find helpful *OSI: A model for Computer Communications* by Uyless Black, published by Prentice Hall.

Figure 11–1 shows the layers and the names of the layers that are invoked across the interface between the mobile and land station. We

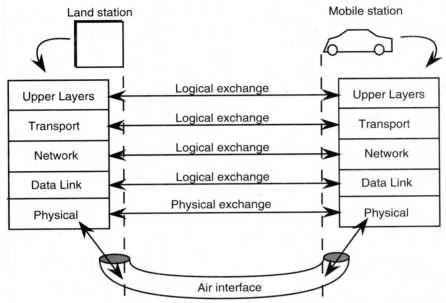

Invocation of network, transport, and upper layers at a land station varies. Each vendor offering should be examined.

Figure 11–1
The mobile air data interface.

will be using this figure throughout Chapters 11 and 12 to illustrate how data traffic is exchanged between the two stations. The next few paragraphs provide an overview of these layers.

A Brief Look at the Layers

The lowest layer in the model is called the *physical layer*. The physical layer is responsible for activating, maintaining, and deactivating a physical circuit between communicating machines. The physical layer's most common operations deal with the creation and reception of physical signals. For example, conventions may exist to represent a binary one with a plus voltage and a binary zero with a minus voltage.

The *data link layer* is responsible for the transfer of data across *one* communications link. It delimits the flow of bits from the physical layer. It also provides for the identity of the bits. It usually (but not always) ensures that the traffic arrives safely at the receiving machine. It often provides for flow control to ensure that the machine does not become over-burdened with too much data at any one time.

One of the most important functions of the data link layer is to provide for the detection of transmission errors. Many data links provide mechanisms to recover from lost, duplicated, or erroneous data. If this operation is supported, traffic is accounted for by the exchange of positive acknowledgments (ACKs) or negative acknowledgments (NAKs) between the sending and receiving stations.

The *network layer* specifies the network/user interface of the user into a network, as well as the interface of two machines with each other through a network. It allows users to negotiate options with the network and each other. For example, the negotiation of throughput, delay, and acceptable error rates are common negotiations. The network layer defines switching/routing procedures within a network. It also includes the routing conventions to transfer traffic between networks (internetworking).

The *transport layer* provides the interface between the data communications network and the upper three layers (generally part of the user's system). The transport layer provides for the end-to-end accountability of user traffic across more than one data link. It also is responsible for end-to-end integrity of users' data in internetworking operations. Therefore, it is a vital layer for sending traffic to users that are attached to different networks.

Invoking the Layers

Be aware that the land station may not execute all the protocols in these layers. The invocation of these layers at the land station depends on the specific implementation. As we shall see in Chapter 12, the network layer at the land station is invoked because it is used to examine a destination network address that was created by the network layer at the mobile station. In contrast, the transport layer may not be invoked at the land station because it may pass this operation and the associated protocol control information (header) to some other component in the network that will process this traffic. Likewise, the box labeled "Upper Layers" may have information that is not processed by the land station. Indeed, this upper layer information may not be processed within the carrier network whatsoever. Usually, the upper layer traffic is passed unaltered to the remote mobile station or end station for invocation. There are many possible scenarios with regard to the invocation of this upper layer information. But it can be stated clearly that the mobile station and the land station must coordinate their activities at least through the physical and data link layers.

MODEMS

About forty years ago, when computers began to be used extensively in businesses, remote sites (offices, campuses, etc.) had to send computer-based information to each other. An important question had to be answered: How are discrete digital bits to be sent over the telephone line, which was designed for the transmission of analog voice signals? As Figure 11–2 shows, the shape and nature of the signals are quite different.

Wire-Based Media

It is possible to redesign an analog, wire-based link so that it will carry the digital signals, but such a redesign is an expensive process. Moreover, the telephone local loops (into homes and most offices) are built for analog transmissions, and it was only logical that early wire-based data communications systems use the ubiquitous telephone system. Can you imagine how great the task would be of replacing all these systems with digital systems? The answer was clear. Some method had to be devised to the current analog system, yet provide a means to send digital traffic (data) over it.

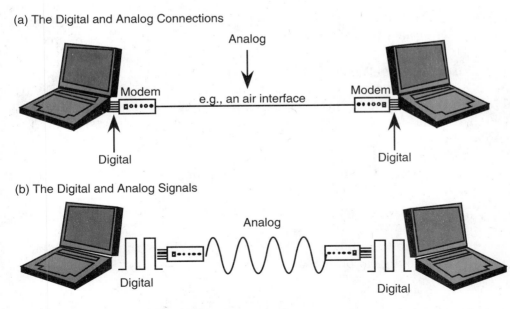

(a) The Digital and Analog Connections

Analog

Modem   e.g., an air interface   Modem

Digital   Digital

(b) The Digital and Analog Signals

Analog

Digital   Digital

Figure 11–2
Interfacing the analog and digital worlds.

Wireless Media

For wireless media, the alternatives are more limited, but more straightforward. Analog signaling must be employed on wireless channels in order to use the FDMA technology, which is an inherent component of many mobile wireless architectures. When we speak of a digital channel on a wireless interface, we mean that digital signals are impressed (modulated) onto an analog carrier.

Wire-Based or Wireless Media

To provide a simple summary of the issue: For wireless links, the principal job of the system is to translate a digital signal to an analog signal at the transmitting side and to translate this analog signal back to a digital signal at the receive side.

These operations are unaware of the type and nature of user data being transferred. There is no checking of user addresses; there is no checking of user syntax. This physical layer has limited control functions. Most of its operations are driven by the communications software, the computer operating system, and the user applications.

The Modem Operations at the Physical Layer

In order to use the analog signal for data transmission (digital transmission), the industry developed a relatively simple device called a modem. The term is a derivative of the words *mo*dulator and *dem*odulator.

Three basic methods of digital-to-analog modulation are employed by modems. Some modems use more than one of the methods (see Figure 11–3). Each method impresses the data on an analog *carrier* signal, which is altered to carry the properties of the digital data stream. The three methods are:

- *Amplitude modulation*—Alters the amplitude of the signal in accordance with the digital bit stream.
- *Frequency modulation*—Alters the frequency of the signal in accordance with the digital bit stream.
- *Phase modulation*—Alters the phase of the signal in accordance with the digital bit stream.

A special extension of phase modulation is *quadrature amplitude modulation* (QAM). Practically all modems today use some form of QAM.

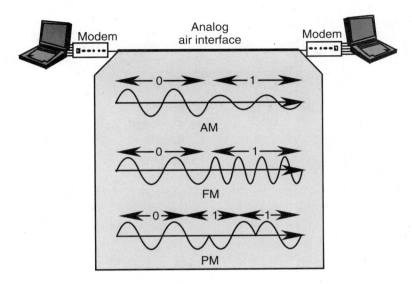

Figure 11–3
Modulation.

Indeed, it is difficult to find a modem that operates in the 9.6 kbit/s range that does not use this technique.

THE ITU-T V-SERIES RECOMMENDATIONS

Since the majority of data transmissions take place over the telephone line, or over lines that are engineered to the telephone line specifications, the standards organizations have published many recommendations defining how these connections and communications are made. The International Telecommunications Union-Telecommunications Standardization Sector (ITU-T) V-Series define these connections. They are the most widely used physical level specifications in the world. Table 11–1 summarizes some of the more widely used V-Series modems.

Enhanced Throughput Cellular (ETC) Modems

AT&T Paradyne has published the Enhanced Throughput Cellular (ETC) modem specification. It uses V.32bis and V.42 technology. Inherent in these standards is the ability to negotiate a variety of options, such as link speed in bit/s (and by association, the modulation

Table 11–1   ITU-T V-Series Interfaces

Series Number	Maximum Line Speed	Modulation Rate	Synchronous or Asynchronous	Modulation- Technique	Bits Encoded
V.17	Varies	2400	Either	QAM	Varies
V.22bis	2400	600	Either	QAM	4:1
V.26bis	1200	1200	Synchronous	PS	1:1
V.26ter	2400	1200	Either	PS	2:1
V.29	9600	2400	Synchronous	QAM	4:1
V.29	7200	2400	Synchronous	PS	3:1
V.29	4800	2400	Synchronous	PS	2:1
V.32	9600	2400	Synchronous	QAM	4:1
V.32	9600	2400	Synchronous	TCM	5:1
V.32	4800	2400	Synchronous	QAM	2:1
V.34	28800	Varies	Synchronous	TCM	Varies
V.35	48000	NA	Synchronous	AM-FM	NA

technique). The V.42 technology also allows modems to negotiate the use or nonuse of V.42 link layer procedures, and V.42bis compression. The ETC modem exploits these capabilities during the handshake, and also determines if the answer modem supports ETC. The ETC modem can perform from 4.8 kbit/s to 28.8 kbit/s, but will fall back to a V.22 rate of 1.2 kbit/s if link conditions are poor.

After the negotiation is complete (which takes about 10 seconds), the modem monitors the received signals to determine if the link is performing satisfactorily. The modem measures phase jitter and the signal-to-noise ratio of the incoming signal. If the signal quality deteriorates below a threshold, the modem reduces its transmission rate (the other modem adjusts as well). The rate is increased if link conditions improve. These features are quite useful on the mobile link, which can experience varying degrees of quality as the mobile unit travels through a cell.

Cellular Modem Providers

Table 11–2 provides the reader with a survey of the cellular modem products. The reader may find the table on V-Series modems (Table 11–1) useful when studying this table. As you can see, most of the products in the market now offer V.32 or V.32bis rates up to 14.4 kbit/s. The

Table 11–2   Examples of Cellular Modems

Vendor	Product	Speed (kbit/s)	Wireless Protocol
Air Communications, Inc.	Aircommunicator	14.4 (V.32bis data)	MNP 10
AT&T Paradyne	Keep In Touch	14.4 (V.32bis data/V.17 fax)	ETC (Enhanced throughput cellular)
Apex Data, Inc.	Internal series	14.4 (V.32bis data/V.17 fax)	MNP 10
	PCMCIA series	14.4 (V.32bis data/V.17 fax)	MNP 10
Compaq Computer Corp.	Speedpak	14.4 (V.32bis) 9.6 (fax)	MNP 10
Data Race	Redicard 1914	14.4 (V.32bis data/ V.17 fax), 19.2 (V.32 terbo data)	None
Megahertz Corp.	CC4144	14.4 (V.32bis data/V.17 fax)	MNP 10
Microcom Inc.	Travelporte Fast	14.4 (V.32bis data/ V.17 fax), 28.8 (proprietary data)	MNP 10
	Travelporte V.32bis	14.4 (V.32bis data/V.17 fax)	MNP 10
Motorola UDS	Cellect 14.4	14.4 (V.32bis data/fax)	Motorola ECC (Enhances Cellular Control)
	Cellect 14.4 PCMCIA	14.4 (V.32bis data/V.17 fax)	Motorola ECC (Enhances Cellular Control)
Powertek Industries, Inc.	CMI-3000	14.4 (V.32bis data)	MNP 10; ETC
Racal-Datacom, Inc.	ALM 3226 portable modem	14.4 (V.32bis data/V.17 fax)	MNP 10
Toshiba America, Inc.	NW192CR	14.4 (V.32bis data/V.17 fax)	MNP 10
U.S. Robotics	Courier HST Dual Standard Cellular Fax	14.4 (V.32bis data/ V.17 fax); 16.8 (proprietary data), 19.2 (V.32 terbo)	U.S. Robotics High Speed Technology (HST)
	Worldport Dual Standard Cellular Fax	14.4 (V.32bis data/ V.17 fax); 16.8 (proprietary data)	U.S. Robotics High Speed Technology (HST)
Western Datacom	Worldcom V.32bis	14.4 (V.32bis data/V.17 fax)	MNP 10

[JOHN94]

MNP 10 protocol is still the link protocol of choice for most of these offerings, but V.42 is gaining in acceptance.

THE DATA LINK LAYER

The transfer of data across the mobile link must flow in a controlled and orderly manner. Since the traffic on mobile links may experience considerable distortions (such as noise and fading), a method must be provided to deal with the occasional errors that occur; that is, the system must provide the mobile and land station with the capability to send data to each other, with the assurance that the data arrives error-free. The sending and receiving stations must maintain complete accountability for all traffic. In the event the data are distorted, the receiver must be able to direct the originator to resend the errored traffic or devise a means to correct the errors.

These operations are taken for granted in voice communications because the human speakers can detect distortions and ask for retransmissions (". . . say again please"). For data, it requires the installation of data link protocols.

Data link protocols manage the flow of data across the mobile link. Their functions are limited to this individual link. That is to say, link control is responsible only for the traffic between adjacent stations on the link. Once the data are transmitted to the adjacent station and an acknowledgment of the transmission is returned to the transmission site, the link protocol task is complete for that particular transmission.

The data link protocol provides the following functions:

- Synchronizing the sender and receiver through a stream of bits called flags.
- Controlling the flow of data to prevent the sender from sending too fast.
- Detecting and recovering from errors that occur on the link.
- Maintaining awareness of link conditions, such as distinguishing between data and control and determining the identity of the communicating stations.

As discussed earlier in this chapter, the data link layer rests above the physical layer in the OSI model. Generally, the data link protocol is medium independent, and relies on the physical layer to deal with the specific media (wire, radio, etc.), and the physical signals (electrical current, laser, infrared, etc.). However, with mobile links, we shall see shortly that the data link layer works in concert with the physical layer to perform some special services that are not needed on a wire-based link.

Many different link protocols are used by the data communications industry. The diversity of methods and offerings complicate the task of explaining them to the reader. Our approach will be to explain some of the major features that are relevant to mobile links.

Data Link Protocol Operations

This section provides a closer look at mobile data link protocols (layer 2 in the OSI model) with a focus on the following interrelated topics:

- Flow control of traffic between the mobile and land station
- Sequencing and accounting of traffic
- Actions to be taken in the event of error detection

Automatic Request for Repeat (ARQ)

When the mobile or land station transmits a frame, it places a send sequence number in a control field in the frame, shown in Figure 11–4 as event 1, where the mobile station sends four frames numbered 0, 1, 2, and 3. The receiving station uses these numbers to determine if it has received all other preceding frames (with lower numbers). It also uses the number to determine its response. For example, after it receives a frame with send sequence number = 3 in event 1, it performs error checks on the frames (event 2) and responds with a positive acknowledgment (ACK) frame that contains a receive sequence number = 4 (event 3). This operation signifies the receiver accepts all frames up to and including 3 and expects 4 to be the send sequence number of the next frame. So, all is well and the mobile station continues to send frames 4, 5, 6, 7, and 0 in event 4. This event is an example of how sequence numbers are reused. A wraparound counter of 0 to 7 is employed to limit the magnitude of the sequence number field in the frame to 3 bits ($2^3 = 8$, with decimal values of 0–7).

The term ARQ (automatic request for repeat) describes the process by which a receiving station requests a retransmission. As an example, the reception of a negative acknowledgment (NAK) with receive sequence

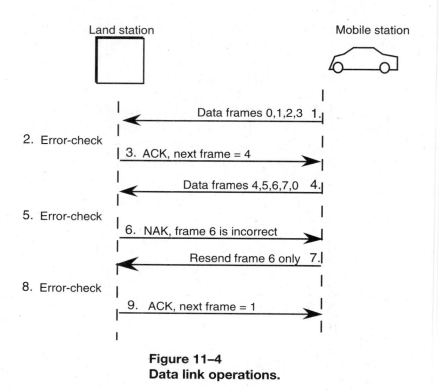

Figure 11–4
Data link operations.

number = 6 in event 6 indicates that frame 6 is in error and must be re-transmitted, which occurs in event 7. In events 8 and 9, frame 6 is checked, and an ACK of 1 is returned to acknowledge all frames. The technique of resending only the errored frame is called selective reject (SREJ). For mobile links, it is gaining in favor over the traditional method called reject (REJ) in which the errored frames and all succeeding frame must be resent.

Inclusive acknowledgement.   Events 3, 6, and 9 illustrate a concept called inclusive acknowledgment. In event 3, the ACK of 4 acknowledges all frames preceding frame 4. That is to say, an ACK of 4 means the station received and acknowledges everything up to and including 3, and the next frame expected should have a 4 in its send sequence field.

In event 6, the NAK of 6 means all frames up to and including 5 are accepted, frame 6 is not acceptable, and "I'll let you know about frames 7 and 0 shortly." In event 9, the ACK of 1 means all frames up to and including 0 are accepted.

Piggybacking.   Most mobile link layer protocols permit the inclusion of the sending and receiving number fields in the same frame. This technique, called piggybacking, allows the protocol to "piggyback" an ACK onto an information frame. As an example, assume a station sends a frame with a receive number of 5 and a send number of 1. The receive number = 5 means all frames up to a number 4 are acknowledged and the send number of = 1 means the station is sending user information in this frame with a sequence of 1.

Functions of timers.   Many link protocols use timers to verify an event occurs within a prescribed time. When a transmitting station sends a frame onto the channel, it starts a timer and enters a wait state. The valve of the timer (usually called T1 [no relation to a digital T1 carrier]) is set to expire if the receiving station does not respond to the transmitted frame within the set period. Upon expiration of the timer, 1 to n retransmissions are attempted, each with the timer T1 reset, until a response is received or until the link protocol's maximum number of retries is met. In this case, recovery or problem resolution is attempted by the link level. If unsuccessful, recovery is performed by a higher level protocol or by manual intervention and troubleshooting efforts.

The number of retries on a mobile link is usually greater than for a wire-based link. The reason is that persistence is important in mobile data communications. For example, we may not be receiving a good signal as our car goes through a tunnel, but on the other side of the tunnel, if the link protocol keeps retrying, the data will eventually be sent to the mobile station without errors.

The T1 timer described earlier is designated as the acknowledgment timer. Its value depends on (1) round trip propagation delay of the signal (usually a small value: except for very long and very high speed circuits); (2) the processing time at the receiver (including queuing time of the frame); (3) the transmission time of the acknowledging frame; and (4) possible queue and processing time at the transmitter when it receives the acknowledgment frame.

The receiving station may use a parameter (T2) in conjunction with T1. Its valve is set to ensure an acknowledgment frame is sent to the transmitting station before the T1 at the transmitter expires. This action precludes the transmitter from resending frames unnecessarily.

Flow control with sliding windows.   Link layer protocols use the concept of transmit and receive windows to aid in link management operations. The concept of a "window" is easy to understand if we think of it as a buffer to hold data link frames. A window is established on the link to provide a reservation of resources (buffers) at the mobile and land stations. In most systems, the window provides both buffer space and sequencing rules. By sequencing, I mean a rule on how large the sequence number may be. In previous examples, it was set to 7 and it is usually configured to range from 7 to 127.

During the initiation of a link session (handshake) between the stations, a window is established. For example, if the mobile and land station are to communicate with each other, each station reserves a receive window (a receive buffer).

The windowing concept is necessary for full duplex protocols because they entail a continuous flow of frames into the receiving site without the intermittent stop-and-wait acknowledgments. Consequently, the receiver must have a sufficient allocation of memory to handle the continuous incoming traffic.

Link Layer Operations of ETC Modems

An earlier section describes the physical layer operations of ETC modems. At the data link layer, the ETC modem has been modified (from a conventional wire-based modem) to optimize its operations over a mobile link. First, the information field in the frame is 32 bytes, which means that only 32 bytes are resent in the event of an error. Second, the transmit window is 15 instead of the conventional window of 7. This expanded window is needed since the frame is small, and a link could idledown if the window is exhausted before the receiving modem sends back acknowledgments of the transmitted frames. Third, the ETC modem uses SREJ and not REJ. Fourth, the retry parameter is 20 (that is, resending the frame at least 20 times until it is acknowledged), which translates to a more reliable service since this persistence means the frame has a good chance of being received correctly.

The ETC supporters claim the SREJ operation works better on a mobile link than REJ. I have not seen their statistics to back this claim, but I am skeptical. An impairment on the mobile link such as noise or a fade will most likely affect more than one frame, especially if the frames are small and operating on a link with a high bit rate.

A pure SREJ becomes a half-duplex protocol in the event of multiple frame errors because multiple SREJs cannot be sent onto the link. That is, the first SREJ must be cleared before the second is issued since a SREJ inclusively acknowledges succeeding frames. For example, refer to Figure 11–4, and assume that frames 6 *and* 7 are incorrect. If the land station sends SREJ=6, followed by SREJ=7, the SREJ=7 indicates that the receiver accepts all frames up to 6 and rejects 7. Thus, the issuance of the second SREJ before the first SREJ would inclusively acknowledge the very frame that the first SREJ is rejecting.

ETC is new, and we shall have to wait and see how it is accepted in the industry. It has some good features, and they are the implementation of parts of V.32bis and V.42.

THE NETWORK LAYER

For mobile links, the Internet Protocol (IP) has become a common network layer implementation, primarily because of its wide use in the public Internet and in many private internets (LANs, for example). It is a simple protocol and employs the ubiquitous IP address to identify source and destination address. IP is quite similar to the ISO 8473 (the Connectionless Network Protocol or CLNP) specification, which is the OSI counterpart to IP. Many of the ISO 8473 concepts were derived from IP.

IP is an example of a connectionless service. It permits the exchange of traffic between two machines without any prior call setup. The IP destination address, which resides in the IP header, is used at switches (routers) to route the traffic to the next node. Figure 11–5 shows that IP is passed by the mobile network to a router, which determines the next node that is to receive the datagram. This router may be part of the mobile network's architecture, and can reside at the land station (not shown in this figure).

It is possible that data could be lost between the two end users' stations. For example, an IP module enforces a maximum queue length size, and if this queue length is violated, the buffers will overflow. In this situation, the additional datagrams are discarded in the network.

IP has no error-reporting or error-correcting mechanisms. It relies on a module called the Internet Control Pessage Protocol (ICMP) to report errors in the processing of a datagram and provide for some administrative and status messages. The ICMP will notify the sending machine if a destination is unreachable. ICMP is also responsible for managing or creating a time-exceeded message in the event that the lifetime of the datagram expires. ICMP also performs certain editing functions to determine if the IP header is in error or otherwise unintelligible, but it does not recover from errors.

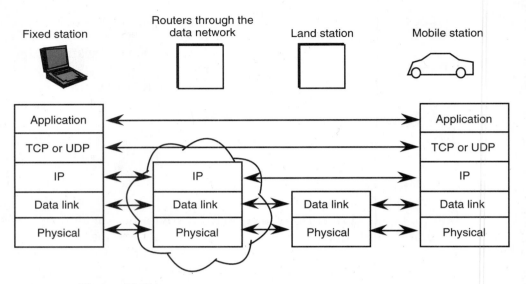

Figure 11–5
One configuration for the fixed and mobile data interface.

THE TRANSPORT LAYER

The Transmission Control Protocol (TCP) is a widely used protocol at the transport layer on mobile links. It is situated above IP and below any upper layers, such as the application layer. As depicted in Figure 11–5, it is designed to reside in the host computer or in a machine that is tasked with end-to-end integrity of the transfer of user data. For mobile links, TCP is usually placed in the computer at the mobile station and in the final computer to which the data is being delivered, which could be a mobile or fixed station.

TCP supports the tasks of end-to-end reliability, flow control, sequencing, and the opening and closing of applications' sessions with each other. Although TCP and IP are tied together so closely that they are used in the same context "TCP/IP," TCP can also support other protocols. For example, another connectionless protocol, such as the ISO 8473 (Connectionless Network Protocol or CLNP), could operate with TCP (with adjustments to the interface between the modules). In addition, the application layer protocols, such as the File Transfer Protocol (FTP) and the Simple Mail Transfer Protocol (SMTP), rely on many of the services of TCP.

Perhaps the best way to think of TCP is that it is a security blanket that provides an end-to-end acknowledgment of all traffic between two user machines. It makes no difference if the traffic is sent, first through a mobile link, second through a fixed network (like the Internet), and third to a receiving computer. TCP will guarantee (with some minor exceptions) that all traffic is received correctly.

The User Datagram Protocol (UDP) is sometimes used in place of TCP in situations where the full services of TCP are not needed. For example, the Trivial File Transfer Protocol (TFTP), and the Remote Procedure Call (RPC) use UDP. UDP serves as a simple application interface to IP. Since it has no reliability, flow control, nor error-recovery measures, it serves principally as a multiplexer/demultiplexer for the receiving and sending of IP traffic to/from an application.

CHOICES FOR MOBILE DATA OPERATIONS

Even though cellular systems were designed initially for the transport of voice signals, data applications are now commonplace, and the data-over-wireless industry is growing very rapidly. Table 11–3 provides a summary of the choices available in some locations for data services. This section describes each of these services.

Private Data Networks

One option for sending data over wireless is to subscribe to a private data network. The two private data networks are Ardis and Ram Mobile Data. More information is provided on these two networks in Table 11–4. As shown in Figure 11–6, data is sent from the mobile station to a private radio base station, which relays the traffic across a private data network [JOHN94]. In turn, some options permit interworking with other private or pubic data networks.

As mentioned, ARDIS and RAM are nationwide private network providers, and CDPD is an emerging public offering. Of course, using a conventional radio-based modem over AMPS is probably the most common means of sending data over wireless media. In addition, a number of vendors offer data services over specialized mobile radio (SMR) and satellite channels.

For the user who is interested in obtaining products for sending data over wireless systems, Table 11–5 describes several vendor products. This description is a general summary of a more detailed examination of the marketplace that is available in [JOHN94].

Table 11–3   Wireless Data Approaches

Technology and Coverage	Applications	Providers
Private packet Local or regional coverage	Short, bursty data: messaging, point-of-sale, telemetry, database queries	Ardis, Ram
Circuit-switched cellular National coverage	Large file transfers, faxes, long messages	Any cellular provider
Cellular Digital Packet Data System (CDPD) Local and spotty coverage	Short, bursty data: messaging, point-of-sale, telemetry, database queries	Ameritech, Bell Atlantic, GTE, McCaw, PacTel
Trunk radio (SMR, Specialized mobile radio)	Paging, file transfers	Racotek, Nextel, and others
Spread spectrum	All types of data	Racotek, Nextel, and others
Satellite (two-way mobile, excluding VSATs)	All types of data	Mobile Telecommunications, Orbital Communications
Enhanced paging services (EPS)	Broadcast information, mobile updates	Mobile Telecommunications, Motorola
Personal communications services (PCS)	Voice, data, fax, e-mail, others	MCI and Nextel offer PCS-like service now; AT&T, Sprint, US West and others will in the future

Public Data and Voice Networks

Figure 11–7 shows two options for the transport of data over public facilities. One option, called circuit-switched data service, uses the conventional telephone network. The other option, called packet-switched data service, uses the emerging Cellular Digital Packet Data System (CDPD) technology that was introduced into the industry in 1994.

Circuit-switched option.   The attractive aspect of the circuit-switched option is that the nation's cellular system is used by a mobile station to connect to 95 percent of the country. Other options discussed in this section cannot match this wide coverage. The down side is that throughput is limited to about 9.6 kbit/s in most situations, unless the user purchases a higher-speed, error-correcting modem, such as V.32bis.

Table 11–4 Private Data Network Providers

Vendor	Data Rate	Protocol	Price
Ardis Company Lincolnshire, IL Coverage: 400 cities	19.2 kbit/s in some cities, 4.8 kbit/s in most locations	Radio data link-access protocol (RD-LAP) at 19.2 kbit/s; Motorola Data Communications (MDC-4800) protocol at 4.8 kbit/s	One-time installation fee of $1,445 per user; charges range from 8.5¢ to 17.6¢ per packet (depending on length and time of day). Custom pricing and volume discounts available.
Ram Mobile Data Inc. New York, NY Coverage: 266 cities	8 kbit/s	Mobitex	From $25/month to $35/month depending on amount of data transmitted.

[JOHN94]

Moreover, the user has no network support or help desk to call in the event of problems; it is the same scenario as a dial-up call on the Public Switched Telephone Network (PSTN). Some cellular providers offer a service called modem pooling in which a bank of high-speed error-correcting modems can be used by the subscriber entering a code prior to entering the called telephone number.

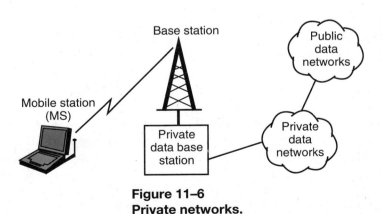

**Figure 11–6
Private networks.**

Table 11–5   Products for Private Packet Networks

Vendor	Product	Description	Data Rate
Ardis			
Motorola Inc.	Infotac	Personal data communicator	4.8 kbit/s 19.2 kbit/s[1]
	MRM 420	Mobile radio modem	4.8 kbit/s 19.2 kbit/s
	9100 product line	Portable data terminal for DOS/Windows	4.8 kbit/s
	PDT220	Stand-alone portable data terminal	4.8 kbit/s 19.2 kbit/s[1]
	RPM 405	Internal modem card and transmitter	4.8 kbit/s 19.2 kbit/s[1]
Itronix Corp.	T5000	Wireless palmtop with integrated modem and radio	4.8 kbit/s 19.2 kbit/s[1]
	T3500	Handheld computer with integrated modem and radio	4.8 kbit/s 19.2 kbit/s[1]
RAM			
Ericsson GE Mobile Communications Inc.	Mobidem	External modem and radio for PCs and laptops	8 kbit/s
Intel Corp.	Intel wireless modem	External modem and radio for PCs and laptops	8 kbit/s

[1]Also works at 8 kbit/s on RAM networks
[JOHN94]

CDPD option.   Strictly speaking , CDPD is not a public network offering because individual carriers such as Ameritech offer the service within their local access and transport areas (LATAs). However, CDPD's strategic goal is to provide a nationwide public data network to support mobile interfaces. Figure 11–7 shows how CDPD is set up with the mobile station and the CDPD fixed network. Due to CDPD's superior throughput (28.8 kbit/s), its provision for data encryption and segmentation services, a 24-hour help desk, attractive prices, and the use of the TCP/IP protocol suite, I think it will be successful. But, it is still new, and not yet available in many cities. Since Chapter 12 is devoted to CPDP, we will defer further discussion at this time.

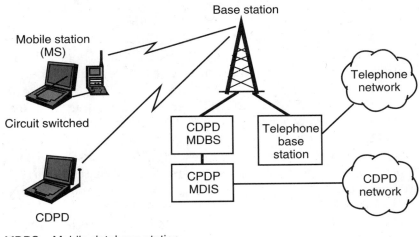

MDBS   Mobile database station
MDIS   Mobile data intermediate system

**Figure 11–7
Public networks and CDPD.**

Other Options

For users who do not need full duplex services, one-way paging is available from a number of vendors. This approach will satisfy a wide range of applications who need to receive information, but do not need to send any traffic. Some systems will down-line load graphics as well. Several paging services are available for dispatch services using the specialized mobile radio (SMR) spectrum. In the not-to-distant future, the narrowband PCS spectrum will be used for two-way paging.

MIDDLEWARE AND APIs

The user who chooses only one of the services and carriers just described for a local service need not be concerned about the details of how the applications operate over the local service. Typically, tailored line drivers and/or software modules are provided by the carrier to support the customer's application interface into the lower layers of the vendor's product. However, we just learned that a wide variety of service options exist in the marketplace. Because the physical and data link layers of these options are different, each service offering requires tailored hardware and software interfaces to a user application.

Moreover, many enterprises need to offer services to their customers (and run the applications over diverse mobile link services) on a regional or national basis. We just learned that not all the mobile data services are available universally. And if they were available, the services may be priced differently and offered with different options (e.g., line speed) in certain cities.

For example, consider a national car rental company. It must take advantage of the local offerings in each city, but it must implement common applications on a conventional AMPS-based air interface, a CDPD air interface, a private network provider interface, and so on. In this situation, when a customer boards the car rental bus that transports the customer to the parking lot where the rented car is located, the bus driver enters a message into a key pad that is sent to the car rental parking lot . This message alerts the personnel at the lot to prepare the car. This application is the same across all of the car rental company's locations, even though a location may be using a different local mobile interface to support the application.

In order to keep these applications transparent to the underlying mobile technology, the industry has implemented a service called *middleware*. As shown in Figure 11–8, middleware rests between the user application and the layers that are specific to the mobile interface. It is the job of middleware to translate the application's application programming interface (API) service requests to operations that are specific to a particular air interface.

The middleware industry is thriving, and over fifteen offerings are available. Most of the products offer interfaces into Ardis, RAM, CDPD, and conventional dial-up. As of this writing , work is underway to develop a standardized API to the middleware. Two efforts are noteworthy. A windows API is being developed by the Winsock 2 Forum, and is called the Windows Sockets 2 API. As the name implies, it will allow an application to connect to middleware in a Microsoft Windows environment. The second effort is sponsored by the Portable Computer and Communications Association (PCCA). This organization is developing a lower layer API into device drivers. It is expected that the PCCA interface will allow an application to work over Microsoft's Network Device Interface Specification (NDIS) and Novell's Open Data Link Interface (ODLI).

Standardized middleware and associated APIs are vital to the mobile communications industry. Their importance can be compared to the standardized Internet socket calls, and the well-known ports that are now available in C/UNIX-based off-the-shelf products.

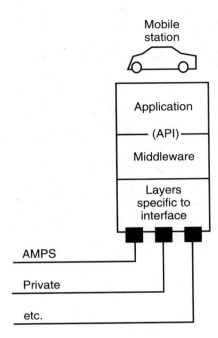

Figure 11–8
Middleware and the API.

SUMMARY

Circuit switched and packet switched services are now available in many cities for the mobile systems user. In the major cities, private data networks are offered by RAM and Ardis, who offer attractive features at a reasonable cost. A mobile station user also has access to the conventional PTSN through a cellular dial-up modem, but the rates are high. Slowly but surely, CDPD is finding its way into the industry, offering high bit rates, low delay, and secure communications.

12

The Cellular Digital Packet
Data System (CDPD)

INTRODUCTION

This chapter introduces the Cellular Digital Packet Data system, better known as CDPD. The CDPD services are analyzed and compared to conventional dial-up operations. We examine how CDPD coexists with voice traffic and how it borrows bandwidth from AMPS voice conversations. The CDPD protocols are explained as well.

INITIAL SPONSORS OF CDPD

In 1993, several mobile carriers published a specification for a wireless extension to the existing AMPS network. It is named the Cellular Digital Packet Data System (CDPD). Its goal is to provide a wireless packet data connectivity to mobile communications users [CDPD93]. The companies that produced this specification are listed in Table 12–1.

The intent of CDPD is to utilize the unused voice capacity of the existing Advanced Mobile Phone Systems (AMPS) to support data transmission. Moreover, CDPD specifies the use of existing data communications protocols, such as the Connectionless Network Protocol (CLNP), the Internet Protocol (IP), the OSI transport layer, and the Transmission Control Protocol (TCP).

Table 12–1 Initial Sponsors of CDPD

Ameritech Mobile Communications, Inc.

Bell Atlantic Mobile Systems

Contel Cellular, Inc.

GTE Mobile Communications, Inc.

McCaw Cellular Communications, Inc.

NYNEX Mobile Communications, Inc.

PacTel Cellular

Southwestern Bell Mobile Systems

In effect, existing protocols running at layers 3 and above use CDPD, which operates at the lower two layers. CDPD also specifies a wide variety of upper-layer protocols for directory management, electronic messaging, home location management, and so on. Many of these services are OSI- and Internet-based, such as X.500, X.400, and the Domain Name System (DNS), although not all these services are available.

TYPICAL CDPD TOPOLOGY

CDPD's architecture is OSI-based, and is derived from ISO 7498 and the ITU-T's OSI X.200 Recommendations. The developers have used OSI concepts and terminology wherever possible, but the protocol stacks that have been implemented thus far are based also on the TCP/IP and related protocols. This chapter describes both protocol suites.

As seen in Figure 12–1, each CDPD service provider supports three interfaces:

1. Airlink interface (A): The interface between the service provider and the mobile subscriber
2. External interface (E): The interface between the service provider and external networks
3. Interservice provider interface (I): The interface between cooperating CDPD service providers.

Two basic network entities exist in this architecture. The mobile end system (M-ES) is the user device, which is called a host in Internet terminology. Each M-ES must be identified with at least one globally unique

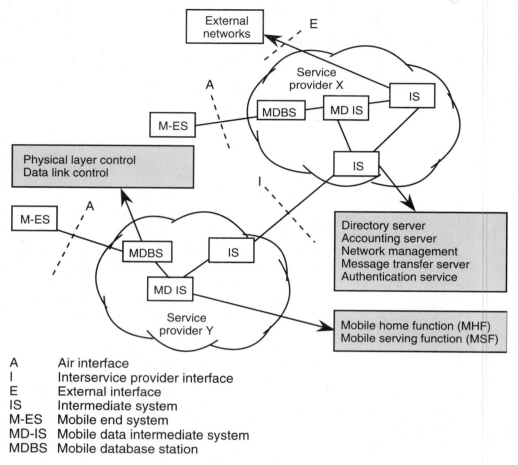

A   Air interface
I   Interservice provider interface
E   External interface
IS   Intermediate system
M-ES   Mobile end system
MD-IS   Mobile data intermediate system
MDBS   Mobile database station

Figure 12–1
The Cellular Digital Packet Data System (CDPD).

Network Entity Identifier (NEI). During the handshake the NEI is verified, otherwise the M-ES cannot decode the data sent from the CDPD network.

The intermediate system (IS) is an internetworking unit, which is called a router in Internet terminology. In addition to supporting conventional protocols, such as TCP/IP, the IS also runs a CDPD-defined operation called the Mobile Network Location Protocol (MNLP), which provides location information in the system. The latter device is called a mobile data intermediate system (MD-IS).

The MD-IS is the only entity that has any knowledge of the mobility of the ESs. It provides mobility management through two routing services. The Mobile Home Function (MHF) provides a packet forwarding function, and supports a database for its serving area (its "home" ESs and ISs). Each M-ES must belong to a fixed home area; and MHF keeps track of this information. The Mobile Serving Function (MSF) handles the packet transfer services for visiting MSs. Like most mobile systems, a visiting M-ES must register with the serving MD-IS, which notifies the visiting ES's MD-IS of its current location.

The mobile database station (MDBS) supports the air interface to the M-ES. It resides at the AMPS cell site, and uses the AMPS transmit and receive equipment. It must translate the data from the M-ES into packets and forward them to the MD-IS for further routing.

SHARING THE AMPS VOICE CHANNELS

As mentioned earlier, CDPD shares the AMPS channels and equipment at the cell site. It uses these channels for a forward channel and a reverse channel. The forward channel is from the MDBS to the M-ES. The reverse channel is from the M-ES to the MDBS. The forward channel is broadcast from the MDBS to all the M-ESs in the cell or cell sector. It is always available and, since it is being sent from the MDBS, it is contentionless. In contrast, the reverse channel must be shared by more than one M-ES. Therefore, it has a contention protocol running on it to manage the traffic. This protocol is discussed later in this chapter.

In Chapter 5, we learned how TDMA channels are dynamically shared through the real-time allocation of time slots. CDPD is a TDMA technology that uses short time slots on an AMPS voice channel when there is no speech activity on that channel. Therefore, data traffic occupies a channel only when a voice system does not need the channel bandwidth.

The MDBS broadcasts the CDPD forward channel on an idle voice channel. Furthermore, when the MDBS detects that this voice channel is becoming active, the MDBS shuts off the forward channel and hops to an idle channel. In turn, the M-ESs are informed that the forward channel has been moved to another channel. This allows the M-ESs to tune to the particular channel, synchronize their activities, and continue ongoing communications.

Figure 12–2 provides a general view of how these activities are coordinated between the MDBS and M-ES. In event 1, the M-ES is sending

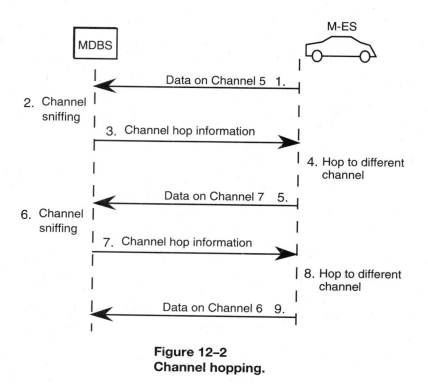

Figure 12–2
Channel hopping.

its data on AMPS channel number 5, shown as event 2. The MDBS, in turn, is monitoring all channels through a channel sniffing procedure. During this activity, the MDBS detects that an AMPS voice connection is starting to use this channel, which is occupied by CDPD traffic. As a result, the MDBS gives the direction through event 3 to the M-ES to hop to a different channel. This hop occurs in event 4.

Channel hopping requires that the M-ES resynchronize its signal and then commence sending data on another channel. This activity is depicted in event 5 where the M-ES has hopped to channel 7. Events 6 to 9 show yet another channel hop.

The MDBS detects the beginning of voice activity by "sniffing" low-level radio frequencies on the transmit side of the AMPS channel. Obviously, the MDBS must work within very tight time constraints since it may be analyzing all the calls in the cell or all the calls in a sector. The sniffers can be either narrowband or wideband devices. A narrowband sniffer scans each 30 kHz channel, one at a time; the wideband receiver analyzes all radio frequencies in the 12.5 MHz spectrum. In either imple-

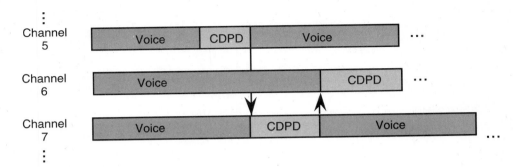

**Figure 12–3
Hopping the channels.**

mentation, the job of the MDBS is to allocate the data traffic to unused voice channels.

Figure 12–3 provides another review of the activity described in Figure 12–2. In this example, the M-ES is hopping from channel 5 to channel 7 and then to channel 6. This allows the intermixing of both the ongoing AMPS voice traffic and the CDPD data traffic.

The M-ES and MDBS have slightly different methods of ramping up and ramping down during channel hops. For the forward RF channel, the MDBS has a ramp-up and ramp-down time of 10 ms. For the reverse channel, the M-ES has a ramp-up and ramp-down time of 2 ms.

Planned and Forced Channel Hops

A forced channel hop is the type of hop we just examined. A planned channel hop occurs at a time specified by the MDBS. Typically, the timer is set to a value less than an AMPS user's perception that the CDPD traffic is interference, which would result in the channel being taken out of use ("sealed").

Since the M-ES and MDBS may be hopping frequently, tight controls are needed for the off-to-on and on-to-off carrier switching. For example, in the off-to-on M-ES operation, the ramp-up time to the desired level is 1.979 ms.

Messages for Channel Configuration and Hopping

In Figure 12–4 some of the major operations between the MDBS and its associated M-ESs were explained. Although this figure shows four serial events, these events do not have to occur in the exact order shown in this figure. The figure does, however, represent a typical invocation of

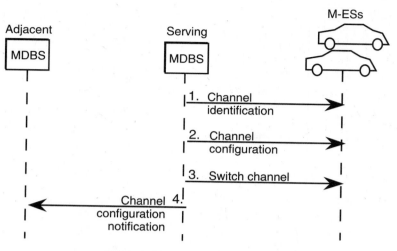

**Figure 12–4
Configuration operations.**

the events. In event 1, the channel identification message is sent by the MDBS to notify all M-ESs of the identity of the serving cell, the current channel stream, and the service provider network that is responsible for the cell. The fields in the message give the M-ESs information on the channel capacity, which indicates if there is spare capacity to support new mobile stations. The message also contains a channel stream identifier (CSI), the local cell identifier (LCI), and the service provider network identifier (SPNI). It also contains the local service area identifier (LSAI) field. All these identifiers are described shortly.

In event 2, the MDBS sends a channel configuration message to associated mobile stations. The purpose of this message is to provide information for the mobile stations for channel hopping and cell transfer. The message contains information on the current cell or an adjacent cell as well as a list of channels currently in use for CDPD and the identified cells. It also contains the local cell identifier and an area color code. This color code is used to determine whether the referenced cell is served by the same MD-IS as the current cell. The message also contains an indication if the associated RF channel is dedicated for CDPD or must be used by AMPS as well. The RF channel numbers are also contained in this message.

In event 3, a channel message is sent to the mobile stations to give them information on the channel to which they should switch. In the message are a list of terminal end point identifiers (TEIs) that identify each mobile station required to process the message. Obviously, the message must also contain the RF channel fields to which the mobile station is to switch. Finally, in event 4, a channel configuration notification message is sent to other MDBSs to bring their information up to date on channel hops or to present new information if a channel stream is brought on-line or taken off-line. This message must be sent to each MDBS controlling an adjacent cell in which a change has occurred.

MOBILITY MANAGEMENT

Mobility management is responsible for the maintenance of location databases and the routing of the protocol data units to the M-ES. It works in conjunction with radio resource management, which is tasked with the selection and use of the optimal radio channel to the M-ES. Mobility management is organized around several key components, which are illustrated in Figure 12–5. The CDPD network service is provided through domains, areas, and cells. The cell, of course, is defined by the geographic area that is covered by either the mobile database station (MDBS) or, if the cell is sectored, by the coverage area within the sector. An MDBS may control multiple cells.

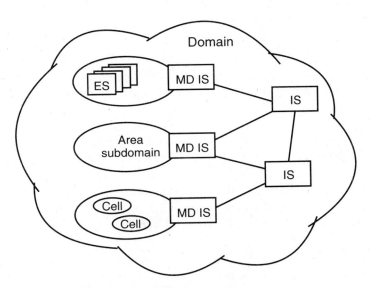

Figure 12–5
CPDP routing architecture.

An MDBS is under the control of a single mobile data intermediate system (MD-IS) and the combined coverage of all the MDBSs under the control of a single MD-IS defines a routing area subdomain. This area may cover multiple cellular geographic service areas (CGSA) or it may be only one CGSA. The CDPD domain is defined by a cohesive set of MD-ISs that are operated and controlled by one CDPD service provider.

A single geographic service area defined by an MD-IS corresponds to the ISO definition of routing domains, which can be obtained in ISO-TR-9575, titled The *OSI Routing Framework,* and ISO-10589, titled *The IS-IS Intradomain Routing Protocol.* Consequently, the MD-IS can be classified as a level 1 intermediate system because it routes directly to the end systems within its own area and it also routes to a level 2 IS when the destination is located in a different area.

The decision made to perform cell transfer, either within an area or between areas, is based on the local cell identifier (LCI), the channel stream identifier (CSI), and the channel stream color code, which is made of the cell group color and the area color. All cells in the same routing area are assigned the same area color code and the comparison of these parameters on the previous RF channel to the current RF channel reveals one of three possible conditions:

1. There is no change in the cell group color or area color or the LCI or CSI; therefore, a channel hop has been performed and no further action is required.
2. The area color is the same, but the LCI and CSI is different; therefore an intra-area cell transfer is performed.
3. Different area colors exist, which means that an inter-area cell transfer procedure must be performed.

CDPD uses several identifiers in many of its messages between the various entities. Each cell is given a local cell identifier (LCI). The LCI must be unique among the cell and all the adjacent cells and it must be unique over all cells controlled by the same MDBS.

The channel stream identifier (CSI) is a unique six-bit number for all channel streams on the cell. The LCI and CSI are concatenated to form a unique identifier for all channel streams on any given cell or its adjacent cells.

Each CDPD service provider network is identified by a 16-bit value called the service provider network identifier (SPNI). The SPNI must be unique among all CDPD service provider networks. The purpose of the SPNI is to allow the M-ES to identify the service provider network.

Finally, the local service area is identified by a 16-bit number called the local service area identifier (LSAI). This value must be unique among all local service areas in the CDPD network.

Intra-Area Cell Transfer

Figure 12–6 shows the operations involved for an intra-area cell transfer; that is to say, from one cell to another cell that is controlled by the same MD-IS. Since this activity involves only the transfer of the M-ES to another physical channel, these operations are transparent to the layers above the physical and data link layers. The M-ES decides to exit a cell if it detects an extended loss of channel synchronization and/or an unacceptable error rate. To assist the M-ES in locating a channel, the MDBS periodically broadcasts the RF channel number in use or as candidates for use in the adjacent cells.

After the M-ES has exited the old cell and made contact with the new cell and its MDBS, it then forwards a link layer receive ready (RR), shown in even 1, to the serving MD-IS. The MD-IS then acknowledges this frame by receive ready back which is (shown in event 2). This activity allows the MD-IS to update the physical media association for the M-ES.

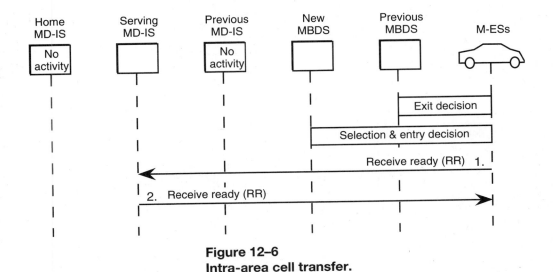

Figure 12–6
Intra-area cell transfer.

Inter-Area Cell Transfer

In the event that the mobile station travels across cells, CDPD provides a set of procedures for the M-ES to reregister into a new MD-IS. These operations are shown in Figure 12–7. The first three boxes labeled exit decision, selection and entry decision, and data link establishment have been described in previous examples in this section. We pick up this discussion with the M-ES sending an end system hello (ESH, shown in event 1) to the new serving MD-IS. The function of this hello message is to inform the new MD-IS of the presence of the mobile station and to register the mobile station's addresses at the new MD-IS. The message must contain the unique address of the M-ES, which is known as the NEI. The NEI is either an OSI network layer address or the conventional Internet

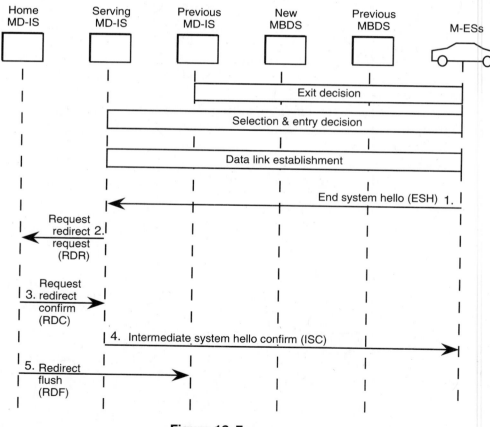

Figure 12–7
Inter-area cell transfer.

IP address. Upon receipt of this message, event 2 shows the new serving MD-IS sends to the home MD-IS the redirect request protocol data unit (RDR). This message contains the source address of the M-ES as well as a forwarding network address. This latter address is the address of the forwarding entity and the serving MD-IS and this is a direction to the home MD-IS to tell it where messages should be redirected. In event 3, the home MD-IS returns the request redirect confirm message to the new serving MD-IS and this tells this receiver if registration has been successful. In event 4, the new serving MD-IS returns to the mobile end system the intermediate system hello confirm (ISC) that is to confirm that registration has indeed occurred. The final activity shown in event 5, is the redirect flush (RDF PDU), which is sent by the home MD-IS to notify a previous serving MD-IS that messages would no longer be forwarded to that location.

The CDPD Layers

Figure 12–8 illustrates one possibility of a full protocol layer stack operating at the mobile end system (M-ES), the mobile database station, the various intermediate stations, and the end stations. We will use this figure to explain the functions of the layers, which will go a long way toward understanding some of the major features of CDPD.

For ease in this analysis I will discuss these layers from the physical layer and work up to the transport layer. The physical layer differs between the forward and reverse channels. We learned earlier that the forward channel is contentionless and the backward channel is contention-oriented. The data link on both physical channels operates at 19.2 kbit/s. The modems employ Gaussian-minimum shift keying (GMSK) with a modulation index of 0.5. The forward channel uses a Reed-Solomon encrypted packets of 378 bits in length. The format for this traffic is explained later in this section.

The ME-S and the MDBS operate with two layer 2 (data link) protocols. The mobile data link protocol (MDLP) and a MAC layer protocol designated in this figure as CDPD-MAC. The MAC layer is designed to provide frame delimiting of the traffic and also provides for error correction and detection on both the forward and backward channels. The MDLP sublayer is derived from HDLC.

The subnetwork dependent convergence protocol (SNDCP) performs several functions. It is responsible for compression operations and also segments traffic into a preconfigured segment length. It is also responsible for the encryption of the traffic at the transmit side and the decryp-

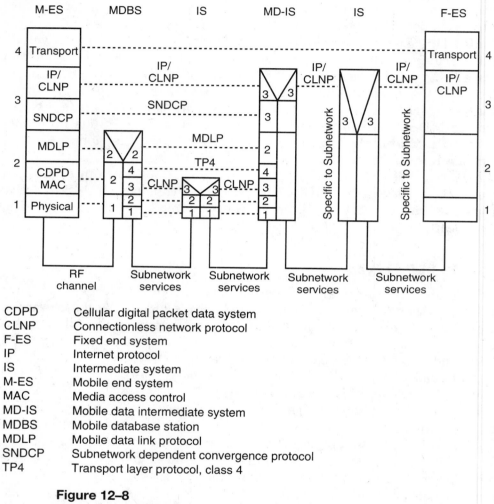

Figure 12–8
Example of CDPD layers and data flow. Dotted lines denote data flow.

CDPD	Cellular digital packet data system
CLNP	Connectionless network protocol
F-ES	Fixed end system
IP	Internet protocol
IS	Intermediate system
M-ES	Mobile end system
MAC	Media access control
MD-IS	Mobile data intermediate system
MDBS	Mobile database station
MDLP	Mobile data link protocol
SNDCP	Subnetwork dependent convergence protocol
TP4	Transport layer protocol, class 4

tion of the traffic at the receive side. Obviously, at the receive side, it is also responsible for reassembly of the segments and for performing decompression on the traffic.

At layer 3 rests either the Internet Protocol (IP) or the ISO Connectionless Network Protocol (CLNP). These protocols provide CDPD with destination and source addresses. For IP, these are the well-known

Internet addresses consisting of 32 bits that are registered through the Internet structure. For CLNP, the address varies but is usually derived from the OSI-based address defined in ITU-T Recommendation X.200.

Finally, at the transport layer rests either the Internet's Transmission Control Protocol (TCP) or the ISO/ITU-T transport layer protocol known as transport layer protocol class 4 (TP4). One of the major functions of these protocols is to provide end-to-end flow control and end-to-end acknowledgment of traffic.

As noted in Figure 12–8, the implementation of the layers within various subnetworks is not defined. For example, the physical layer, data link layers, and some transport services are unique to a specific subnetwork. Since we are dealing with an air interface in this chapter, those layers need not concern us.

Intended Services

Since CDPD is new, and deployment and development are still in their embryonic states, not all services have been developed. But it is important to keep in mind that if CDPD meets its goals of a nationwide connectivity, services will be quite important, just as they are in the fixed Internet.

Eventually, the intent is for service provider to provide a number of "servers" for its domain. These servers reside in an IS and are called fixed end systems (F-ESs). The servers perform the operations that are summarized in the next paragraphs. Most of the services are based on layer 7 of the OSI model. As a practical matter, more Internet-based layer 7 services are used in the industry, so the initial thrust of CDPD has concentrated on offering Internet applications. Figure 12–9 shows an abstract view of where the services can be provided. Bear in mind vendors vary in the placement (or inclusion) of these services. In addition, network providers vary in how these services are distributed and/or combined.

The directory server provides X.500 directory services for name-to-address translation, information on subscribers, and other "yellow" and "white" page functions. Lower layer access to a directory server must adhere to a specific CDPD protocol, and ISO's Connection Oriented Transport Service (COTS), and optionally, ISO's Connectionless Network Service (CLNS), X.25, PVC frame relay, point-to-point, or a LAN profile.

The accounting server provides a repository for accounting information, including the collection and distribution of this information to interested (and authorized) parties. Lower layer access to an accounting server must adhere to the same conventions as the directory server.

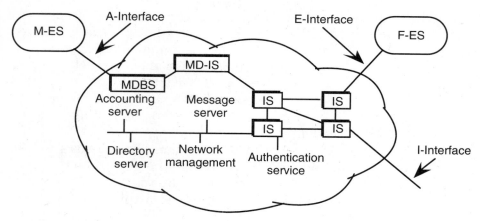

Figure 12–9
Eventual service provider network fixed end systems (F-ES).

Network management provides network management services through the use of either common management information protocol (CMIP), or simple network management protocol (SNMP). The ITU-T/OSI system management functional areas (ITU-T M.3400) must be supported (fault management, configuration management, accounting management, performance management, security management). Lower layer access to network management must adhere to the same conventions as the directory server.

The message transfer server provides an electronic messaging service through the use of ITU-T's X.400 Recommendation. Lower layer access to the message transfer server must adhere to the same conventions as the directory server, except ISO's Connectionless Network Service (CLNS) is not allowed.

The authentication service provides an authentication service for a home MD-IS to verify a M-ES's credentials by the use of secret key encryption and decryption. The authentication protocol must run on top of OSI's association control service element (ACSE, X.217) and the remote operations service element (ROSE, X.219). Authentication is explained in more detail later.

CDPD Layer Relationships

CDPD provides a wide variety of services at the various layers of a conventional OSI model. Figure 12–10 shows the layers as well as the protocol entities residing in the layers. The subnetwork subprofiles in-

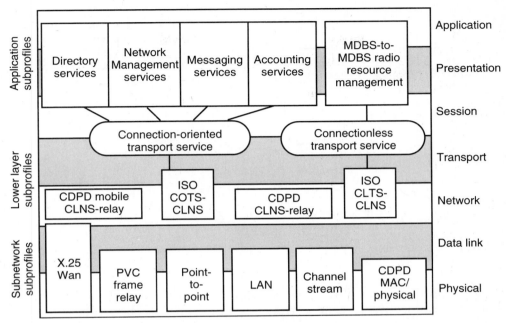

Figure 12–10
CDPD support services profiles.

clude conventional layer 1 and layer 2 protocols such as X.25, frame relay, point-to-point, and of course the CDPD MAC physical layer. The lower layer subprofiles include several combinations of connection-oriented and connectionless services residing at the network and transport layers. The upper layers contain the services described earlier in this chapter.

Network management profiles. The CDPD network management profiles are illustrated in Figure 12–11. The I subprofile refers to an OSI-based protocol stack and the A subprofile refers to the Internet protocol subprofile. Due to the overhead in the OSI stacks, initial implementations have focused on the A subprofile.

The OSI stack runs the common management information protocol (CMIP) over the association control service element (ACSE) and the remote operations service element (ROSE). CMIP performs conventional management operations such as the issuance of GET and SET messages to an agent. The agent, in turn, responds to these messages in accordance with the rules of the protocols and additional information stored in

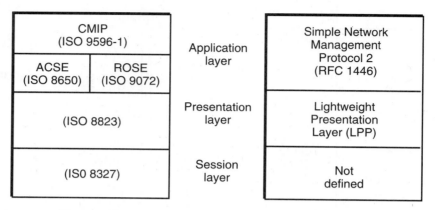

Figure 12–11
CDPD network management I and A subprofiles.

a management information base (MIB). ACSE is somewhat of a house-keeping protocol in the sense that it sets up an association between two CMIP entities in two different machines. After ACSE performs these functions, it is no longer invoked until the association is to be taken down. ROSE is a remote procedure call specification that was described in Chapter 8; therefore, we shall not repeat this description in this chapter. The presentation and session layers are the conventional ISO, or ITU-T protocols. They are bound closely to the activities of the application layer and support syntax transfer and session management.

The Internet network management profile is much simpler. The simple network management protocol (SNMP) is used at the application layer. It too performs function such as GETs and SETs. It operates over a sparse presentation layer known as the light weight presentation protocol (LPP). It does not invoke any session layer functions at this time.

CMIP and SNMP each allow an agent to send messages to a managing process. CMIP calls this message an event report and SNMP calls the message a trap. Generally, the protocols are similar in how they perform functions except CMIP is an object-oriented protocol which allows the use of inheritance, managed object classes, as well as the creation and deletion of instances of objects. SNMP is not object-oriented.

The internet profiles. Figure 12–12 shows a more commonly implemented protocol stack that uses the Internet specifications. The network layer contains the Internet Protocol (IP) and the Internet Control

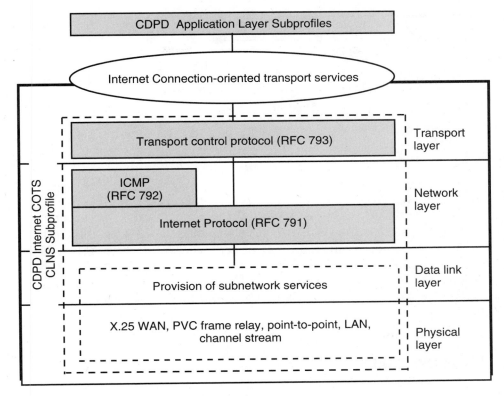

Figure 12–12
The Internet stack.

Message Protocol (ICMP). The transport layer contains the well-known Transmission Control Protocol (TCP). TCP/IP was described in Chapter 11, so it is not repeated here.

PHYSICAL LAYER INTERFACES

The unit transmitted over the channel stream is a fixed length block of 378 bits (see Figure 12–13). This burst is interleaved with a variety of control and synchronization bits, which are encoded using a systematic Reed-Solomon error correcting code. The encoding operation generates 47 6-bit symbols and a parity field of 16 6-bit symbols, yielding a block of 378 bits.

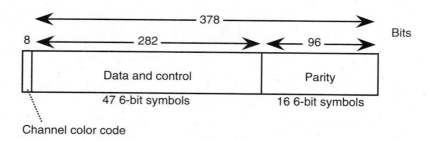

Figure 12–13
The CDPD burst.

Each channel stream is assigned an 8-bit channel color code. This code has two fields: the 5-bit cell group color identifies a cell group and the 3-bit area color identifies a set of cells controlled by a given MD-IS. The color code is used by an M-ES to detect co-channel interference from a remote MDBS or to note that a cell transfer has involved a change of MD-IS. The MDBS uses it to detect co-channel interference from a remote M-ES.

DATA FLOW EXAMPLE

Figure 12–14 shows the flow of data from the network layer through the sublayers down to the physical layer. The figure shows where compression occurs, where encryption and decryption operations are implemented, as well as where segmentation operations are performed. Note the names of the layers and sublayers are shown on the right side of the figure. The illustration is self-explanatory, so I will not comment on it any further.

CDPD DEPLOYMENT

The status of CDPD deployment is changing frequently. Table 12–2 represents some of the current systems that are in place, or due to come online shortly. The prices for the services vary. The rates are based on volume of traffic sent. Presently, the costs range from 12 to 19 cents per kilobyte of data transmitted.

With the rapid rise of data transmission services, it is only a matter of time before data over wireless becomes as common place as data over

quired percentage of total time available, this time should be enough to get the message through. If so, then the communicator wins. However, the jammer wins if the jammer's transmitters operate on the communicator's frequency enough of the time to prevent the message from getting through to the receiver.

To increase the chances of a communicator avoiding a jammer, the communicating sender and receiver agree upon a procedure where, at specific periods, the frequencies change for the transmission. This arrangement decreases the chances of the jammer transmitting with the frequency that the communicator is using. In addition, a technique known as fast frequency hopping further increases the communicator's chances. With this approach, the communicator reduces the length of each burst of the transmission to be equal or less than the propagation time from the communicator's transmitter to the receiver. This approach also overcomes the possibility that the jammer might learn the sequence of the frequency hops because the hopping is done through a randomizing sequence. Assuming that the randomizing algorithm is random (orthogonal), the jammer will not be able to predict the location of the hopping. Consequently, with frequency hopping using spread spectrum, wideband channels are divided into a large number of smaller channels and the communicator uses a randomizing approach to hop from one channel to another while transmitting very short bursts to the receiver.

DIRECT SEQUENCE SPREAD SPECTRUM

Direct sequence spread spectrum was introduced in Chapter 5. With this approach, a voice signal has other signals added to it that have noise-like characteristics (see Figure 13–2). The effect of this addition is the production of a noise modulated signal that resembles noise. The receiver is designed to subtract the noise signals from the transmission, resulting in the replica of the original voice signal that was "buried" in the noise transmission. The added signal contains the unique orthogonal (code) and operates at a much faster rate and over a wider bandwidth than the signal that carries the user traffic.

PREFERRED METHODS FOR MOBILE SYSTEMS

Until recently, the preferred method for obtaining security and privacy in a wireless system has been to scramble or encrypt the signals with private encryption keys. As examples, GSM, DECT, and IS-54 stipulate pri-

(a) At the transmitter:

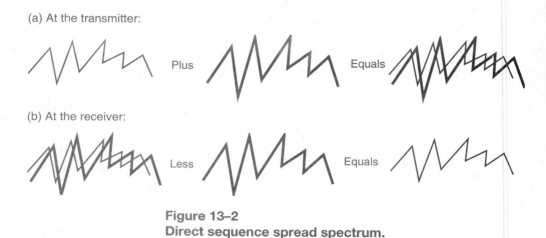

(b) At the receiver:

Figure 13–2
Direct sequence spread spectrum.

vate key technology. This approach has been used because it is simple and fast. Public key encryption has not seen much use because of the time required to set up a call and establish the keys for the communicating parties. However, some proposals have surfaced that claim to be able to exploit public key technology on wireless systems. The reader can find information on this research and proposals in various issues of the *IEEE Journal on Selected Areas in Communications* (specifically, Vol. 11, No. 6, August 1993 contains some useful articles).

PRIVATE KEY ENCRYPTION

In its simplest form, private key encryption requires that the sender and receiver of a message use one value (key) to scramble and unscramble the traffic respectively. These keys are called private keys, because they are known and shared only between the sender and receiver, or (usually) between a known and trusted community of senders and receivers. Figure 13–3 shows the operations for private key encryption.

The Data Encryption Standard (DES)

In 1977, the U.S. government published the Data Encryption Standard (DES). It was established in conjunction with IBM and released to the general public with the goal of providing a standardized cryptography algorithm for the industry.

The Direct Debit Guarantee

* This Guarantee is offered by all Banks and Building Societies that take part in the Direct Debit Scheme. The efficiency and security of the Scheme is monitored and protected by your own Bank or Building Society.

* If the amounts to be paid or the payment dates change, you will be told of this in advance by at least 14 days as agreed.

* If an error is made by the London Borough of Enfield or your Bank or Building Society, you are guaranteed a full and immediate refund from your branch of the amount paid.

* You can cancel a Direct Debit at any time by writing to your Bank or Building Society. Please also send a copy of your letter to the London Borough of Enfield.

DIRECT Debit

CTDD05/3/280597

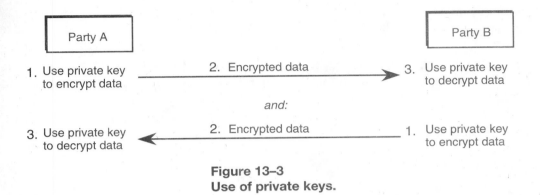

Figure 13–3
Use of private keys.

DES is based on an encryption algorithm that changes the plaintext with so many combinations that a cryptoanalyst should not be able to figure out the plaintext even if numerous copies were available. The idea of the DES is shown in Figure 13–4(a). The encryption begins with the permutation function (P function)—in this case 8 bits are input into the P function. As seen inside the box, the bits are changed in relation to the output. The P box can consist of wires or use programmable software to perform various kinds of permutation. The second function, the substitution function, is shown in Figure 13–4(b). In this situation, a 5-bit input (decoder) selects one of the eight possible lines into an S box. The S function performs the substitution of the lines, resulting in the encoding (encoder) of the 8 lines back to the 5 input bits. The idea of the DES is to

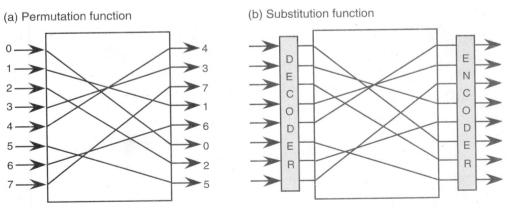

Figure 13–4
DES and permutation/substitution.

provide for several stages of permutation and substitution as illustrated in Figure 13–5.

The DES provides a key of 64 bits, of which 56 bits are used directly by the DES algorithm and 8 bits are used for error detection. There are over 70 quadrillion (70,000,000,000,000,000) possible keys of 56 bits in length. Obviously, a tremendous amount of computer power is needed to break this key. However, it can be done: High-speed computers can find the key. Notwithstanding, the objective of the DES is not to provide absolute security, but rather to provide a reasonable level of security for business-oriented networks.

As shown in Figure 13–5, in the DES approach plaintext to be enciphered is subjected to an initial permutation (IP) with a 64-bit input block permuted as:

58	50	42	34	26	18	10	2
60	52	44	36	28	20	12	4
62	54	46	38	30	22	14	6
64	56	48	40	32	24	16	8
57	49	41	33	25	17	9	1
59	51	43	35	27	19	11	3
61	53	45	37	29	21	13	5
63	55	47	39	31	23	15	7

That is, the permuted input has bit 58 of the input as its first bit, bit 50 as its second bit, and so on, with bit 7 as its last bit. The permuted input block becomes the input to a complex *key-dependent computation* consisting of sixteen stages. The stages are the same in actual operation, but the cipher function uses the key (K) in different ways.

The final calculation is then subjected to the following permutation (IP^{-1}), which is the inverse for the initial permutation.

40	8	48	16	56	24	64	32
39	7	47	15	55	23	63	31
38	6	46	14	54	22	62	30
37	5	45	13	53	21	61	29
36	4	44	12	52	20	60	28
35	3	43	11	51	19	49	27
34	2	42	10	50	18	58	26
33	1	41	9	49	17	57	25

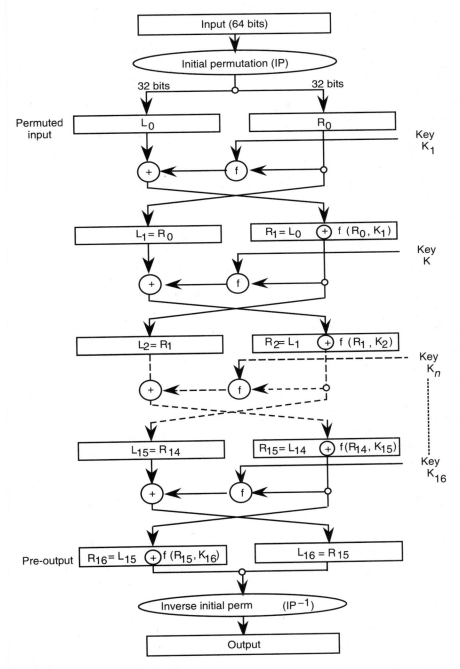

Figure 13–5
DES and permutation/substitution.

The sixteen stages use the two blocks (L and R) of 32 bits to produce two 32-bit blocks of output. The left and right copies are exchanged before each stage. The function (F) performs four steps on the right output through an *exclusive or* transposition (in Figure 13–5, + denotes bit-by bit addition).

1. The 32-bit R is expanded by a transposition and duplication rule to a 48-bit number E.
2. E and K are combined together by *exclusive or*. At each stage, a different block K of key bits is chosen from the 64-bit key.
3. The 48 bits produced in step 2 are divided into eight 6-bit groups and input into S boxes, each of which produces 4 output bits.
4. The resulting 32 bits are input into a P box.

The 56-bit key is too short for some applications. For example, a high-speed computer can search all 2^{56} possible keys (72,057,594,037,927,936) in less than four hours [WEIN94]. However, systems are now available that use longer keys. One system, called triple DES, performs three encryptions with the DES, by using two keys. Triple DES yields a key of 112 bits [SIMM91].

Secret Key Distribution Problems

The problem with a private key is just that: It must be held privately between the two communicating parties. Party A and party B have a shared key that no one else knows. However, if these parties need to communicate with another party, say party C, then two more secret keys are needed: A $\leftrightarrow$ C, and B $\leftrightarrow$ C.

With n parties to be "fully meshed", $n(n - 1)/2$ keys are needed. To place this problem into perspective, the Internet has over 20 million users. For any two Internet users to communicate with each other would require the use of 200 trillion keys [ODLY94]. Each user would have to keep a file of 20 million keys, or somehow exchange in secret the secret key with selected parties—clearly an impossible task. This problem gave rise to public key systems.

PUBLIC KEY ENCRYPTION

In contrast, public key encryption allows one of the keys, the public key, to be made known to the public—hence, its name, public key encryption. This public key is created during the same invocation of an algorithm that creates another value, which is called a private key. Actually, more than two keys are created, but this generic example will focus on two keys. Therefore, the public and private keys are the result of the same function instance.

Because of this relationship, public key encryption permits the sharing of a public key, yet security is obtained by limiting the "knowledge" of the private key to the entity that invoked the algorithm that produced the private key. The private key and public key can be used to encrypt and decrypt traffic (see Figure 13–6).

Distribution of Keys

Public encryption systems can be used to distribute private keys. For example, assume party A chooses a secret key and sends it to party B by encrypting it with the public part of party B's key, which is stored in a public directory. In turn, party B decrypts the message with party B's private part, thus obtaining party A's private key. The process is reversed for A to obtain B's private key.

RSA Technique

The best known public key system is the RSA algorithm, named after its inventors, Ron Rivest, Adi Shamir, and Len Adleman of MIT. It works as follows (see Figure 13–7[a]). Party A selects two large prime numbers p and q and calculates $n = p \times q$. Next, party A chooses a random integer e, $1 <e> n$. The value e must have no integer divisors > 1 that are in common with $p - 1$ or $q - 1$. Party A publishes the (n,e) pair, but not the (p,q) pair. Thus, (n,e) is the public key, and (p,q) is the private key.

We assume that party B now has A's public key (n,e). Party B encrypts a message m into a cipher c to send to party B:

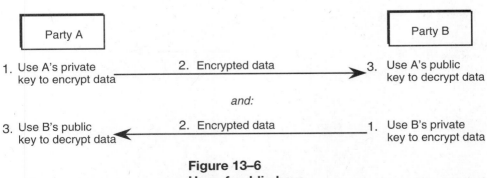

Figure 13–6
Use of public keys.

$$c = m^e \quad (\text{mod } n) \quad 0 \le c < n$$

Party A decrypts the ciphered message c as follows:

$$m = c^d (\text{mod } n),$$

where d is A's secret decryption exponent. The value d is computed correctly from e only if p and q are known:

$$ed = 1 \ (\text{mod } p - 1)$$
$$ed = 1 \ (\text{mod } q - 1),$$

because c and d are multiplicative inverses:

$$(m^e)^d = m^{ed} = m^1 = m$$

Therefore, party B's original message is recovered. Again, this activity is shown in Figure 13–7(a).

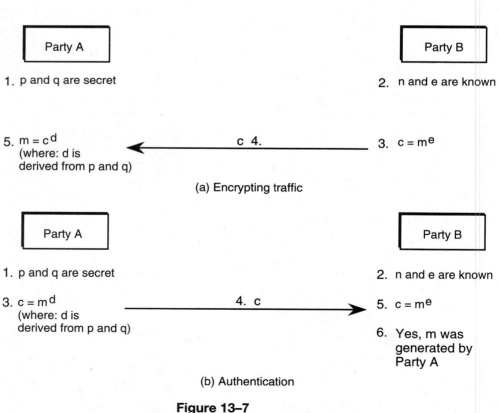

Figure 13–7
Public key operations.

Figure 13–7(b) shows another way in which public keys are employed. Party A signs a message (a digital signature) in order to verify to party B that party a is really party A. Once again, party A creates the ciphered signature m with A's secret exponent d. At the receiving end, party B uses e to decrypt the message, and to determine if the signature is valid. This method is used often in authentication operations, a subject discussed later in this chapter.

Breaking the RSA Code

In 1977, Rivest, Shamir, and Aldeman issued a challenge to the industry to break the RSA 129-digit code. The expectation was that the code could not be broken for many years. In 1994, a task force organized by Bellcore broke the code. The team was able to find two prime numbers multiplied together that resulted in the 129-digit key value. Bellcore claims that is close to breaking 155-digit keys, which is of considerable concern to companies that moved away from the 129-digit code to the 150-digit code [MESS94]. As of this writing, efforts are focused on using more digits in the key, and 150- to 230-digit sizes are ranges that are recommended.

AUTHENTICATION MODEL

This section explains a model used by many systems for authentication. For example, it is used in X.32 dial-up procedures, X.400, X.500, and GSM. This discussion is based on X.32, tailored to the subject of authenticating a mobile station user. The rule in the model is that the challenged party (a mobile station) must identify itself. In a mobile, wireless system, this operation entails the mobile station sending a signature to the network.

The model describes the roles of the *questioning* party and the *challenged* party. Obviously, the questioning party is the one that is challenging the challenged party to provide correct identification and authentication. Before explaining this protocol, several definitions are in order:

- *Identity element* (ID): A string of octets representing the identity of the challenged party
- *Signature element* (SIG): A string of octets representing the identity, such as a password, or a result of an encryption process
- *Random number* (RAND): An unpredictable range of octets

- *Signed response element* (SRES): The reply of the challenged party to the questioning party
- *Diagnostic element* (DIAG): The result of the identification process; transmitted by questioning party at the end of the identification process

The authentication model defines two security options: security grade 1, and security grade 2. Security grade 1 involves two messages exchanged between the challenged and challenging party. Both options are in effect for the call. Any new identification process must first be preceded with a disconnect of the link.

As depicted in Figure 13–8(a), the challenged party must first send its identity (ID) and, if required, some type of signature (SIG). In turn, the questioning party responds with the diagnostic message (DIAG), which contains the result of the process. If it is not successful, security grade 1 permits up to three retries before a disconnect occurs.

The security grade 2 procedure involves a more enhanced authentication exchange (see Figure 13–8[b]). Basically, if the initial identification and signature of the challenged party are valid, the questioning party will return a message with a random number (RAND), which the challenged party must encipher and return as its signed response (SRES). The questioning party then is required to decipher the SRES, and, if the result of its deciphering equals the value in the RAND, an ap-

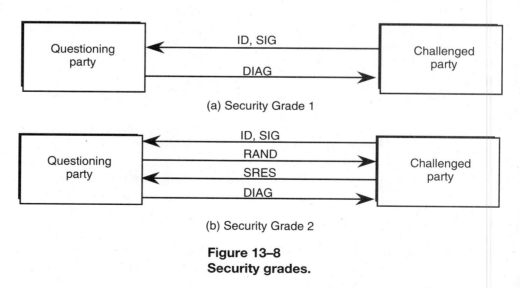

(a) Security Grade 1

(b) Security Grade 2

Figure 13–8
Security grades.

propriate diagnostic message (DIAG) is sent to the challenge party and the two parties have completed the authentication and identification process. If the encryption and identification process does not succeed, the error diagnostic message is returned and a connection is not made. X.32 permits only one attempt when the network is the questioning party.

Using the Authentication Model in the Mobile Environment

This part of the chapter shows an example of how GSM uses the authentication model. To begin the discussion, remember that GSM uses an alias for identification across the air interface. It does not send the IMSI, but the TMSI.

GSM enciphers its information bursts. This burst consists of a 114 bits of a normal burst. Ciphering is accomplished by applying an exclusive OR operation to the 114 bits. The operation is performed with a pseudo random bit sequence as shown in Figure 13–9. This operation is performed at the transmitter with a complementary operation performed at the receiver. The deciphering also uses the exclusive OR operation. By doing this at the transmitter and receiver, the 114 bits will retain their original value. GSM uses an algorithm called A5 to perform this opera-

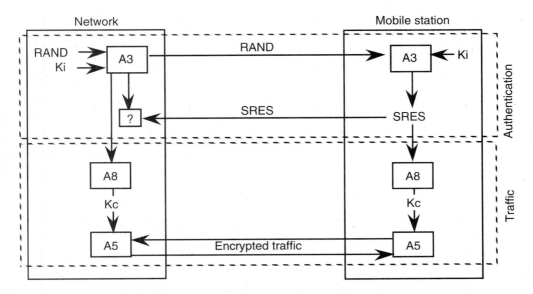

Figure 13–9
Example of GSM authentication and traffic transfer.

tion. The A5 algorithm is implemented in both the mobile and authentication stations. We shall have more to say about A5 shortly.

One of the most important operations in the handshake of any mobile system is the proper authentication of the user. GSM provides authentication by checking the validity of a subscriber's SIM card. This authentication is based on what is called the A3 algorithm which is stored in both the SIM card and access control (AC).

By using Figure 13–8 as a starting point, we can redo this figure to show the specific operations of GSM in Figure 13–9. As this figure illustrates, the network sends to the mobile subscriber a randomly generated number called RAND, discussed earlier. The message is a "challenge" to the user. The mobile station uses RAND as input to the A3 calculation along with the authentication key, Ki. This value is stored only on the SIM card and by the network. The input of Ki and RAND into the A3 algorithm produces the signed response (SRES). This value is returned to the authentication center (AC) and checked to determine if it has been decoded properly. In this manner, the network is able to verify the proper identify of the user. Obviously, if SRES does not equal the predicted value by the network, then the user is not authenticated.

The RAND value can range between 0 and 2^{128-1}, thus RAND is 128 bits long. The SRES is 32 bits in length.

Typically, a set of RAND and SRES values are stored by the network (at the HLR and VLR) for use at the AC. This approach allows different values to be used with each authentication. If the HLR exhausts the list of numbers, additional values can be requested from the AC. As we learned earlier in this chapter, the important aspect of authentication is that parameters A3 and Ki are never sent across any of the communications channels, but are stored in secured places.

The A5 algorithm works with a preliminary step as shown in Figure 13–9. It uses a key designated as Kc. This key is calculated from RAND and from Ki through an algorithm designated as A8. The result of this operation is a ciphering key Kc. The A8 algorithm is stored at the mobile station on the SIM card. The Kc key is then used with the ciphering algorithm A5. As discussed in the GSM chapter, the network instructs the mobile station to begin a ciphering sequence and upon this instruction, the mobile station transmits ciphered data (unless directed otherwise by the network). This idea is also shown in Figure 13–9.

The idea of these operations is to make the production of SRES an easy affair if Ki and RAND are known. In contrast, deriving Ki from RAND and SRES is quite complex, and computationally expensive, which is the essence of this approach.

THE SMART CARD

Several references have been made in this book to the smart card. We now explain it in more detail in relation to authentication. I will use the AT&T smart card as the example during this discussion [SHER94].

The smart card is shown in Figure 13–10. It looks like an ordinary credit card, except it houses a computer and memory. Also, its front and back covers are made of material to provide a stiff, strong housing for the inside components.

Inside the card is a single-chip microprocessor, an operating system, read only memory (ROM), erasable electronic programmable read only memory (EEPROM), and random access memory (RAM). Additionally, the AT&T card has an inductive power coil, which means it does not need an exposed external interface that is subject to damage and requires a mechanical reader. This "contactless" interface uses the inductive coil for power transfer and capacitive plates for information transfer. The transfer rate is 19.2 kbit/s.

Support for Multiple Applications

For a smart card to be exploited to its fullest, it should support more than one application. As part of this support, a PIN should be used to "in-lock" the card, and a unique key should be tied to each application and

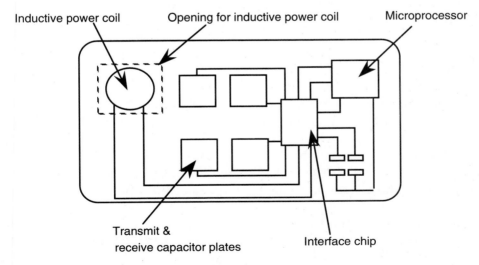

Figure 13–10
Inside a smart card.

the files/directories for the application. With this approach, the smart card can support multiple applications such as PCS, credit cards, travel portfolios, and bank debit/credit records.

Each application has read/write privileges, so a corporation issuing the card can control levels of access and functions—perhaps tailored for each employee. Security keys can be stored within the card, which means a user need not know the key.

It is only a matter of time before the smart card becomes as commonplace as the credit card. But it too has some security problems. After all, a person carrying a smart card becomes a potential walking ATM machine.

PIN VERSUS BIOMETRIC AUTHENTICATION

Most systems use a PIN as the basic building block for security operations. We have discussed the PIN several times in this book, so we shall not repeat the material here.

Another security method, called biometric authentication, is gaining in acceptance. It uses some physical aspect of a person to validate that person's authenticity, such as a voice or video template, a signature, or a fingerprint.

Biometric authentication can be used with smart cards if compression operations are applied to the authentication images. For the present, the PIN will remain the choice for mobile systems.

SUMMARY

Frequency hopping with spread spectrum was developed from the U.S. Department of Defense (DOD) systems to avoid jamming, and it can provide for privacy. Gradually, it will be employed in mobile systems.

Encryption with private or public keys remains the most frequently used technique to secure communications signals. In the past public keys had not seen much use in wireless systems, but research is leading to their use.

Smart cards are gaining in use and will become a standard means for providing people and applications portability across different machines.

14

Network Management

INTRODUCTION

This chapter describes how network management is provided across the air interface and on the network side. It introduces the subject by explaining why integrated standardized network management is beneficial, and why network management standards are needed.

The OSI approach is described with an examination of the common management information protocol (CMIP). The Internet approach is also described with an examination of the simple network management protocol (SNMP). Object libraries and management information bases (MIBs) are also described.

The chapter concludes with a description of Bellcore's network management model for a PCS system, the Wireless Access Communications System (WACS) radio port control unit (RPCU).

VALUE OF NETWORK MANAGEMENT STANDARDS

A mobile network is of little long-term value if it cannot be managed properly. One can imagine the difficulty of trying to interconnect and communicate among different machines such as mobile and land stations if the conventions differ for managing the use of alarms, performance indicators, traffic statistics, logs, accounting statistics, and other vital elements of a network. The difficulty of managing these resources is becoming increasingly complex as networks add more components, more functions, and more users.

In recognition of this fact, the ISO and ITU-T have been working on the development of network management standards for a number of years. Another major thrust into network management standards has been through the Internet activities. In the last few years, the Internet Activities Board (IAB) has assumed the lead in setting standards for the Internet, and have fostered a protocol called the *Simple Network Management Protocol (SNMP)*.

Figure 14–1 illustrates the principal problem that occurs when management standards are not used, as well as the potential benefit that can be derived from their use. In the past, each vendor has developed and sold proprietary network management packages. A number of these systems are functionally rich and perform well within the vendor's network. With some exceptions, they are designed to interact with a specific vendor's hardware and software. Consequently, the use of these network management products to "oversee" other vendor's architectures is quite difficult.

The top part of the figure shows the typical approach without the use of network management standards. The enterprise is tasked with developing five different interfaces for the five vendors illustrated in this figure. The cost to develop and maintain these interface systems can be extraordinary, often resulting in complex software and unpredictable performances.

In contrast, network management standards (illustrated at the bottom of the figure) allow an organization to use one set of software to interact with the vendors' network management packages. Of course, the benefit to the organization is that this approach forces these vendors to place the standardized software and databases in their own machines.

The approach still allows the different vendors to communicate with each other in a more transparent manner. Therefore, the benefits of decreased costs and simpler operations are reaped by the network management center, the individual vendors, and the customers.

KEY TERMS AND CONCEPTS

The OSI, Internet, and IEEE network management standards define the responsibility for a *managing process* (called a network management system in some vendor's products) and a *managing agent* (also known as an

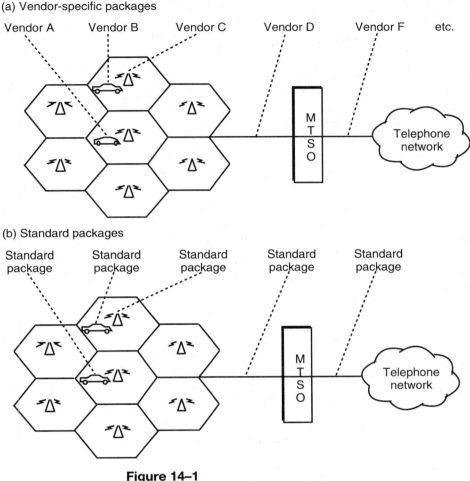

Figure 14–1
Network management alternatives.

agent process). In the strictest sense, a network management system really contains nothing more than protocols that convey information about network elements back and forth between various agents in the system and the managing process.

One other component is vital to a network management system. It is called the *management information base* or *library* (hereafter called a MIB). This conceptual object is actually a database that is shared between managers and agents to provide information about the managed network elements.

THE TELECOMMUNICATION MANAGEMENT
NETWORK (TMN) MODEL

Like most of ITUT-T's recommendations, the TMN is a generic model that describes the functions, interfaces, and reference points of a management system. In this case, the TMN is organized around OSI concepts, insofar as possible. The TMN also is organized around object-oriented techniques, which makes it supportive of CMIP and CMISE. In addition, TMN employs the five management functional areas of OSI: security management, performance management, accounting management, configuration management, and fault management. The major objectives of TMN are summarized in Table 14–1.

The TMN architecture is organized around TMN functions (and function blocks). These function blocks describe the activities that TMN performs in its management responsibilities. The function blocks are also further organized into functional components. Any pair of function blocks that exchange information between them are separated by reference points (much like the CCITT ISDN reference model).

Figure 14–2 shows the function blocks that are directly related to the management operations of TMN. The circles in the figure symbolize the functions—some of which are not completely in the TMN (explained below).

The function blocks are responsible for the following:

- *Operations systems function (OSF) block:* Provides overall management responsibilities for the entire TMN.
- *Network element function (NEF) block:* Communicates with TMN in order to allow the managed network to be managed. Responsible for representing the managed functions to the TMN; as such these functions are not part of TMN.

Table 14–1   Objectives of TMN

- Provide a framework (a generic model) for management
- Describe the appropriate functions that exist in the parts of the TMN
- Define the interfaces between the TMN and the actual networks
- Make use of OSI-based services, where appropriate
- Employ the object-oriented approach to represent TMN architecture
- Employ the OSI five management functional areas (X.700 Recommendations)

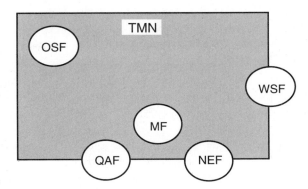

**Figure 14–2
TMN function blocks.**

- *Workstation function (WSF) block:* Acts as the interface to the human user, and as such, has part of it operating on the outside of the TMN.
- *Mediation function (MF) block:* Acts as a converter for convergence operator between an OSF and NEF (or a QAF) in the event that these function blocks have some differences that need to be resolved.
- *Q adapter function (QAF) block:* Acts as a converter between TMN functions and non-TMN functions that are somewhat similar to NEF and OSF. It translates between a TMN reference point and a proprietary reference point.

OSI NETWORK MANAGEMENT MODEL

The OSI network management model is consistent with the overall OSI application layer architecture (Figure 14–3). Layer 7 creates and uses the protocol data units (PDUs) transferred between the management processes of the two machines. The management protocol (such as fault management) may use the communications services of application services elements (ASEs) or the common management information protocol (CMIP). As depicted in the figure, the use of CMIP implies the use of ROSE and ACSE.

In accordance with OSI conventions, two management applications in two open systems exchange management information after they have established an application context. The application context uses a name

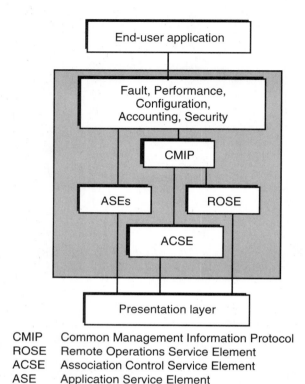

CMIP   Common Management Information Protocol
ROSE   Remote Operations Service Element
ACSE   Association Control Service Element
ASE   Application Service Element

Figure 14–3
The OSI network management structure.

that identifies the service elements needed to support the association. ISO 10040 states that the application context for OSI management associations implies the use of ACSE, ROSE, and CMIP.

THE INTERNET MODEL

The layering for the Internet suite is simpler than the OSI suite (Figure 14–4). The simple network management protocol (SNMP) forms the foundation for the Internet architecture. The network management applications are not defined in the Internet specifications. These applications consist of vendor specific network management modules such as fault management, log control, and security and audit trails. As illustrated in the figure, SNMP rests over the User Datagram Protocol (UDP). UDP in

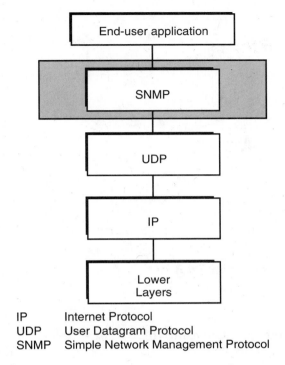

IP   Internet Protocol
UDP   User Datagram Protocol
SNMP Simple Network Management Protocol

Figure 14–4
The internet network management layers.

turn rests on top of IP, which then rests upon the lower layers (the data link layer and the physical layer).

MIBs AND OBJECT LIBRARIES

The management information base (MIB) is one of the most important parts of a network management system (Figure 14–5). The MIB identifies the network elements (managed objects) that are to be managed. It also contains the unambiguous names that are to be associated with each managed object.

From the conceptual viewpoint, MIBs are really quite simple. Yet, if they are not implemented properly, the network management protocol (such as CMIP or SNMP) is of little use. These network management protocols rely on the MIB to define the managed objects in the network.

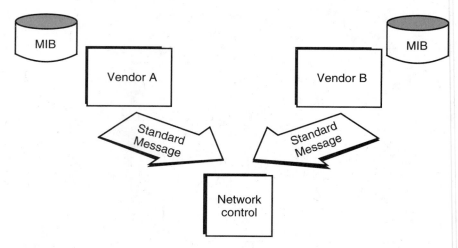

Figure 14–5
Use of MIB for standardizing network management messages.

It should be emphasized that the MIB represents the managed objects. After all, the MIB is a database that contains information about the managed objects. For example, a MIB can contain information about the number of packets that have been sent and received across an X.25 interface; it can contain statistics on the number of connections that exist on a TCP port, and the like.

The MIB defines the contents of the information carried with the network management protocols. It also contains information that describes each network management user's ability to access elements of the MIB. For example, user A might have read-only capabilities to a MIB while another user may have read/write capabilities.

Network management protocols (with few exceptions) do not operate directly on the managed object, they operate on the MIB. In turn, the MIB is the reflection of the managed object. How this reflection is conveyed is a proprietary decision. The important aspect of the MIB is that it defines the (1) elements that are managed, (2) how the user accesses them, and (3) how they can be reported.

This figure shows how the MIB defines the structure and contents of the network management message. Since the MIB contains the elements that are managed as well as their names, the network management software can access the MIB for guidance on how to formulate the network management message.

SNMP AND CMIP OPERATIONS AND MESSAGES

Figure 14–6 shows the messages that are exchanged between a manager and an agent. The interface is achieved by passing protocol data units (PDUs) between the two entities. Conceptually, even though the flow of some of the PDUs could proceed in either direction, it makes little sense for (say) traps to be issued by a manager. But this general model may not be relevant to all systems.

Nonetheless, if the reader chooses to obtain code from well-known sources, the flow of the SNMP messages proceeds as shown in this figure. Two other PDUs are used with SNMPv2: the Get Bulk and the Inform Request. The Get Bulk is used to access multiple variables in a MIB—for example, a table. It is somewhat equivalent to the CMIP scoping operation. The Inform request is used only between managing processes for their own internal operations. (SNMPv2 has not seen much use in the industry.)

Figure 14–7 shows the CMIP operations and PDUs. The event report service is used to report an event to a service user. Since the operations of network entities are a function of the specifications of the managed objects, this event is not defined by the standard but can be any event about a managed object that the user chooses to report. The service provides the time of the occurrence of the event as well as the current time.

The get service is used to retrieve information from an agent. The service uses information about the managed object to obtain and return a set of attribute identifiers and values of the managed object or a selection of managed objects. It can only be used in a confirmed mode and a reply is expected.

The set service requests the modification of attribute values (the properties) of a managed object. It can be requested in a confirmed or nonconfirmed mode. If the confirmed mode is used, a reply is expected.

The action service is used by the user to request that another user perform some type of action on a management object, other than those associated with attribute values (state changes, etc.). It can be requested in a confirmed or nonconfirmed mode. If confirmed, a reply is expected.

The create service is used to create a representation of another instance of a management object, along with its associated management information values. It can only be used in a confirmed mode and a reply is expected.

The delete service performs the reverse operation of the create service. It deletes an instance of a managed object. It can only be used in a confirmed mode and a reply is expected.

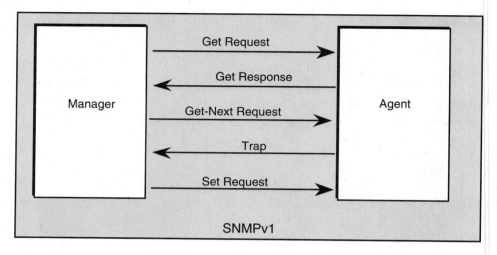

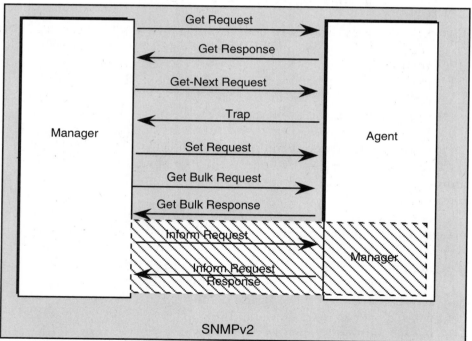

Figure 14–6
SNMP protocol data units (PDUs).

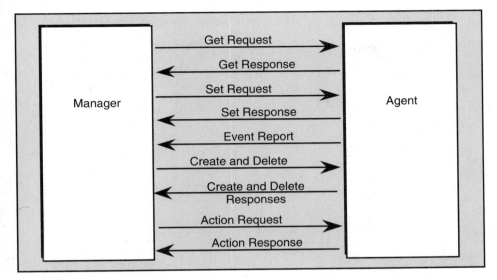

Figure 14–7
The CMIP protocol data units (PDUs).

THE BELLCORE WIRELESS NETWORK MANAGEMENT MODEL

This section describes Bellcore's view of an information model that is used for network management across the Wireless Access Communication System (WACS) radio port control unit (RPCU). Since the subject matter revolves around a model, some of the material is relatively abstract. The model uses object-oriented techniques and abstract syntax notation one (ASN.1). Figures 9–7 and 9–8 in Chapter 9 should be reviewed prior to reading this material.

The WACS operation's architecture is illustrated in Figure 14–8. The local exchange carrier (LEC) provides a variety of OSI functions, which are organized around the OSI five functional areas of fault, performance, configuration, security, and accounting management. These operate through the telecommunication management network (TMN).

As the figure depicts, TMN is a grouping of the operations system, the element manager, the data communications network, and the network management workstation. The RPCU can be connected into the operations, administration, and maintenance (OAM) functions through an ISDN switch or through an X.25 interface. There are no direct connec-

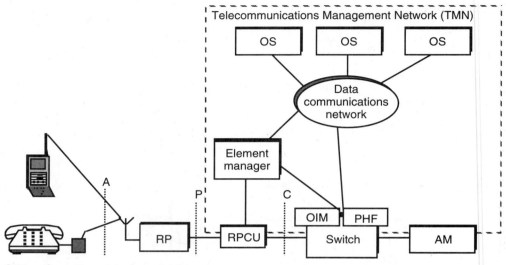

OIM: Operations interface module
PHF: Packet handler function

Figure 14–8
WACS and TMN.

tions between the subscriber unit or the radio port and the TMN. All operations of the TMN take place through the RPCU. Bellcore supports the common management information protocol (CMIP) described earlier in this chapter. The TMN and RPCU exchange CMIP messages. In turn, the RPCU communicates with the RP.

OSI Information Modeling

Bellcore uses the OSI model for modeling information on frame relay interfaces. This section provides a review of the concepts of information modeling. The resources that are supervised and controlled by OSI network management are called *managed objects (MO)*. A managed object can be anything deemed important by organizations using the OSI network management standards. As examples, hardware such as switches, workstations, PBXs, PBX port cards, and multiplexers can be identified as managed objects. But be aware that an MO is a representation of how the resource can be managed by a management protocol—it is not a thing unto itself. It is an abstraction of a physical or logical entity (the latter clause is how Bellcore views an MO).

A managed object is completely described and defined by four aspects of OSI network management:

- Its *attributes* (characteristics or properties) that are known at its interface (visible boundary)
- The *operations* that may be performed on it
- The *notifications* (reports) it is allowed to make
- Its *behavior* that is exhibited in response to operations performed on it

Managed objects have certain properties that distinguish them from each other. These properties are called *attributes*. The purpose of an attribute is to describe the characteristics, current state, and conditions of the operation of the managed objects. Associated with the attributes are attribute values. For example, an object (such as a PBX line card) may have an attribute called status and a value of "operational."

Each attribute consists of one type and one or more values. For example, a type might be labeled the operational state of a packet switch. The values for this type could be disabled, enabled, active, or busy.

Like other OSI models, the WACS RPCU model defines several managed object classes (MOCs). The names of the MOCs are listed in Table 14–2 and a brief discussion of each of these classes follows. Be aware that each object class is defined by standard OSI templates. It is beyond the scope of this book to explain the details of templates. The interested reader can consult Bellcore document GR-2835-Core for a detailed description of MOCs and their associated packages. Table 14–2 contains a "definition" column that explains the MOC. Note that if the definition column contains no indication of default values, then they are not defined.

Functional Areas

As mentioned earlier, this network management model is organized around OSI and the OSI five functional areas. Table 14–3 summarizes the five areas, their major functions, and the components found in the WACS RPCU model.

Table 14–2 Managed Object Classes for PCS

Managed Object Class	Definition
wACSRadioChannel	Bandwidth allocation on the air interface channel
radioTermination	Termination point for portable or fixed unit
antennaSystem	Antenna and cable to antenna that serves one or more transceivers
fixedRadioTermination	CPE radio termination containing a hybrid circuit, converting a 2-wire loop drop
handoverCurrentData	Performance data collected for handover operations. Current:
handoverHistoryData	default value of 15 minutes; History: default value of 8 hours
managedFunction	Class of managed objects within a managed element
powerSupply	A component that provides power to the object
qSAFATransceiverCurrentData qSAFATransceiverHistoryData	Performance data collected during quasi—static autonomous frequency assignment operations
rPCUCurrentData	Performance data collected on an RPCU basis
rPCUEquip	Usage, operational and administrative information on a piece of equipment
rPCUF	Radio port controller unit function (RPCUF) is interface between RPs and PCS switching center; allocates activities with center
rPEquipment	The radio port (RP)
rPF	Radio port function (RPF) provides interface between subtending transceivers and RPCU
rPFLoopbacktestobject	Information on RP loop back tests
returnToNormLogRecord	Information stored in log reflecting a return to normal notification
transceiverAccessCurrentData transceiverAccessHistoryData	Performance data about wireless link. Current: default value of 15 minutes; History: default value of 8 hours
transceiverEquip	Alarm and fault information pertaining to transceiver equipment
transceiverF	RF transmit and receive functions
transceiverMap	Information on which transceivers have non-empty cell coverage intersection with cell of this node
transceiverUtilizationCurrentData transceiverUtilizationHistoryData	Attributes that record channel utilization within radio port receiver
wACS Radio ChannelCurrentData wACS Radio ChannelHistoryData	Performance data collected per radio channel; Current: default of 3 seconds
wACS Radio Channel	Values for threshold settings of the performance monitoring parameters

Table 14–3   Bellcore TMN Functional Areas for PCS

TMN Functional Area	Components
Configuration management	• Provisioning management • Status and control management
Fault management	• NE alarm surveillance • Fault localization • Fault correction • Testing • Trouble administration
Accounting management	• Measuring network service usage • Determining related costs
Performance management	• Performance monitoring • Network data collection • Network traffic management
Security management	• Ensuring security of transactions • Managing security-related information

SUMMARY

Prevalent network management standards are published by ISO, CCITT, IEEE, and the Internet Activities Board (IAB). The ISO/ITU-T is responsible for the OSI network management standards, which includes CMIP and CMISE. The IAB is responsible for SNMP and the Internet MIBs. Bellcore has developed an extensive OSI-based model for PCS, with a full definition of managed object classes, objects, and object attributes.

15

Conclusions

Today, we find ourselves in the flat part of the S-curve for first-generation mobile systems. Eventually, AMPS will play itself out, and digital TDMA and CDMA second-generation systems will become prominent. But the second-generation mobile users and vendors cannot rest on their laurels. Even though the second-generation mobile systems are not yet firmly in place, work is underway for a third-generation system. This work is spearheaded in Europe and sponsored by the European Commission, the Comité Consultif International Radio (CCIR), and the ETSI.

The European Commission sponsors this work through the Research on Advanced Communications for Europe (RACE). The goal of RACE is to create a third-generation mobile system by the year 2000. This system is called the Universal Mobile Telecommunications System (UMTS).

Significant progress has been made on RACE with the support by the World Administrative Radio Congress (WARC) in allocating 230 MHz of spectrum space for the UMTS efforts. In addition, the CCIR is providing support for a parallel effort called the Future Public LAN Mobile Telecommunications System (FPLMTS).

As depicted in Figure 15–1, the likely topology for these new systems will be what is called a mixed cell architecture in which variable-sized cells will be tailored to meet specific geographical areas and traffic demands—with one handset.

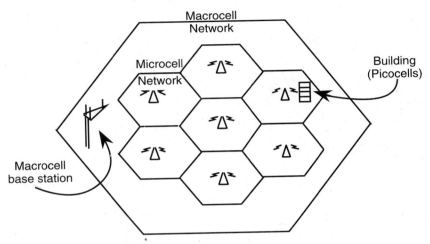

Figure 15–1
Mobile cells for third generation systems.

A mixed-cell architecture must deal with the problems of short battery life, electromagnetic emission constraints, weight and size of the handset, antenna placement, handoff between small and large cells, and so on.

We know better to say that these problems cannot be solved. So, as we say in the radio world, stay tuned, for more is yet to come.

Appendix **A**

Signaling System Number 7 (SS7)

INTRODUCTION

Early signaling systems used a technique called per-trunk, in-band signaling. With this approach, the call control path is the same physical circuit as the speech path. Consequently, call control competes with voice traffic for use of the channel.

In contrast to per-trunk signaling, common channel signaling divides the call control path from the speech path. As a consequence, call control does not compete with voice traffic for use of the channel. Moreover, this approach reduces call set up time and provides the opportunity to build redundant links between offices which improves reliability. Another advantage is the ability to look ahead when setting up a connection. Therefore, resources do not have to be reserved until it is determined that a connection can be made. Thus, the high reliability coupled with faster operations and increased capabilities provides both local exchange carriers and interchange carriers with a powerful tool for enhancing telephone operations.

SS7 FUNDAMENTALS

Common channel signaling (CCS) systems were designed in the 1950s and 1960s for analog networks and later adapted for digital telephone switches. In 1976, AT&T implemented the Common Channel Interoffice Signaling (CCIS) into its toll network. This system is referred to as CCS6 and was based on the CCITT Signaling System No. 6 Recommendation. SS6 and CCS6 were slow and designed to work on low-bit rate channels. Moreover, these architectures were not layered which made changing the code a complex and expensive task.

Consequently, the CCITT began work in the mid-1970s on a new generation signaling system. These efforts resulted in the publication of SS7 in 1980 with extensive improvements published in 1984 and again in 1988. Today, SS7 and variations are implemented throughout the world. Indeed, SS7 has found its way into other communications architectures such as personal communications services (PCS) and global systems for mobile communications (GSM).

SS7 defines the procedures for the set-up, on-going management, and clearing of a call between telephone users. It performs these functions by exchanging telephone control messages between the SS7 components that support the end users' connection. This table provides a summary of the major functions of SS7.

The SS7 signaling data link is a full duplex, digital transmission channel operating at 64 kbit/s. Optionally, an analog link can be used with either 4 or 3 kHz spacing. The SS7 link operates on both terrestrial and satellite links. The actual digital signals on the link are derived from pulse code modulation multiplexing equipment, or from equipment that employs a frame structure. The link must be dedicated to SS7. In accordance with the idea of clear channel signaling, no other transmission can be transferred with these signaling messages and extraneous equipment must be disabled or removed from an SS7 link.

Figure A–1 depicts a typical SS7 topology. The subscriber lines are connected to the SS7 network through the service switching points (SSPs). The SSPs receive the signals from the CPE and perform call processing on behalf of the user. SSPs are implemented at end offices or access tandem devices. They serve as the source and destination for SS7 messages. In so doing, SSP initiates SS7 messages either to another SSP or to a signaling transfer point (STP).

The STP is tasked with the translation of the SS7 messages and the routing of those messages between network nodes and databases. The STPs are switches that relay messages between SSPs, STPs, and service control points (SCPs). Their principal functions are similar to the layer 3 operations of the OSI model.

The SCPs contain software and databases for the management of the call. For example, 800 services and routing are provided by the SCP.

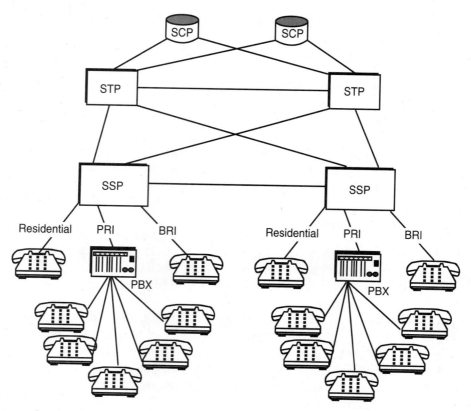

Another node called the signaling point (SP) may exist between user and SSP

BRI   Basic rate interface
PBX   Private branch exchange
PRI   Primary rate interface
SCP   Service control point
SSP   Service switching point
STP   Signaling transfer point

Figure A–1
Typical SS7 topology.

They receive traffic (typically requests for information) from SSPs via STPs and return responses (via STPs) based on the query.

Although Figure A–1 shows the SS7 components as discrete entities, they are often implemented in an integrated fashion by a vendor's equipment. For example, a central office can be configured with a SSP, a STP, and a SCP or any combination of these elements. These SS7 components are explained in more detail later in this section.

THE SS7 LEVELS (LAYERS)

Figure A–2 shows the levels (layers) of SS7. The right part of the figure shows the approximate mapping of these layers to the OSI model. Beginning from the lowest layers, the message transfer part (MTP) layer 1 defines the procedures for the signaling data link. It specifies the functional characteristics of the signaling links, the electrical attributes, and the connectors. Layer 1 provides for both digital and analog links although the vast majority of SS7 physical layers are digital. The second layer is labeled MTP layer 2. It is responsible for the transfer of traffic between SS7 components. It is quite similar to an HDLC-type frame and

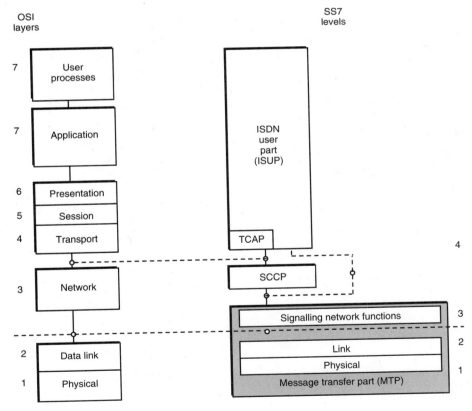

SCCP   Signaling connection control point
TCAP   Transaction Capabilities Applications Part

Figure A–2
SS7 Levels (layers).

indeed was derived from the HDLC specification. The MPT layer 3 is somewhat related to layer 3 of ISDN and X.25 in the sense that this layer provides the functions for network management, and the establishment of message routing as well as the provisions for passing the traffic to the SS7 components within the SS7 network. Many of the operations at this layer pertain to routing, such as route discovery and routing around problem areas in an SS7 network.

The signaling connection control part (SCCP) is also part of the network layer, and provides for both connectionless and connection-oriented services. The main function of SCCP is to provide for translation of addresses, such as ISDN and telephone numbers to identifiers used.

The ISDN user part (ISUP) is responsible for transmitting call control information between SS7 network nodes. In essence, this is the call control protocol, in that ISUP sets up, coordinates, and takes down trunks within the SS7 network. It also provides features such call status checking, trunk management, trunk release, calling party number information, privacy indicators, detection of application of tones for busy conditions, etc. ISUP works in conjunction with ISDN Q.931. Thus, ISUP translates Q.931 messages and maps them into appropriate ISUP messages for use in the SS7 network.

The transaction capabilities application part (TCAP) is an OSI application layer. It can be used for a variety of purposes. One use of TCAP is the support of 800 numbers (in North America) transferred between SCP databases. It is also used to define the syntax between the various communicating components and it uses a standard closely aligned with OSI transfer syntax, called the basic encoding rules (BER). Finally, the OAM and ASEs are used respectively for (a) network management and (b) user-specific services.

References

[ARNO95] Arnold, P. (1995). "Digital Portable Communications, Background/ Propagation," *Bellcore PCS Video Series,* Document LP-PXD.

[ASTH95] Asthana, P. (June 1995). "Jumping the Technology S-Curve," *IEEE Spectrum.*

[BAHI91] Bahia, G. S. (April 1991). "UK Cellular Radio Development," A paper from BNR, UK.

[BELL92] (April 1992). "PCS Network Access Service Alternatives," SR-INS-002245, Issue 1.

[BLAC89] Black, U. (1989). *Data Networks, Concepts, Theory and Practice,* Prentice Hall.

[BLAC91] Black, U. (1991). *X.25 and Related Protocols,* IEEE Computer Society Press.

[BNR92] Bell Northern Research (1992). Global Systems for Mobile Communications, *Telesis,* 92.

[BNR95] Bell Northern Research (1995). "Overview of PCS," Document DT7010, Learning Resource Center, Dept. 2J32, Richardson, Texas.

[CALH92] Calhoun, G. (1992). *Wireless Access and the Local Telephone Network*, Artech House, Inc.

[CDPD93] (July 19, 1993). "Cellular Digital Packet Data System Specification," Release 1.0.

[COOP81] Cooper, R. B. (1981). *Introduction to Queuing Theory*, 2nd ed., North Holland Press.

[COVE89] Covey, S. R. (1989). *The 7 Habits of Highly Effective People*, Simon and Shuster.

[CRAW94] Crawford, T. R. (January 10, 1994). "CDMA is Ready to Go," *Telephony.*

[FLAN90] Flanagan, W. A. (1990). "The Guide to T-1 Networking," The Telecom Library.

[JOHN94] Johnson, J. T. (March 21, 1994). "Wireless Data: Welcome to the Enterprise," *Data Communications.*

[KLEI86]   Klein, L. (ed.) (1986). "Digital Switching Systems," Ottawa, Ontario, Canada, Bell Northern Research.

[MASO94]   Mason, C. F. (June 20, 1994). "A Niche Market in the U.S.," *Telephony.*

[MESS94]   Messmer, E. (May 2, 1994). "Bellcore leads team effort to crack RSA encryption code," *Network World.*

[MOUL92]   Mouly, M., and Pautet, M-B. (1992). "The GSM System for Mobile Communications," Published by the authors.

[ODLY94]   Odlyzko, A. M. (Sept./Oct. 1994). "Public Key Cryptography," AT&T Technical Journal, vol. 73, no. 5.

[PAPO84]   Papaoulis, A. (1984). *Probability, Random Variables, and Stochastic Processes,* 2nd, ed. McGraw-Hill, Inc.

[REDL95]   Redl, S. M., Weber, M. K., and Oliphant, M. W. (1995). *An Introduction to GSM,* Artech House, Norwood, MA.

[REY83]   Rey, R. F., (Technical ed.) (1983). "Engineering and Operations in the Bell System," 2nd ed., Murray Hill, NJ, AT&T.

[SHER94]   Sherman, S. R., Skibo, R., and Murray, R. S. (Sept./Oct. 1994). "Secure Network Access using Multiple Applications of AT&T's Smart Card," AT&T Technical Journal, vol. 73, no. 5.

[SHER95]   Sherry, H. (1995). "PCS Network Issues," Bellcore Personal Communications Issues, document number LP-PXD.

[SIMM91]   Simmons, G. (ed.) (1991). "Contemporary Cryptology," *IEEE Press.*

[VISO95]   Visockis, T. (1995). "Personal conversation on the future of the handset."

[VITE95]   Viterbi, A. J. (1995). *CDMA: Principles of Spread Spectrum Communications,* Addison Wesley.

[WEIN94]   Wiener, M.J. (May 1994). "Efficient DES Key Search," TR-244, School of Computer Science, Carlton University, Ottawa, Canada. Paper presented at the Rump Session on Crypto '93.

[YOUN95]   Younge, M. (December 1995). "GSM as a Standard in North America," Presentation at the PCS-1900 in North America Conference, OMNI Shoreham Hotel, Washington, D.C.

Acronyms

A interface: Air (A) interface
A: Airlink interface
A/D: Analog-to-digital
AC: Access control
AC: Authentication center
ACKs: Positive acknowledgments
ACSE: Association control service element
ADPCM: Adaptive DPCM
AGCH: Access grant channel
AIN: Advanced intelligence network
ALT: Automatic link transfer
AM: Access manager
AM: Amplitude modulation
AMI: Alternate mark inversion
AMPS: Advanced Mobile Phone Systems
ANSI: American National Standards Institute
AP DPCM: Adaptive predictive DPCM
API: Application programming interface
ARQ: Automatic request for repeat
ASEs: Application service elements
ASN.1: Abstract Syntax Notation One
ATM: Asynchronous transfer mode
AUC: Authentication center
BCC: Bellcore client company
BCC: Block calls cleared
BCCH: Broadcast control channel
BER: Basic encoding rules
BOCs: Bell Operating Companies
BRI: Basic rate interface
BSC: Base station controller
BSC: Base station system
BSS: Base station subsystem
BSs: Base station(s) (BSs)
BTAs: Basic trading areas
BTS: Base transceiver station
CATV: Cable television
CCIR: Comite Consultatif International Radio
CCIS: Common Channel Interoffice Signaling
CCS: Common channel signaling
CDMA: Code division multiple access
CDPD: Cellular Digital Packet Data
CELP: Code-excited linear predictive coding
CGSA: Cellular geographic service area
CHAN: Channel number
CKSN: Ciphering key sequence number
CLNP: Connectionless Network Protocol
CLNS: Connectionless Network Service
CM: Communication management
CMI: Coded mark inversion
CMIP: Common management information protocol
CMISE: Common management information service element
CO: Central office
COTS: Connection Oriented Transport Service
CPE: Customer premises equipment
CRC: Cyclic redundancy check
CSI: Channel stream identifier

CT2: Cordless telephone or cordless communications system
CTS: Cell transmitter stations
CVSD: Continuously variable slope delta modulation
D/A: Digital-to-analog
DCA: Dynamic channel assignment
DCC: Digital color code
DCE: Data circuit-terminating equipment
DCS or DCS1800: Digital Cellular System-1800
DECT: Digital European Cordless Telecommunications
DES: Data encryption standard
DIAG: Diagnostic message
DM: Delta modulation
DNS: Domain Name System
DOD: Department of Defense
DPCM: Differential PCM
DQDB: Distributed queue dual bus
DS3: Digital signallevel 3
DSI: Digital speech interpolation
DSL: Digital subscriber line
DSU: Digital service unit
DTAP: Direct transfer application part
DTE: Data terminal equipment
DTS: Digital termination systems
DTX: Discontinuous transmission
E: External interface
E-TDMA: Extended TDMA
EC: European Commission
EIA: Electronic Industries Association
EIR: Equipment identity register
EPS: Enhanced paging services
ERP: Effective radiated power
ESH: End system hello
ESN: Electronic serial number
ESs: End system(s)
ETC: Enhanced throughput cellular
ETSI: European Telecommunications Standards Institute
F-ESs: Fixed end systems
FAC: Final assembly code
FACCH: Fast associated control channel
FCC: Federal Communications Commission
FCCH: Frequency correction channel
FDD: Frequency division duplex
FDM: Frequency division multiplexing
FDMA: Frequency division multiple access
FEC: Forward error control
FM: Frequency modulation
FOCC: Forward control channel
FPLMTS: Future Public LAN Mobile Telecommunications Systems
FSK: Frequency shift key
FTP: File Transfer Protocol
FVC: Forward voice channel
GMSC: Gateway mobile switching center
GMSK: Gaussian-minimum shift keying
GP: Guard period
GSM: Global system for mobile communications
GSM: Group Speciale Mobile

HDLC: High level data link control
HDSL: High-bit-rate DSL
HLM: Home location manager
HLR: Home location register
IAB: Internet Activities Board
ICMP: Internet Control Message Protocol
ID: Identity
ID: Identity element
IMEI: International mobile station equipment identity
IMSI: International mobile subscriber identity
IMSN: International mobile subscriber number
IMTS: Improved Mobile Telephone Service
Interface DN: 228
IP: Initial permutation
IP: Internet Protocol
IS: Intermediate system
ISC: Intermediate system hello confirm
ISDN: Integrated Services Digital Network
ITU-T: International Telecommunications Union-Telecommunications Standardization Sector
IVDS: Interactive video and data service
JTC: Joint Technical Committee
Key (K): 306: 308
LAI: Location area identity
LANs: Local area networks
LAP: Link access procedure
LAPD: Link access procedure for the D channel
LAPDm: LAPD for mobile link
LATAs: Local access and transport areas
LCDM: Logarithmic companded delta modulation
LCI: Local cell identifier
LEC: Local exchange carrier
LEO: Low earth orbit
LEO: Low-earth orbiting satellite
LLC: Logical link control
LOCREQ: Location request message
LPC: Linear predictive coding
LPP: Light weight presentation protocol
LSAI: Local service area identifier
LSB: Least significant bit
M-ES: Mobile end system
MAC: Medium access control
MAN: Metropolitan Area Network
MAP: Mobile application part
MAS: Multiple address systems
MCC: Mobile country code
MD-IS: Mobile data intermediate system
MDBS: Mobile database station
MDLP: Mobile data link protocol
MEO: Medium-earth orbiting satellite
MF: Mediation function
MFR: Manufacturer's code
MHF: Mobile Home Function
MIBs: Management information base(s)

MIN: Mobile identification number
MM: Mobility management
MNC: Mobile network code
MNLP: Mobile Network Location Protocol
MO: Managed objects
MOCs: Managed object classes (MOCs)
MS: Mobile station
MSC: Mobile services switching center
MSF: Mobile Serving Function
MSIC: Mobile subscriber identification code
MSISDN: Mobile system ISDN
MSN: Mobile serial number
MTAs: Major trading area(s)
MTP: Message transfer part (MTP)
MTSO: Mobile Telephone Switching Office
NAKs: Negative acknowledgments
NBT: Nordic Mobile Telephone system
NEF: Network element function (NEF)
NEI: Network Entity Identifier (NEI)
NPAG: North American PCS 1900 Action Group
NRZ: Nonreturn to zero
OAM: Operations: administration: and maintenance
ODLI: Open Data Link Interface
OFS: Operational-fixed microwave service
ORDQ: Order qualification
OSF: Operations systems function
OSI: Open Systems Interconnection
P function: Permutation function
PACS: Personal access communications system
PAM: Pulse amplitude modulation
PASC: PCS access service for controllers
PASD: PCS access service for data
PASE: PCS access for service for external service providers
PASN: PCS access service for networks
PASP: PCS access service for ports
PC: Pseudo-random code
PCC: Power control channel
PCCA: Portable Computer and Communications Association
PCH: Paging channel
PCM: Pulse code modulation
PCNs: Personal communications networks
PCS: Personal communications service
PIN: Personal identification number
PLMN: Public land mobile network
PMR: Private land mobile radio
PROFREQ: Profile request
PSP: PCS service provider

PSTN: Public switched telephone network
PTOs: Public telecommunications operators
PWP: PCS wireless providers
QAF: Q adapter function
QAM: Quadrature amplitude modulation
QUALREQ: Qualification request
R: Reserved
RACE: Research on Advanced Communications for Europe
RACH: Random access channel
RAND: Random number
RBOCs: Regional Bell Operating Companies
RCID: Radio call identifier
RECC: Reverse control channel
REF: Reference
REGNOT: Registration notification
REJ: Reject
RF: Radio frequency
RN: Routing number
ROSE: Remote operations service element (ROSE)
RP(s): Radio port(s)
RPC: Remote Procedure Call
RPCU: Radio port control unit
RR: Radio resource management
RR: Receive ready
RSA: for Rivest: Shamir: Adleman algorithm
RTU: Response transmitter unit
RVC: Reverse voice channel
SABM: Set asynchronous balanced mode
SACCH: Slow associated control channel
SAPs: Service access points
SAT: Supervisory audio tone
SCC: Satellite communications controller
SCC: Set color code
SCCP: Signaling connection control part
SCH: Synchronization channel
SCM: Station class mark
SCPs: Service control point(s)
SDDCH: Stand-alone dedicated control channel
SID: System identification (SID) number
SIG: Signature element
SIM: Subscriber identity module
SMDS: Switched Multimegabit Data Service
SMR: Specialized mobile radio
SMTP: Simple Mail Transfer Protocol
SN: Serial number
SNDCP: Subnetwork dependent convergence protocol

SNMP: Simple network management protocol
SNR: Serial number
SPNI: Service provider network identifier
SREJ: Selective reject
SRES: Signed response
SS7: Signaling System Number 7
SSPs: Service switching points
ST: Signaling tone
STDMs: Statistical TDM multiplexers
STP: Signaling transfer point
SU: Subscriber unit
SWID: Switch identification
SWNO: Switch number
TAC: Type approval code
TACS: AMPS-based system
TACS: Technical ad hoc groups
TACS: Total Access Communications System
TAD: Total average delay
TASI: Time-assigned speech interpolation (TASI): 99
TCAP: Transaction capabilities application part
TCH: Traffic channels
TCP: Transmission Control Protocol
TDD: Time division duplex
TDM: Time division multiplex(ing) (ed)
TDMA: Time division multiple access
TEIs: Terminal end point identifiers
TFTP: Trivial File Transfer Protocol
TIA: Telecommunications Industry Association
TID: Terminal identifier
TMN: Telecommunication management network
TMSI: Temporary mobile subscriber identity
TP4: Transport layer protocol class 4
UDP: User Datagram Protocol
UMTS: Universal Mobile Telecommunications System
UPT #: UPT number
UPT: Universal personal telecommunication (UPT)
VAC: Voice activity compression
VAD: Voice activity detector
VDR: Voice digitization rate
VLM: Visitor location manager
VLR: Visitor location register
VMAC: Voice mobile attenuation code field
VSATs: Very-small aperture
WACS: Wireless Access Communications System
WARC: World Administrative Radio Congress
WCDMA: Wideband CDMA
WSF: Workstation function

Index

Note to readers: Page numbers referring to a figure are marked with an italic *F*, page numbers referring to a table are marked with an italic *T*, and page numbers referring to a calculation are marked with an italic *C*.

343